FRANCIS FORD COPPOLA

INTERVIEWS

CONVERSATIONS WITH FILMMAKERS SERIES
PETER BRUNETTE, GENERAL EDITOR

Photo credit: courtesy Gene D. Phillips

FRANCIS FORD COPPOLA

INTERVIEWS

EDITED BY GENE D. PHILLIPS AND
RODNEY HILL

UNIVERSITY PRESS OF MISSISSIPPI / JACKSON

To
Stanley Kubrick

www.upress.state.ms.us

The University Press of Mississippi is a member of
the Association of American University Presses.

Manufactured in the United States of America

12 11 10 09 08 07 06 05 04   4 3 2 1

∞

Library of Congress Cataloging-in-Publication Data

Coppola, Francis Ford, 1939–
    Francis Ford Coppola : interviews / edited by Gene D. Phillips and
Rodney Hill.
        p. cm.—(Conversations with filmmakers series)
    Includes filmography.
    Includes bibliographical references and index.
    ISBN 1-57806-665-4 (alk. paper)—ISBN 1-57806-666-2 (pbk. : alk. paper)
    1. Coppola, Francis Ford, 1939– —Interviews. 2. Motion picture producers
and directors—United States—Interviews. I. Phillips, Gene D. II. Hill, Rodney,
1965– . III. Title. IV. Series.

PN1998.3.C67A3   2004
791.43′0233′092—dc22   2004043548

British Library Cataloging-in-Publication Data available

CONTENTS

INTRODUCTION

Visionary director, writer, producer, one-time movie mogul, patron saint of the film-school generation, renaissance man—Francis Coppola has been called everything from "maverick" to "megalomaniac." His career so far has been dominated by extremes, from the phenomenal successes of the 1970s (*The Godfather*, 1972, and *The Godfather Part II*, 1974, spring immediately to mind) to some bitter disappointments in the 1980s (notably *One from the Heart*, 1982). This pronounced duality extends to what Joseph Gelmis has termed Coppola's "love-hate relationship" with the Hollywood system, in which his artistic vision often has been compromised for the sake of "the bottom line," if not for his own economic survival. Furthermore, one can spot a similar gulf between some of the glowing critical acclaim Coppola has received, on the one hand, and the brutal attacks he has sustained on the other.

As he tells Gelmis, in the first interview that appears in this volume: "I'm trying not to believe all the baloney publicity written about me. There is no intermediate in this business. They either say, 'Here he is, the boy wonder, the best young filmmaker . . .' or they say, 'Ah, he's just a load of crap.' Why doesn't someone ever say, 'Well, he's a promising guy and he's somewhat intelligent and he's really trying and maybe in ten years he might be a really . . . '? No one ever says that." This rather early (1970) observation by Coppola has rung true for most of his career.

On the positive side, he has enjoyed some of the top honors in the business: two Golden Palm Awards at Cannes, five Oscars, two Golden Globes, three Directors' Guild of America Awards, three Writers' Guild of

America Awards, the BAFTA Film Award, Best Director from the National Society of Film Critics, and a career Golden Lion from the Venice Film Festival, among others. Journalists in *Time, Newsweek,* and elsewhere have likened Coppola to wunderkind directors Orson Welles and Stanley Kubrick; and in interviews reprinted here, Robert Lindsey and Gene Phillips would seem to agree. Of course such praise has its sting, given the well-known turbulence of Welles's career and the gross misrepresentations that Kubrick suffered in the press. Regrettably, the same has held true for Coppola.

His worst publicity was dished out around two of his most daring, personal projects, *Apoclaypse Now* (1979) and *One from the Heart.* During the filming of *Apocalypse Now* in the Philippines, a production that was running long and over budget, the press depicted Coppola as a megalomaniacal madman, inventing what Tony Chiu labels as hostile, "sarcastic nicknames like . . . 'Ayatollah Coppola.' " Similarly, even well before *One from the Heart* was released, the press largely had deemed it a fiasco, an excessive vanity project by a director who had perhaps gotten too big for his britches. Coppola even admits, in an interview with Lindsey, "The success of *The Godfather* went to my head like a rush of perfume. I thought I couldn't do anything wrong."

Coppola later tells Breskin, "I was so destroyed when I saw the perception of me in the press as a wild man, ridiculing what I was doing. . . . I was starting to be portrayed as a megalomaniac surrounded by 'yes men,' when in fact that's never been what this company [American Zoetrope] has been. Never."[1] Lillian Ross's extensive profile on Coppola, conducted during the release of *One from the Heart,* not only provides an excellent primer for those unfamiliar with distribution deals and strategies, it also adds credence to Coppola's objections noted above. During several staff meetings to which Ross was privy, the director seems quite open to the doubts, reservations, and suggestions of his associates, who come across as anything but "yes men."

Such unfair portrayals of Coppola and his films have continued sporadically, as with *Bram Stoker's Dracula* (1992), which—even before its release—garnered a "sarcastic nickname" of its own. Journalists dubbed

---

1. David Breskin, *Inner Views: Filmmakers in Conversation* (New York: De Capo, 1992).

it "The Bonfire of the Vampires," referring to the (perhaps exaggerated?) debacle surrounding Brian De Palma's film adaptation of *The Bonfire of the Vanities*. By that time, though, as Maslin points out, Coppola had endured so much from the press that he no longer seemed to be fazed by it. As he tells Breskin, "I've never been portrayed as anything but a guy on a tightrope, which is an interesting story, but it's not the whole story. I've been on a tightrope for twenty-five years."

An incurable dreamer (as if dreaming were a condition of which to be cured), Coppola has always looked forward to a day when he and other artists of the cinema would be able to make films according to their own inspired visions. Indeed, since the late 1960s he has been threatening (or promising) to leave Hollywood altogether and make low-budget, amateur, even experimental films.

As he tells Chiu, "I dream of being part of a really scintillating world cinema; it would be nice for movies to again become special events. . . . If I ever got the bucks that, say, George Lucas got from *Star Wars* [1977], I'd put every penny into changing the rules."

Still, Coppola understands the need to come to terms with Hollywood, as he explains to Murray: "People like myself, who decide that it's necessary to work within a system in order to be able either to change it or eventually to go off on their own to subsidize the kind of work they believe in, inevitably become changed by the process, if they go along with it."

So it seems that Coppola would not agree entirely that he has a "love-hate" relationship with the system. As he tells Breskin: "It's not that I don't love the system, it's that I *do* love the system. And it seems like it would be so easy to have it be right. It's a frustration I can't get my hands on."

His desire to change the system for the better, coupled with his frustration at the stubborn resistance the system puts up to such potential change, has stayed with Coppola throughout his career. According to Lindsey, "He is an outsider at once angry with the industry moguls who stifle 'creative people' and unsure of himself in the world they dominate."

One advantage of a collection such as this, with interviews spanning nearly three full decades, is that it allows the reader to spot such constant concerns—as well as variations—in Coppola's outlook over the years. So even though there may be considerable overlap in the subject matter covered across the interviews, the editors of this volume see that as a strength rather than a liability.

Francis Coppola's career in entertainment began—as he has said he would like it to end up—as an amateur. During a childhood illness that kept him in bed for almost a year, he occupied himself with various gadgets and puppets, making up stories and shows. As a child he also edited home movies and added sound to them. (Coppola's early affinities for puppetry and film oddly parallel those of another great visionary filmmaker, Jacques Demy.) Coppola was influenced by the films of Sergei Eisenstein at a young age, and he was inspired to pursue the study of theatre at Long Island's Hofstra University, where he directed and wrote numerous plays. Then he enrolled in the masters program at UCLA's film school, where he studied with Dorothy Arzner. While at UCLA he became an assistant to B-movie king Roger Corman, for whom he made his first commercial feature, the low-budget horror movie *Dementia 13* (1963).

In the mid-1960s, Coppola wrote a number of scripts for Seven Arts, including an adaptation of Carson McCullers's *Reflections in a Golden Eye*, eventually filmed by John Huston in 1967. Around the same time he wrote *Patton*, a screenplay that would win him the first of several Academy Awards.

In 1969, already frustrated by his experience making the studio musical *Finian's Rainbow*, Coppola founded his own production company, American Zoetrope. Through it, he helped launch the careers of other young filmmakers like George Lucas, John Milius, and Carroll Ballard. Milius tells Michael Sragow: "[Francis] always said we were the Trojan horse, but that wasn't quite true, because he was inside opening the gate. None of those other guys—Lucas, Spielberg, all of them—could have existed without Francis's help." Furthermore, as Lindsey points out, films produced by American Zoetrope over the years have introduced at least two generations of new stars to Hollywood: Al Pacino, Diane Keaton, Robert De Niro, Robert Duvall, Harrison Ford, Rob Lowe, Emilio Estevez, and others.

Ironically, Francis Coppola (a moniker he prefers over "Francis Ford Coppola") was reluctant to take on the project that was to become his breakthrough film: *The Godfather*. His initial impression of Mario Puzo's best-seller was unfavorable to say the least, but after a second look at the novel, he saw the appeal in its fundamental study of family and power, two subjects that have always interested Coppola immensely. After a series of uphill battles over casting decisions, cinematographic style, and other issues, the resulting film met with staggering critical and financial success.

Oddly enough, according to Coppola's own view, that success may have been the worst thing that ever happened to him, as he tells Sragow: "In some ways [*The Godfather*] ruined me. It just made my whole career go this way instead of the way I really wanted it to go, which was into doing original work as a writer-director. . . . The great frustration of my career is that nobody really wants me to do my own work."

On the other hand, *The Godfather* did bring about the chance for Coppola to do exactly the kind of film he wanted to make. When Paramount asked Coppola to make *The Godfather: Part II*—an idea that he says initially "seemed horrible to me"—he agreed on the condition that the studio finance what remains his favorite among his own films, *The Conversation* (1974). In his interview with Phillips, Coppola characterizes *The Conversation* as "a personal film based on my own original screenplay; it represents a personal direction I wanted my career to take."

In the mid- to late-1970s, Coppola produced and directed what remains his most notorious film, *Apocalypse Now*, a project plagued by negative rumors for much of its production. As Coppola tells Maslin, "I guess when I was in the Philippines, people thought of me as a crazy person, and then it became the thing to do just to make fun of me." A seemingly chaotic series of preview screenings only added grist to the rumor mill, perhaps predisposing critics and audiences alike to beware of the film. Despite winning the prestigious Palme d'Or at the Cannes International Film Festival—making Coppola the first director ever to win the award twice—*Apocalypse Now* took several years to break even on its $31 million budget. Its status today as an acknowledged masterpiece gives one pause to consider the usefulness of popular "criticism" and entertainment "journalism."

Among Coppola's personality traits that emerge from these interviews, perhaps the most outstanding are his determination and resiliency. In speaking with Scott Haller, Coppola aptly likens the movie business to high-stakes gambling: "It's like I'm at a poker table with five guys, and they're all betting two or three thousand dollars a hand, and I've got about eighty-seven cents in front of me. So I'm always having to take off my shirt and bet my pants. Because I want to be in the game. I want to play." He continues the metaphor in his interview with Ross: "If you don't bet, you don't have a chance to win. It's so silly in life not to pursue the highest possible thing you can imagine, even if you run the risk of losing it all, because if you don't pursue it you've lost it anyway. You can't be an artist and be safe."

Riding high on his success with *The Godfather* and *The Godfather: Part II*, Coppola took some of the biggest chances of his career in the late 1970s and early '80s. In 1979, largely with money he had earned from his profit-participation in the *Godfather* films, Coppola purchased the old Hollywood General Studios and formed Zoetrope Studios. The idea was to create an updated studio system, with a stable of players, writers, and technicians, along with a few old-school consultants and "artists in residence," such as Gene Kelly and Michael Powell.

The first (and only) film that Coppola would produce and direct at Zoetrope Studios was his ill-fated musical fantasy, *One from the Heart*, probably the biggest disappointment of his career. In her extensive profile on Coppola, Ross chronicles the problems with that film's distribution, compounded by reports in the press about the perceived excesses of the production—echoes of *Apocalypse Now*. Coppola expresses his frustrations with these misrepresentations in his interview with Breskin: "*One from the Heart* suffered from the perception of me as some wild, egomaniac Donald Trump type of guy, and once they think about you that way, it's just so many months before you're brought down."

The commercial failure of *One from the Heart*, along with the disappointing box-office performance of other films produced at Zoetrope Studios, left Coppola saddled with tremendous debt by the mid-1980s. He had bet big and lost big, and in 1984 he was forced to sell the studio real estate at auction. Still, determined as ever to stay in the game, he took on the role of director-for-hire on a number of films (already familiar territory from the *Godfather* films), with the aim of pulling out of debt and resurfacing to make his own kind of pictures.

When Lindsey asks point-blank, "Have you become sort of a hired gun?" the director replies without hesitation, "Very definitely." A few of these works for hire have enjoyed considerable commercial and even critical success, notably *Peggy Sue Got Married* (1986). Although these were not the kind of personal films that Coppola would have preferred to make, he tells Murray that he "never took on anything with the attitude that it was going to be terrible. It may have turned out that way, but I thought it was great while I was doing it." Coppola puts it a bit more bluntly in his marathon interview with Breskin: "I didn't care much for the *Peggy Sue* project or *Gardens of Stone* [1987], but . . . I never did anything, even *Peggy Sue*, that I disrespected."

A curious trend in Francis Coppola's career, one to which these interviews refer repeatedly, is that his films often bear uncanny parallels to his own life. For example, Lindsey summarizes *Tucker: The Man and His Dream* (1988) in terms that could describe Coppola's problematic relationship with the Hollywood system: "A creative, if perhaps impractical, dreamer comes forth with a better idea that is quashed by a powerful establishment in order to maintain the status quo."

Most strikingly, though, at the time when Coppola was shooting *Gardens of Stone* (a film about the loss of young soldiers in the Vietnam war), his oldest son, Gian Carlo (Gio), was killed in a boating accident. One of the most poignant aspects of any of the interviews included here is the candor with which Coppola discusses this most personal tragedy. He tells Phillips: "I was doing a movie about the burying of young boys and suddenly found that my own boy died right in the midst of it; and his funeral was held in the same chapel where we shot similar scenes of deceased veterans in *Gardens of Stone*. My son is gone, but his memory is not."

Ross also notes Coppola's candid, open approach to the interview process: "He does not measure his words. He is not cautious in expressing his ideas or his uncertainties about them. He likes to throw out his ideas—to try them out on people who he thinks might share his deep interest in motion pictures."

Murray would seem to agree: "The minute I switched on my tape recorder, Coppola came to life. . . . All you have to do with Coppola is get him going. After that, the problem is slowing him down, much less stopping him. I got the feeling he could have been a tremendous politician or an eloquent preacher."

According to Chiu, "In conversation, his mood ranges from defiant pride tinged with insecurity . . . to off-the-wall whimsy. . . . Compelling on almost any subject, he is never more passionate than when he discusses his work."

Phillips found Coppola to be "cordial and cooperative. . . . During a conversation he always listens intently to the person with whom he is talking, as if he stood to gain as much from the interchange as his interviewer."

In his interview with Breskin, Coppola offers the following self-analysis of his conversational style: "First of all, understand that the things I say—a lot of times, and maybe you can see this in my talking to you—as I discover things in talking, I get excited about them. And I may say, 'And I tell you without any doubt!' because I myself am in the moment of discovery. I'm an emotional person. I speak and I say things without thoughtful consideration. And nine times out of ten there's truth in what I say, because it does come from intuition."

In his working methods, Coppola also relies heavily on intuition. As he tells Breskin, "Everything I do is because of my feelings." Another refutation of the "megalomaniac" rumor lies in the fact that Coppola tries to foster an improvisatory, collaborative atmosphere for his actors. Extensive rehearsals are crucial for this approach, and Coppola always asks for at least three weeks' worth, although he usually has to make do with two. He explains to Breskin, "I add scenes in rehearsals—not in the shooting script—to give the actors 'memories.' One thing I often do is have a scene where two characters meet for the first time, even though in the story they've already known each other for a while. I find that giving the cast sensual memories always helps them. As artists, as they're playing a scene, just the fact that they share a memory—it becomes a little emotional deposit in their bank account that enables them to better know each other."

Of course to some, too much reliance on improvisation and spontaneity can seem like a dangerous thing. Cinematographer Gordon Willis has clashed with Coppola more than once when it comes to working methods. Willis tells Michael Sragow, "I like to lay a thing out and make it work, with discipline. Francis's attitude is more like, 'I'll set my clothes on fire—if I can make it to the other side of the room it'll be spectacular.'"

Fascinated with gadgetry since childhood, Coppola has tended to employ the latest technology in his work. For example, he had an image-and sound-control van custom-designed, with audio-video recorders, playback, and editing bays, to facilitate the directorial process. As he tells Ross,

"I'm rarely in the van during an actual take, but in the van afterward I can review each shot, make immediate cuts, and know right away whether I want to shoot additional material or make a change in a scene."

Indeed, for most of his career Coppola has been just as interested in new cinematic technologies as he has been in narrative techniques, if not more so. His forward-thinking hopes for an "electronic cinema," articulated numerous times in these interviews as far back as the 1970s, may finally be fulfilled with the current, ongoing digital revolution.

Coppola offers some astonishingly prescient remarks to Chiu in 1979: "I believe we'll be the first all-electronic movie studio in the world. . . . We won't shoot on film or even on tape; it'll be on some other memory—call it electronic memory. And then there's the possibility of synthesizing images on computers, of having an electronic facsimile of Napoleon playing the life of Napoleon."

In 1992, he tells Breskin that, in the early 1980s, he "was just sure that the motion picture industry was going to turn into a worldwide electronic communications industry, that television was going to be international, that satellites were going to make any part of the world as viable as any other part of the world, that advanced editing and forms of high-definition television were going to allow filmmakers to cook up what they had in their heads cheaper and easier, and there was going to be a great golden age of communication. And I wanted to be in on that. And I wanted that studio!" At the time, Breskin noted that Coppola's hopes for such technology had not been realized; but now, more than a decade later, at least some of Coppola's predictions have come to pass, and with the benefit of hindsight one can see more clearly the potential that Coppola foresaw a generation ago.

In May of 2002, Coppola tells an audience gathered for Lincoln Center's gala tribute to him that "some extraordinary new technology" was enabling him to pursue his current (and yet to be realized) pet project, one that has occupied his imagination for decades: *Megalopolis*. In 1992, he describes the story to Breskin as "very ambitious. It's a dramatic piece about society and the city of the future. . . . It's based on republican Rome and contemporary America: debt was the plague of both societies, both have a patrician class, but they are republics. And I've tried to imagine the Catiline conspiracy as happening in contemporary New York, and I've evolved an original screenplay based on that." In his Lincoln Center address (not reprinted here), Coppola adds, "A film director has to do many things, but he also has to earn the money to make the film. I have found that it's easier for me to make $50 million to make my film than it is to ask someone to allow me to make it. So that's what I'm doing. I hope I don't let you down."

As he has for many years, Coppola has been earning those millions as a director-for-hire on such films as *Jack* (1996), starring Robin Williams, and *The Rainmaker* (1997), a compelling David-and-Goliath courtroom drama starring Matt Damon and Danny DeVito.

So it seems that Coppola is still "walking that tightrope" some thirty-five years into his career, trying to keep his balance economically in the fiercely competitive industry within which he must function, while simultaneously keeping his eyes fixed on his perennial goal: to create fresh, personal, rewarding films, such as *Megalopolis* may well turn out to be. Perhaps Haller sums it up best in his 1981 interview: "Expert story-teller that he is, Coppola has turned his own career into the best cliff-hanger in Hollywood." For our part, the editors of this volume hope that the denouement is a long time in coming.

RH

GP

CHRONOLOGY

1939   Born April 7 in Detroit, Michigan, to Carmine and Italia Coppola.

1957   Attends Hofstra University on a drama scholarship.

1960   Earns a Bachelor of Arts degree at Hofstra and enters the film school of the University of California at Los Angeles, where he studies on campus for two years.

1962   Hired by Roger Corman, an independent producer, and works on *Battle Beyond the Sun, The Young Racers*, and other films.

1963   Directs his first feature, *Dementia 13*, a low budget movie made for Corman. The assistant art director is Eleanor Neil, whom Coppola marries after completing the movie.

1966   As scriptwriter for Seven Arts, an independent production unit, he is given a screen credit for co-scripting *This Property Is Condemned* and *Is Paris Burning?*

1967   Directs *You're a Big Boy Now*, his first film for a major studio; it enables him to earn his Master of Arts degree at U.C.L.A., which is conferred the following year.

1968   *Finian's Rainbow*, a musical with Fred Astaire.

1969   *The Rain People* wins the Grand Prize and the Best Director Award at the San Sebastian International Film Festival. Inaugurates American Zoetrope, an independent production unit in San Francisco.

1970   *Patton*, for which he co-authors the screenplay, wins him his first Academy Award, for Best Screenplay.

1972   *The Godfather* wins him an Academy Award for co-authoring the screenplay of the film, which he also directed; the picture is also voted the Best Picture of the Year.

1974   *The Conversation* wins the Grand Prize at the Cannes International Film Festival. *The Great Gatsby*, the last picture for which he wrote a script without directing the film, is released. *Godfather II* wins him Academy Awards for Best Director and for co-authoring the screenplay; the film becomes the only sequel up to that time to be voted Best Picture of the Year.

1979   *Apocalypse Now*, which had an unprecedented shooting period of 238 days, wins him his second Grand Prize at the Cannes International Film Festival; one of the first major films to deal with the Vietnam War.

1980   Inaugurates Zoetrope Studios in Hollywood.

1982   *One from the Heart*, a commercial failure, forces him to close his independent studio in Hollywood; he continues to run an independent production unit, American Zoetrope, in San Francisco, producing films for release by major studios in Hollywood.

1983   *The Outsiders* and *Rumble Fish* are made back-to-back in Oklahoma.

1984   Assumes direction of *The Cotton Club*, a film with a troubled production history up to that point.

1985   *Rip Van Winkle*, a telefilm, is first broadcast.

1986   *Peggy Sue Got Married* becomes a major hit.

1987   *The Gardens of Stone*, his second film set during the Vietnam War.

1988   *Tucker: The Man and His Dreams*, after some false starts, is finally made.

1989   *New York Stories*, an anthology film with segments by Martin Scorsese, Woody Allen, and Coppola.

1990   *Godfather III*, the final sequel to *The Godfather*.

1991   Fax Bahr and George Hickenlooper's feature-length documentary *Hearts of Darkness*, about the making of *Apocalypse Now*.

1992   *Bram Stoker's Dracula* is a commercial success; he receives a Golden Lion as a Life Achievement Award at the Venice International Film Festival.

1995   The National Film Registry of the Library of Congress, which preserves films of enduring quality, includes *The Godfather*, *Godfather II*, and *The Conversation* in its collection.

1996   *Jack*, a vehicle for Robin Williams.

1997   *The Rainmaker*, from the John Grisham novel.

1998   Recipient of the Life Achievement Award, the highest honor that can be bestowed by the Directors Guild of America. A jury orders Warner Bros. to pay him $80 million for reneging on a deal to film *Pinocchio*—the largest victory by a filmmaker over a major studio up to that time.

1999   American Zoetrope, Coppola's production unit, releases *The Virgin Suicides*, written and directed by his daughter Sofia.

2000   He edits (uncredited) the release version of *Supernova*, after the director, Walter Hill, departs the project.

2001   Theatrical release of *Apocalypse Now Redux*, with fifty minutes of additional footage added to the film as originally released. Release on DVD of *The Godfather Trilogy*, with a documentary about the making of the three films.

2002   Gala tribute by the Film Society of Lincoln Center of New York for his lifetime achievement in the cinema, May 7. American Zoetrope releases *CQ*, written and directed by Coppola's son Roman. *Sight and Sound*'s international poll of film directors and film critics chooses Coppola as one of the top ten directors of all time and *Godfather I* and *Godfather II* among the top ten films of all time.

2003   *Premiere* magazine conducts a nationwide poll for the 100 greatest films, and *Godfather II* leads the list in first place. In a TV special aired on June 3, the American Film Institute honors the best 100 heroes and villains in cinema history, including Michael Corleone in *Godfather II* as a legendary villain. The Motion Picture Academy sponsors a screening of *One from the Heart*, with Coppola leading a discussion of the film. Francis Coppola serves as an executive producer for American Zoetrope on Sofia Coppola's second feature, *Lost in Translation*.

2004   A nationwide poll published by *Premiere* magazine names *The Godfather* as one of the seventy-five most influential films of all time, because it raised the gangster film to the level of the cinematic epic. *One from the Heart*, which had not been available to the public for two decades, is released on DVD, with a documentary about the making of the film.

FILMOGRAPHY

1961
TONIGHT FOR SURE
Producer: **Francis Ford Coppola**
Director: **Francis Ford Coppola**
Screenplay: Jerry Shaffer and **Francis Ford Coppola**
Photography: Jack Hill
Music: Carmine Coppola
Editor: Ronald Waller
Art Director: Albert Locatelli
Length: 75 minutes

1962
THE BELLBOY AND THE PLAYGIRLS
Producer: Wolfgang Hartwig and Harry Ross
Director: **Francis Ford Coppola**, Jack Hill, and Fritz Umgelter
Screenplay: **Francis Ford Coppola**, Dieter Hildebrandt, and Margh Malina
Photography: Paul Grupp
Art Director: Walter Dorfler
Length: 94 minutes

1963
DEMENTIA 13
Production Company: Roger Corman Productions

Producer: **Francis Ford Coppola**
Director: **Francis Ford Coppola**
Screenplay: **Francis Ford Coppola** and Jack Hill
Photography: Charles Hannawalt
Music: Ronald Stein
Editors: Morton Tubor, Stuart O'Brien
Art Director: Albert Locatelli
Cast: William Campbell (Richard Haloran), Luana Anders (Louise
Haloran), Bart Patton (Billy Haloran), Mary Mitchel (Kane), Patrick Magee
(Justin Caleb), Eithne Dunne (Lady Haloran), Peter Read (John Haloran),
Karl Schanzer (Simon), Ron Perry (Arthur), Derry O'Donovan (Lillian),
Barbara Dowling (Kathleen)
Length: 97 minutes

1966
YOU'RE A BIG BOY NOW
Production Company: Seven Arts
Producer: Phil Feldman
Director: **Francis Ford Coppola**
Screenplay: **Francis Ford Coppola**, based on the novel by
David Benedictus
Photography: Andrew Laszlo
Music: Robert Prince; songs by John Sebatian, performed by the
Lovin' Spoonful
Editor: Melvin Shapiro
Art Director: Vassilis Photopoulos
Costumes: Theoni V. Aldredge
Choreography: Robert Tucker
Cast: Peter Kastner (Bernard Chanticleer), Elizabeth Hartman
(Barbara Darling), Geraldine Page (Margery Chanticleer), Julie Harris
(Miss Thing), Rip Torn (I. H. Chanticleer), Tony Bill (Raef), Karen Black
(Amy), Michael Dunn (Richard Mudd), Dolph Sweet (Francis Graf),
Michael O'Sullivan (Kurt Dougherty)
Length: 96 minutes
Distributor: Warner Brothers

1968
FINIAN'S RAINBOW
Production Company: Warner Brothers/Seven Arts
Producer: Joseph Landon
Associate Producer: Joel Freeman
Director: **Francis Ford Coppola**
Screenplay: E. Y. Harburg and Fred Saidy, based on the Broadway play
(book by E. Y. Harburg and Fred Saidy, lyrics by E. Y. Harburg, music by
Burton Lane)
Photography: Philip Lathrop
Music: Ray Heindorf
Associate Music Supervisor: Ken Darby
Editor: Melvin Shapiro
Sound: M. A. Merrick and Dan Wallin
Costumes: Dorothy Jeakins
Choreography: Hermes Pan
Cast: Fred Astaire (Finian McLonergan), Petula Clark (Sharon
McLonergan), Tommy Steele (Og), Don Francks (Woody Mahoney),
Barbara Hancock (Susan the Silent), Keenan Wynn (Senator "Billboard"
Rawkins), Al Freeman, Jr. (Howard), Ronald Colby (Buzz Collins),
Dolph Sweet (Sheriff), Wright King (District Attorney), Louis Silas
(Henry), Brenda Arnau (Sharecropper), Avon Long, Roy Glenn, Jester
Hairston (Passion Pilgrim Gospellers)
Length: 145 minutes
Distributors: Warner Brothers/Seven Arts

1969
THE RAIN PEOPLE
Production Company: American Zoetrope
Producers: Bart Patton and Ronald Colby
Associate Producers: George Lucas, Mona Skager
Director: **Francis Ford Coppola**
Screenplay: **Francis Ford Coppola**
Photography: Bill Butler
Music: Ronald Stein

Editor: Barry Malkin
Sound: Nathan Boxer
Sound Montage: Walter Murch
Art Director: Leon Ericksen
Cast: James Caan (Kilgannon), Shirley Knight (Natalie Ravenna), Robert
Duvall (Gordan), Marya Zimmet (Rosalie), Tom Aldredge (Mr. Alfred),
Laurie Crews (Ellen), Andrew Duncan (Artie), Margaret Fairchild
(Marion), Sally Gracie (Beth), Alan Manson (Lou), Robert Modica
(Vinny)
Length: 101 minutes
Distributor: Warner Brothers/Seven Arts

1972
THE GODFATHER
Production Company: Paramount Pictures
Producer: Albert S. Ruddy
Associate Producer: Gray Frederickson
Director: **Francis Ford Coppola**
Screenplay: Mario Puzo and **Francis Ford Coppola**, based on the novel
by Mario Puzo
Photography: Gordon Willis
Music: Nino Rota, with additional music by Carmine Coppola
Editors: William Reynolds and Peter Zinner
Sound: Christopher Newman
Art Director: Warren Clymer
Production Designer: Dean Tavoularis
Costumes: Anna Hill Johnstone
Cast: Marlon Brando (Don Vito Corleone), Al Pacino (Michael Corleone),
James Caan (Sonny Corleone), Richard Castellano (Clemenza), Robert
Duvall (Tom Hagen), Sterling Hayden (McCluskey), John Marley (Jack
Woltz), Richard Conte (Barzini), Al Lettieri (Sollozzo), Diane Keaton (Kay
Adams), Abe Vigoda (Tessio), Talia Shire (Connie), Gianni Russo (Carlo
Rizzi), John Cazale (Fredo Corleone), Rudy Bond (Cuneo), Al Martino
(Johnny Fontane), Morgana King (Mama Corleone), Lenny Montana
(Luca Brasi), John Martino (Paulie Gatto), Salvatore Corsitto (Bonasera),
Richard Bright (Neri), Alex Rocco (Moe Greene), Tony Giorgio (Bruno
Tattaglia), Vito Scotti (Nazorine), Tere Livrano (Theresa Hagen),

Victor Rendina (Philip Tattaglia), Jeannie Linero (Lucy Mancini),
Julie Gregg (Sandra Corleone), Ardell Sheridan (Mrs. Clemenza),
Simonetta Stefanelli (Apollonia), Angelo Infanti (Fabrizio), Corrado Gaipa
(Don Tommasino), Franco Citti (Calo), Saro Urzi (Vitelli)
Length: 175 minutes
Distributor: Paramount Pictures

1974
THE CONVERSATION
Production Company: American Zoetrope
Producers: **Francis Ford Coppola** and Fred Roos
Director: **Francis Ford Coppola**
Screenplay: **Francis Ford Coppola**
Photography: Bill Butler and Haskell Wexler (uncredited)
Music: David Shire
Editor: Richard Chew
Supervising Editor: Walter Murch
Technical Advisors: Hal Lipset, Leo Jones, and Jim Bloom
Cast: Gene Hackman (Harry Caul), John Cazale (Stan), Allen Garfield
(Bernie Moran), Frederic Forrest (Mark), Cindy Williams (Ann), Michael
Higgings (Paul), Elizabeth MacRae (Meredith), Harrison Ford (Martin
Stett), Robert Duvall (the Director), Mark Wheeler (Receptionist),
Teri Garr (Amy), Robert Shields (Mime), Phoebe Alexander (Lurleen)
Length: 113 minutes
Distributor: Paramount Pictures

1974
THE GODFATHER, PART II
Production Company: American Zoetrope
Producers: **Francis Ford Coppola**, Gray Frederickson, and Fred Roos
Associate Producer: Mona Skager
Screenplay: **Francis Ford Coppola** and Mario Puzo, based on the events
in the novel by Mario Puzo
Photography: Gordon Willis
Music: Nino Rota and Carmine Coppola
Editors: Peter Zinner, Barry Malkin, and Richard Marks

Art Director: Angelo Graham
Set Direction: George R. Nelson
Production Design: Dean Tavoularis
Costumes: Theadora Van Runkle
Cast: Al Pacino (Michael Corleone), Robert Duvall (Tom Hagen), Diane
Keaton (Kay Corleone), Robert De Niro (Vito Corleone), John Cazale
(Fredo Corleone), Talia Shire (Connie Corleone), Lee Strasberg (Hyman
Roth), Michael V. Gazzo (Frank Pentangeli), G. D. Spradlin (Senator Pat
Geary), Richard Bright (Al Neri), Gaston Moschin (Fanucci), Tom Rosqui
(Rocco Lampone), Bruno Kirby, Jr. (Clemenza), Frank Sivero (Genco),
Francesca de Sapio (Young Mama Corleone), Leopoldo Trieste (Signor
Roberto), Dominic Chianese (Johny Ola), Amerigo Tot (Bodyguard), Troy
Donahue (Merle Johnson), John Aprea (Tessio), Joe Spinell (Willi Cicci)
Length: 200 minutes
Distributor: Paramount Pictures

1979
APOCALYPSE NOW
Production Company: American Zoetrope
Producer: **Francis Ford Coppola**, Fred Roos, Gray Frederickson, and
Tom Sternberg
Director: **Francis Ford Coppola**
Screenplay: John Milius and **Francis Ford Coppola**, based on the
novel *Heart of Darkness* by Joseph Conrad (uncredited); narration by
Michael Herr
Photography: Vittorio Storaro
Music: Carmine Coppola, **Francis Ford Coppola**, Mickey Hart
Editors: Walter Murch, Gerald B. Greenberg, Lisa Fruchtman, Richard
Marks, and Barry Malkin (uncredited)
Sound: Walter Murch
Art Director: Angelo Graham
Production Design: Dean Tavoularis
Creative Consultant: Dennis Jakob
Cast: Marlon Brando (Col. Walter E. Kurtz), Robert Duvall (Lt. Col. Bill
Kilgore), Martin Sheen (Capt. Benjamin L. Willard), Frederic Forrest
("Chef" Hicks), Albert Hall (Chief Phillips), Sam Bottoms, (Lance B.
Johnson), Larry Fishburne ("Clean"), Dennis Hopper (Photojournalist),

G. D. Spradlin (General Corman), Harrison Ford (Colonel Lucas), Jerry
Ziesmer (Civilian), Scott Glenn (Capt. Richard Colby)
Length: 153 minutes
Distributor: United Artists

1982
ONE FROM THE HEART
Production Company: Zoetrope Studio
Producers: Gray Frederickson, Fred Roos, Armyan Bernstein
Executive Producer: Bernard Gersten
Director: **Francis Ford Coppola**
Screenplay: Armyan Bernstein and **Francis Ford Coppola**, from the
original screenplay by Armyan Bernstein
Photography: Vittorio Storaro, Ronald Victor García
Music: Tom Waits, sung by Tom Waits and Crystal Gayle
Editors: Anne Goursaud, with Rudi Fehr and Randy Roberts
Sound: Richard Beggs
Art Director: Angelo P. Graham
Production Design: Dean Tavoularis
Costumes: Ruth Morley
Choreography: Kenny Ortega
Cast: Frederic Forrest (Hank), Teri Garr (Frannie), Raul Julia (Ray), Nastassja
Kinski (Leila), Lainie Kazan (Maggie), Harry Dean Stanton (Moe), Allen
Garfield (Restaurant Owner), Jeff Hamlin (Airline Ticket Agent), Italia
Coppola (Woman in Elevator), Carmine Coppola (Man in Elevator)
Length: 101 minutes
Distributor: Columbia Pictures

1983
THE OUTSIDERS
Production Company: Zoetrope Studios
Producers: Fred Roos and Gray Frederickson
Associate Producer: Gian-Carlo Coppola
Director: **Francis Ford Coppola**
Screenplay: Kathleen Knutsen Rowell and **Francis Ford Coppola**
(uncredited), based on the novel by S. E. Hinton
Photography: Stephen H. Burum

Music: Carmine Coppola
Editor: Anne Goursaud
Sound: Jim Webb
Production Designer: Dean Tavoularis
Costumes: Marge Bowers
Cast: Matt Dillon (Dallas Winston), Ralph Macchio (Johnny Cade),
C. Thomas Howell (Ponyboy Curtis), Patrick Swayze (Darrel Curtis),
Rob Lowe (Sodapop Curtis), Emilio Estevez (Two-Bit Mathews),
Tom Cruise (Steve Randle), Glenn Withrow (Tim Shepard), Diane Lane
(Cherry Valance), Leif Garrett (Bob Sheldon), Darren Dalton (Randy
Anderson), Michelle Meyrink (Marcia), Gailard Sartain (Jerry), Tom Waits
(Buck Merrill), William Smith (Clerk)
Length: 91 minutes
Distributor: Warner Brothers

1983
RUMBLE FISH
Production Company: Zoetrope Studios, Universal
Producers: Fred Roos and Doug Claybourne
Executive Producer: **Francis Ford Coppola**
Screenplay: S. E. Hinton and **Francis Ford Coppola**, based on the novel
by S. E. Hinton
Photography: Stephen H. Burum
Music: Stewart Copeland
Editor: Barry Malkin
Sound Design: Richard Beggs
Production Design: Deal Tavoularis
Costumes: Marge Bowers
Cast: Matt Dillon (Rusty James), Mickey Rourke (the Motorcycle Boy),
Diane Lane (Patty), Dennis Hopper (Father), Diana Scarwid (Cassandra),
Vincent Spano (Steve), Nicolas Cage (Smokey), Christopher Penn
(B. J. Jackson), Larry Fishburne (Midget), William Smith (Patterson),
Michael Higgins (Mr. Harrigan), Glenn Withrow (Biff Wilcox), Tom Waits
(Benny), Herb Rice (Pool Player), Maybelle Wallace (Late Pass Clerk),
Nona Manning (Patty's Mother), Domino (Patty's Sister), Gio (Cousin
James), S. E. Hinton (Hooker)
Length: 94 minutes
Distributor: Warner Brothers

1984
THE COTTON CLUB
Production Company: Zoetrope Studios
Producers: Robert Evans, Silvio Tabet and Fred Roos
Executive producer: Dyson Lovell
Screenplay: William Kennedy and **Francis Ford Coppola**, from a story
by William Kennedy, **Francis Ford Coppola**, and Mario Puzo, suggested
by a pictorial history of James Haskins
Photography: Stephen Goldblatt
Music: John Barry and Bob Wilber
Editor: Barry Malkin and Robert Q. Lovett
Sound: Edward Beyer
Art Directors: David Chapman and Gregory Bolton
Production Design: Richard Sylbert
Costumes: Milena Canonero
Choreographer: Michael Smuin
Tap Choreographer: Henry LeTang
Cast: Richard Gere (Dixie Dwyer), Gregory Hines (Sandman Williams),
Diane Lane (Vera Cicero), Lonette McKee (Lila Rose Oliver), Bob Hoskins
(Owney Madden), James Remar (Dutch Schultz), Nicolas Cage (Vincent
Dwyer), Allen Garfield (Abbadabba Berman), Fred Gwynne (Frenchy),
Gwen Verdon (Tish Dwyer), Lisa Jane Persky (Frances Flegenheimer),
Maurice Hines (Clay Williams), Julian Beck (Sol Weinstein), Novella
Nelson (Madame St. Clair), Larry Fishburne (Bumpy Rhodes), John Ryan
(Joe Flynn), Tom Waits (Irving Stark)

1985
RIP VAN WINKLE
Production Company: Home Box Office
Producers: Fred Fuchs and Bridget Terry
Executive producer: Shelley Duvall
Director: **Francis Ford Coppola**
Screenplay: Mark Curtis, Ros Ash, and **Francis Ford Coppola** (uncredited)
from the story by Washington Irving
Photography: George Riesenberger
Music: Carmine Coppola
Editor: Murdo Laird, Arden Rynew
Artistic Consultant: Eiko Ishioka

Production Designer: Michael Erler
Cast: Harry Dean Stanton (Rip Van Winkle), Talia Shire (Wilma Van
Winkle), Henry Hudson (John P. Ryan), Mayor (Tim Conway), Ed Begley, Jr.,
Christopher Penn, Roy Dotrice, Sofia Coppola
Length: 48 minutes

1986
PEGGY SUE GOT MARRIED
Production Company: American Zoetrope
Producer: Paul R. Gurian
Executive Producer: Barrie M. Osborne
Director: **Francis Ford Coppola**
Screenplay: Jerry Leichtling and Arlene Sarner
Photography: Jordan Cronenweth
Music: John Barry
Editor: Barry Malkin
Art Director: Alex Tavoularis
Production Design: Dean Tavoularis
Costumes: Theadora Van Runkle
Cast: Kathleen Turner (Peggy Sue Kelcher), Nicolas Cage (Charlie
Bodell), Barry Miller (Richard Norvik), Catherine Hicks (Carol Heath),
Joan Allen (Maddie Nagle), Kevin J. O'Connor (Michael Fitzsimmons),
Jim Carrey (Walter Getz), Lisa Jane Persky (Dolores Dodge), Lucinda
Jenney (Rosalie Testa), Wil Shriner (Arthur Nagle), Barbara Harris
(Evelyn Kelcher), Don Murray (Jack Kelcher), Sofia Coppola (Nancy
Kelcher), Maureen O'Sullivan (Elizabeth Alvorg), Leon Ames (Barney
Alvorg), with Helen Hunt and John Carradine
Length: 104 minutes
Distributor: TriStar Pictures

1987
GARDENS OF STONE
Production Company: TriStar Pictures, ML Delphi Premier Productions,
and Zoetrope Studios
Producers: Michael I. Levy and **Francis Ford Coppola**
Executive Producers: Stan Weston, Jay Emmett, and Fred Roos, and
David Valdes
Director: **Francis Ford Coppola**

Screenplay: Ronald Bass, based on the novel by Nicholas Proffitt
Photography: Jordan Cronenweth
Music: Carmine Coppola
Editor: Barry Malkin
Sound: Richard Beggs
Art Director: Alex Tavoularis
Production Design: Dean Tavoularis
Costumes: Willa Kim and Judianna Makovsky
Cast: James Caan (Clell Hazard), Anjelica Huston (Samantha Davis),
James Earl Jones (Sgt. Maj. Goody Nelson), D. B. Sweeney (Jackie Willow),
Dean Stockwell (Homer Thomas), Mary Stuart Masterson (Rachel Feld),
Dick Anthony Williams (Slasher Williams), Lonette McKee (Betty Rae),
Sam Bottoms (Lieutenant Webber), Elias Koteas (Peter Deveber), Larry
Fishburne (Flanagan), Casey Siemaszko (Wildman), Peter Masterson
(Colonel Feld), Carlin Glynn (Mrs. Feld), Erik Holland (Colonel Godwin),
Bill Graham (Don Brubaker)
Length: 111 minutes
Distributor: TriStar Pictures

1988
TUCKER: THE MAN AND HIS DREAM
Production Company: Lucasfilm Ltd.
Producers: Fred Roos and Fred Fuchs
Executive Producer: George Lucas
Associate Producer: Teri Fettis
Director: **Francis Ford Coppola**
Screenplay: Arnold Schulman and David Seidler
Photography: Vittorio Storaro
Music: Joe Jackson, Carmine Coppola, Harry DeCosta, Edward Farley,
and Edwin B. Edwards
Editor: Priscilla Nedd
Sound: Richard Beggs
Art Director: Alex Tavoularis
Production Design: Dean Tavoularis
Costumes: Milena Canonero
Cast: Jeff Bridges (Preston Tucker), Joan Allen (Vera Tucker),
Martin Landau (Abe Karatz), Frederic Forrest (Eddie), Mako (Jimmy),
Elias Koteas (Alex), Christian Slater (Junior), Nina Siemaszko (Marily Lee),

Anders Johnson (Johnny), Corky Nemec (Noble), Marshall Bell (Frank), Jay O. Sanders (Kirby), Peter Donat (Kerner), Lloyd Bridges (Senator Ferguson), Dean Goodman (Bennington), John X. Heart (Ferguson's Aide), Don Novello (Stan), Patti Austin (Millie), Sandy Bull (Stan's Assistant), Joe Miksak (Judge), Scott Beach (Floyd Cerf), Roland Scrivner (Oscar Beasley), Dean Stockwell (Howard Hughes), Bob Safford (Narrator), Larry Menkin (Doc), Ron Close (Fritz), Joe Flood (Dutch)
Length: III minutes
Distributor: Paramount Pictures

1989
NEW YORK STORIES, SEGMENT TWO, LIFE WITHOUT ZOE
Production Company: Touchstone Pictures
Producers: Fred Roos and Fred Fuchs
Director: **Francis Ford Coppola**
Screenplay: **Francis Ford Coppola**, Sofia Coppola
Photography: Vittorio Storaro
Music: Carmine Coppola
Songs: Kid Creole and the Coconuts
Editor: Barry Malkin
Sound: Frank Graziadei
Art Director: Speed Hopkins
Production Design: Dean Tavoularis
Costumes: Sofia Coppola
Cast: Heather McComb (Zoe), Talia Shire (Charlotte), Gia Coppola (Baby Zoe), Giancarlo Giannini (Claudio), Paul Herman (Clifford), James Keane (Jimmy), Don Novello (Hector), Bill Moor (Mr. Lilly), Tom Mardirosian (Hasid), Jenny Bichold (Lundy), Gina Scianni (Devo), Diane Lin Cosman (Margit), Selim Tlili (Abu), Robin Wood-Chappelle (Gel), Celia Nestell (Hillary), Alexandra Becker (Andrea), Adrien Brody (Mel), Michael Higgins (Robber), Chris Elliott (Robber), Thelma Carpenter (Maid), Carmine Coppola (Street Musician), Carole Bouquet (Princess Soroya), Jo Jo Starbuck (Ice Skater)
Length: 34 minutes
Distributors: Buena Vista Pictures

1990
THE GODFATHER, PART III
Production Company: Zoetrope Studios, Paramount Pictures
Producer: **Francis Ford Coppola**
Executive Producers: Fred Fuchs and Nicholas Gage, Fred Roos, Gray
Frederickson, and Charles Mulvehill
Director: **Francis Ford Coppola**
Screenplay: Mario Puzo and **Francis Ford Coppola**
Photography: Gordon Willis
Music: Carmine Coppola and Nino Rota
Editors: Barry Malkin, Lisa Fruchtman, and Walter Murch
Sound: Richard Beggs
Art Director: Alex Tavoularis
Production Design: Dean Tavoularis
Costumes: Milena Canonero
Cast: Al Pacino (Michael Corleone), Diane Keaton (Kay Adams), Talia
Shire (Connie Corleone-Rizzi), Andy Garcia (Vincent Mancini), Eli
Wallach (Don Altobello), Joe Mantegna (Joey Zasa), George Hamilton
(B. J. Harrison), Bridget Fonda (Grace Hamilton), Sofia Coppola (Mary
Corleone), Raf Vallone (Cardinal Lamberto), Franc D'Ambrosio
(Anthony Corleone), Donal Donnelly (Archbishop Gliday), Richard
Bright (Al Neri), Helmut Berger (Frederick Keinszig), Don Novello
(Dominic Abbandando), John Savage (Andrew Hagen), Franco Citti
(Calo), Mario Donatone (Mosca), Vittorio Duse (Don Tommasion), Enzo
Robutti (Don Licio Lucchesi), Michele Russo (Spara), Al Martino
(Johnny Fontane), Robert Cicchini (Lou Pennion), Rogerio Miranda
(Armand), Carlos Miranda (Francesco), Jeannie Linero (Lucy Mancini)
Length: 161 minutes; 170 minutes (final version, 2001)
Distributor: Paramount Pictures

1992
BRAM STOKER'S DRACULA
Production Company: American Zoetrope, Columbia Pictures
Producers: **Francis Ford Coppola**, Fred Fuchs, Charles Mulvehill,
Michael Apted, and Robert O'Connor
Co-producer: James V. Hart

Associate Producer: Susie Landau
Director: **Francis Ford Coppola**
Screenplay: James V. Hart, based on the novel by Bram Stoker
Photography: Michael Ballhaus
Music: Wojciech Kilar, Annie Lennox
Editors: Nicholas C. Smith, Glenn Scantlebury, and Anne Goursaud
Sound: David Stone
Art Director: Andrew Precht
Production Design: Thomas Sanders
Cast: Gary Oldman (Dracula), Winona Ryder (Mina/Elisabeta), Anthony
Hopkins (Abraham Van Helsing), Keanu Reeves (Jonathan Harker),
Sadie Frost (Lucy Westernra), Richard E. Grant (Dr. Jack Seward), Cary
Elwes (Arthur Holmwood), Billy Campbell (Quincey Morris), Tom Waits
(Renfield), Monica Bellucci (Dracula's Bride), Jay Robinson
(Mr. Hawkins), I. M. Hobson (Hobbs), Laurie Frank (Lucy's Maid)
Length: 123 minutes
Distributor: Columbia Pictures, Columbia TriStar, and Criterion
Collection

1996
Jack
Production Company: American Zoetrope, Hollywood Pictures
Producers: Ricardo Mestres, Fred Fuchs, and **Francis Ford Coppola**
Executive Producer: Doug Claybourne
Director: **Francis Ford Coppola**
Screenplay: James DeMonaco and Gary Nadeau
Photography: John Toll
Music: Michael Kamen, Bryan Adams
Editor: Barry Malkin
Sound: Agamemnon Andrianos
Art Director: Angelo Graham
Production Design: Dean Tavoularis
Costumes: Aggie Guerard Rodgers
Cast: Robin Williams (Jack Powell), Diane Lane (Karen Powell), Jennifer
Lopez (Miss Marquez), Brian Kerwin (Brian Powell), Fran Drescher
(Dorlores Durante), Bill Cosby (Lawrence Woodruff), Michael McDean
(Paulie), Don Novello (Bartender), Allan Rich (Dr. Benfante), Adam Zolotin

(Louis Durante), Todd Bosley (Edward), Seth Smith (John-John), Mario
Yedidia (George), Jermy Lelliott (Johnny Duffer), Rickey D'Shon Collins
(Eric), Hugo Hernandez (Victor)
Length: 113 minutes
Distributor: Buena Vista Pictures

1997
THE RAINMAKER
Production Company: American Zoetrope
Producers: Michael Douglas, Steven Reuther, Fred
Fuchs and Georgia Kacandes
Director: **Francis Ford Coppola**
Screenplay: **Francis Ford Coppola**, based on the novel by John
Grisham; narration by Michael Herr
Photography: John Toll
Music: Elmer Bernstein
Editor: Barry Malkin
Sound: Nelson Stoll
Art Director: Robert Shaw
Production Design: Howard Cummings
Costumes: Aggie Guerard Rodgers
Cast: Matt Damon (Rudy Baylor), Claire Danes (Kelly Riker), Jon Voight
(Leo F. Drummond), Mary Kay Place (Dot Black), Mickey Rourke (Bruiser
Stone), Danny DeVito (Deck Schifflet), Dean Stockwell (Judge Harvey
Hale), Teresa Wright (Miss Birdie), Virginia Madsen (Jackie Lemanczyk),
Andrew Shue (Cliff Riker), Red West (Buddy Black), Johnny Whitworth
(Donny Ray Black), Danny Glover (Judge Tyrone Kipler), Wayne Emmons
(Prince Thomas), Adrian Roberts (Butch), Roy Scheider (Wilfred Keeley),
Randy Travis (Billy Porter), Michael Girardin (Everett Lufkin), Randall
King (Jack Underhall), Justin Ashforth (F. Franklin Donaldson), Michael
Keys Hall (B. Bobby Shaw)
Distributor: Paramount Pictures

2001
APOCALYPSE NOW (REDUX)
An expanded version of *Apocalypse Now*, with fifty-three minutes of
additional footage

Production Company: Zoetrope Studios
Producers: Kim Aubry, Shannon Lail
Editor: Walter Murch
Sound: Michael Kirchberger
Cast: The French Plantation: Christian Marquand (Hubert DeMarais),
Aurore Clément (Roxanne Surrault)
Length: 202 minutes
Distributor: Miramax Films, United Artists

FRANCIS FORD COPPOLA

INTERVIEWS

Francis Ford Coppola: Free Agent within the System

JOSEPH GELMIS / 1970

Francis Ford Coppola was probably the first graduate of a university film school in America to direct a Hollywood movie. Certainly he was the first to offer a commercial film as his thesis for a degree.

You're a Big Boy Now, made for $800,000 in twenty-nine days, established the twenty-seven-year-old Coppola (born 1939) as a whiz kid at his studio. Though he had had to bully Hollywood into letting him make the film, his willingness to work within the system alienated him from the student filmmakers whose heroes are rebels like Godard.

In some ways, Coppola's love-hate relationship with Hollywood is the archetypal one felt by many young filmmakers. He sentimentally accepted the job of adapting a creaky 1940s musical, *Finian's Rainbow*. Yet before the film had opened, he had coerced the studio into bankrolling a personal film he would make during a unique odyssey on the road across eighteen states in a semiscripted *cinéma vérité* style.

The Rain People was shot for $750,000 over a period of about three months of traveling with a company of twenty in a caravan of seven vehicles equipped with two-way radios. It was edited en route, with the film being processed and returned from the lab in New York within three days. The idea was to capture the actual regional character of the country while filming a pregnant young Long Island housewife going AWOL, in her station wagon, from the responsibilities of marriage.

And then Coppola's ambivalence expressed itself in still another odd decision. He announced that his next movie would be another Hollywood project, *Heaven Can Wait*, starring Bill Cosby in a remake of the 1940s fantasy *Here Comes Mr. Jordan*. And he simultaneously disclosed that he was leaving Hollywood to set up his own small independent production studio in a warehouse in San Francisco where he could experiment and make noncommercial personal films.

"I don't dislike L. A.," he told *Variety*, "but I figure at this age I should find out where I'm going. I'm from New York, but I wouldn't want to live there. Los Angeles, I like it—but I want to do what Jack Warner and Harry Warner did forty years ago. Find the place."

The first film he wants to make in his own studio is *The Conversation*, which he is writing himself. "It's about a man on his fiftieth birthday," he said.

My interview with Coppola was held in his suite at the Plaza Hotel in New York on October 9, 1968, a few hours before the world première of *Finian's Rainbow*. He was nervous and under great emotional stress.

GELMIS: *What experience with filmmaking had you had before UCLA?*
COPPOLA: I used to play with film like a lot of kids. My father, Carmen, was a flutist with Toscanini and a conductor and composer himself. So we had a tape recorder. And I had sound back as early as 1949 or so. I used to have synchronized movies. Most of them I cut together from home movies my family had shot. I'd make myself the hero. I made money out of them, too. I'd show them to other kids in the neighborhood. I had a little movie company there on 212th Street in Queens.

When I was about eighteen, I became very interested in Eisenstein. I became a disciple. I read all of his work and went to see his films at the Museum of Modern Art. And I was really dying to make a film. Taking my example from him, I went to theater school, and worked very hard. I directed lots of plays and I studied theater and I could light a set, build a set. I wanted to be very well rounded, very complete, to have that kind of background, because Eisenstein had started like that.

And I stayed away from film because I knew it would seduce me. I think most young filmmakers in the schools get so hung up—handling film is so much fun, so exciting—that they tend to bypass content and acting, the other things which eventually the film will make use of.

They go into it with just technique. So I tried to stay away from film for four years just so I would really have something to bring to it.

But, in my third year at Hofstra, I sold my car and bought a 16-mm camera. I just couldn't wait. I went out to make a short, which I never finished. It was a subjective piece about a woman who takes her children out for a day in the country and she shows them all these beautiful things. And then she falls asleep in an orchard with them.

When she wakes up they're gone and she goes looking for them. The idea was that everything that had seemed so beautiful before now becomes ugly to her because it represents a possible danger to the missing children. I wanted to experiment with this kind of looking at the same thing two ways. I shot part of it but never finished it. I just didn't have the technical expertise. Then I went to UCLA directly from Hofstra, on graduation. I had done lots of musical comedies and had a pretty rounded stage experience—so much so that the first short I made for the film school was too theatrical.

While I was going to UCLA I became one of Roger Corman's assistants. He'd call me when he wanted cheap labor. I was a dialogue director on *The Tower of London.* And I was Roger's sound man on *The Young Racers.* Roger has one major weakness. When he pays the money to bring a film crew somewhere, he can't resist making a second film with them because he's already paid for their travel.

We were in Ireland with a movie crew that was just begging to be utilized. I was dreaming up an idea for a story, while everybody else just talked about making a film. The secret of all my getting things off the ground is that I've always taken big chances with personal investments. While the other guys my age were all pleading, "Roger, let me make a film," I simply sat down and wrote a script.

Then I took the little money I had and went out and bought some odds and ends I needed for the film. I talked Roger into putting up $20,000 by raising the matching $20,000 myself. I met an English producer in Dublin and he heard we were making a movie—which we weren't, really, yet—and he was willing to buy the English rights. So, essentially, I sold the English rights for a movie which did not exist to this man. And with the $20,000 he paid me and the $20,000 Roger put up, I was able to direct my first feature film—based on a script it had taken me three nights to write.

I shot it with a nine-man crew and some of the actors who were in *The Young Racers*. At the time, I was twenty-two and still just a student at the film school. Some people—including friends of mine—paid their own way to come over to Dublin and work on the film. That's how I met my wife.

The film *Dementia 13* was meant to be an exploitation film, a *Psycho*-type film. *Psycho* was a big hit and William Castle had just made *Homicidal* and Roger always makes pictures that are like other pictures. So it was meant to be a horror film with a lot of people getting killed with axes and so forth.

G: *How would you rate it now?*
C: I think it showed promise. It was imaginative. It wasn't totally cliché after cliché. Very beautiful visuals. In many ways, it had some of the nicest visuals I've ever done. Mainly, because I composed every shot. In the present circumstances, you never have the time. So you just leave it to others. *Dementia 13* got very good reviews and I made money on it. In England, it was released as *The Haunted and the Hunted*.

I came back from *Dementia 13* and I got married and a week later I got this chance, really on the basis of the Samuel Goldwyn screenwriting award I won at school, to write *Reflections in a Golden Eye* for Seven Arts (later Warner Bros.-Seven Arts). They liked it very much and gave me a contract for three years at $500 a week, so I left school. The reaction was such a load of baloney. Everyone read the *Reflections* script and said, "Fantastic, who's this genius? It must be Dalton Trumbo writing under another name." They gave me all that junk. Everything is either one hundred percent or nothing. I'm really fed up.

G: *What happened to your script for* Reflections?
C: What very simply happened to all of them. They finally got placed with a director and actors who brought in their own writers and nothing was used of them. I never saw the film they made. But I know that none of my eleven scripts—*Reflections*, *This Property Is Condemned*, or any of the films I wrote—ever got on the screen very much like I wrote them.

I was twenty-three and I was making about $1000 a week after the first year. I lost it all, by the way. I wanted to make a film so desperately that I saved all my money. And I had about $20,000 cash. I was really frustrated, because I could buy a Ferrari or I could buy a sailboat but I couldn't make a film. So I decided I was going to risk it all on the stock market and either have $100,000 and make a film, or have nothing. I lost it, every penny of it. In one stock. Scopitone. That jukebox with the little films. Lost every penny on it.

A lot of guys are very lazy. Let me tell you. I meet a lot of young film-makers, because I'm interested in them. And they're all very lazy. They come and they want you to pay them to write the scripts. The first job I did for Roger I was paid $250 to do a dub on a Russian space picture (*Battle Beyond the Sun*) and I worked six months for that $250. No one's willing to do that anymore. I would have done anything. That's the difference.

G: *Your screenwriting stint for Seven Arts ended badly, didn't it?*
C: It was traumatic. I was one of ten writers on *Is Paris Burning?*, but Gore Vidal and I got the full screen credit for that fiasco. I quit and was fired at the same time. I was broke. I'd lost all my money. I owed the bank $10,000. And I had two kids and a wife to support. I went to Denmark for some reason. I can't remember why, but I wanted to move there. I was very depressed. Then it turned out that Seven Arts had appropriated my script of *You're a Big Boy Now*, which I had written nights in Paris to stay sane. They maintained that since I wrote it on their time they had the right to keep it. I had nothing. I had *nothing*. Not even a friend. I had lost all my friends because I was such a success.

G: *How did you survive?*
C: Somehow, 20th Century-Fox hired me to write the life of General Patton for $50,000. (Director Franklin Schaffner finally began work on *Patton*, with George C. Scott in the title role, in Spain in January 1969.) I had a little bit of a reputation as a screenwriter that I didn't know about, apparently. So, with that money, I girded myself, as they say, and I made *Big Boy*. I made very little money on the film. I made only $8000 for both writing and directing it, even though I had been offered $75,000 to just write a script for a different film. So, again, I took the risk. Why did I make *Big Boy* for just $8000? Because that's what they could get me for. I would have done it for nothing. I saw *Big Boy* recently, by the way. I really hated it.

And yet I really had to hustle to get that film made. I buffaloed the whole thing through. I got everyone committed before they even realized there was a package I'd put together. Nobody wanted me to direct a film. I was writing films and I was filling a very definite, awful need in the film business, which was to write scripts quickly and anonymously and have them so they could shop them around and get other directors and have other writers rewrite them. I was filling a real function. And I was being paid for it. And I was being paid more than other twenty-three-year-old guys.

But I wanted to make a film. I wanted to make *You're a Big Boy Now* years before I made it. I finally got to make it after this big uphill fight. I bought the book with my own money. I wrote the screenplay. I rewrote the screenplay. I begged people to read it. I got actors to say they would do it. The whole game. I flew to New York. All that stuff.

I paid $1000 for an option on the film rights, against $10,000. It was a big thing for a young guy. I never had anything much. If it makes the people who think I'm in such a great situation feel any better, I never had anything. I lived on ten dollars a week which my father sent me for expenses when I went to graduate school. I earned the tuition. I haven't been pampered. No one helped me do this.

The important thing is that nobody was interested in making the film, literally nobody. The secret of our society is that it's based on the fact that people should pretty much stay where they are, because then everything works. I was a victim of that, I thought. So I went through all of this energy and I got to make *You're a Big Boy Now*. And by the time I got to make it, I didn't know whether I wanted to make it anymore. Because one of the great pities was that I had written *You're a Big Boy Now* before Dick Lester's *The Knack* came out and yet everyone said it was a copy. It was definitely influenced by *A Hard Day's Night*. But it was all there already before I even saw *Hard Day's Night*. One of the troubles of the film business is that you're always sort of forced to do things three years later, like with *Big Boy*.

When I finished *Big Boy*, I resolved I wouldn't make the same mistake as a lot of guys—to suddenly get into projects over their head, films they didn't have complete control over, to take other people's raps, so to speak. And then *Finian's Rainbow* came along and I took it, though I didn't know the play, the book. I only knew the score. When I read the book, I was amazed. I thought it was sort of ridiculous, a cocka-mamy story.

I was hired because they wanted to zip it up and do it à la *Big Boy*, the direction that maybe that was going in. I tried to be very faithful, and to do all of the work underneath so it wouldn't come out like what they did to *A Funny Thing Happened on the Way to the Forum* and films like that. I really tried to show some discipline, to try to make it work on its own terms and not to make a big thing out of myself—you know, to get fancy. I tried to lay low, and give it a lot of warmth and affection and make it work in a timeless way.

I knew there were pitfalls. If I did it faithfully it was going to look like a twenty-two-year-old show. So I tried to make it faithful and yet make it acceptable for contemporary audiences. I think I always knew that the show, critically, was going to be received ungenerously. A lot of lib-eral people were going to feel it was old pap, because of its dated civil rights stance. And they were going to say, "Oh, the real *Finian's Rainbow* we remember was wonderful." If they were to look at the material today, they might not love it so much. And the conservatives were going to say it was a lot of liberal nonsense. I knew I was going to get it from both ends. And it sort of hurt my feelings.

G: *Why did you take on the burden of a twenty-two-year-old musical?*
C: Because I thought it was a lovely old show. I thought there was something warm about it. And I thought that maybe if I could do it right, that if I could find the balance, I could make it timeless. It'd be like *Snow White*. I had always loved musical theater.

G: *Why hadn't it been made in the past twenty years?*
C: There were political reasons, partly. It came out right before the McCarthy era. I guess lots of people felt there were leftist radical things in it. And the people who wrote it wanted lots of money for it. And by the time that subsided, it was already an old show. People had tried to make it, on and off. John and Faith Hubley were planning to make a full-length cartoon out of it back in the '50s.

And another thing, it's being released now as a big fancy roadshow. It wasn't that when it started. It was just a movie musical. It was not expensive. It cost about $3,500,000. You know, it's competing with

$10,000,000 musicals like *Funny Girl* and *Star!* But we rehearsed it in three and a half weeks and shot it in just twelve weeks. It was not a luxury production. I'll tell you honestly, after the second week of this picture I was out of what I had prepared. I was faking it.

The choreography was abysmal, let's be honest. We fired the choreographer halfway through the picture. I staged all the musical numbers, eventually. I didn't know I was going to end up doing quite that. And most of those numbers are faked. For example, after the song "If This Isn't Love" we were supposed to go into a big production number. Well, it was so awful that I finally got little Barbara Hancock (Silent Susan, in the film) and we went back and I shot her with a 500-mm lens going in and out of the trees. She was just faking it. And that's the way the numbers were done. I felt very unhelped in the area of choreography, and I needed help.

I wanted to do the musical numbers. I dreamed up the way the numbers were going to be done. I said, "Grandish." I'll shoot it on a hill and have Petula Clark hanging white bed sheets. And "If This Isn't Love" will be done with children's games. And "On That Great Come and Get It Day" they're going to throw away all their old furniture in big piles. And for every number I had an idea. I figured it out. And I wanted to. But for the dance steps, the "combinations" as they're called, I needed a choreographer.

The whole picture was made on the Warners' back lot, the "jungle." I shot just eight days out of the studio. The location footage was carefully interspersed in the film and used with the titles. Yet look what we're competing with. *The Sound of Music*, where they go and sit on the Alps for a month. Any other picture really took the time to do it right. And, even in fairness to our choreographer—who I think was a disaster and was hired at Fred Astaire's insistence—do you know the months that Herb Ross rehearsed those *Funny Girl* numbers? I mean, that's what we're being compared to.

Do you realize that when *Finian's Rainbow* was first assembled it ran two hours and thirty minutes? And this final print runs two hours and twenty-five minutes. That means that only five minutes were wasted. I'd like to see what the rough cut of one of those other shows ran. William Wyler (*Funny Girl*) and Robert Wise (*Star!*) are perfectionists. I'm really annoyed about the whole thing.

There's a reason why this picture was shot in twelve weeks while *Star!* was made in six months. I'm not so much faster and cleverer than those people. Obviously the reverse. So there was a degree of tolerance in terms of what I could go for in the time allocated. I would shoot a scene eight times. And it would be different every time. And then I'd jump-cut mismatched bits together. In other words, I'd never try to match a picture.

If you look at the chorus during this movie you'll see lots of miscues or flutterings. As you know, kids are very hard to program. And the more you get kids that are programable, the more phony they are. Also, there wasn't lots of time to keep going after every detail. Very often I was going for what I felt was the essence of a scene. I always feel a director directs his movie before it's even done. If the vision is right, then you'll forgive a lot of this other stuff. More time will help alleviate the rough details. But I feel if the audience didn't enjoy it, it's because of the vision.

G: *In the case of a musical, the performance is almost everything. There were problems with the performances of several of your people. Do you think it's possible for a director to control such things?*

C: Yes. Don Francks never did improve, as an actor. The one I'm really unhappy about was Tommy Steele, because I think I could have done better with him. When we were doing the rehearsal, Tommy was doing his *thing.* And I said to him that I really felt we were going in the wrong direction. Everyone loved him and told Tommy he was so great. But I felt the leprechaun should be more shy and timid and bewildered. When I first came into the picture, I wanted Donal Donnelly to play the part. I wanted it to be an introvert leprechaun, a guy who speaks in this quiet voice and then suddenly becomes a human being.

And at my insistence Tommy started to do just that in the rehearsal, and he really was good at it. But actors are funny people. They have certain crutches that they rely on. And they're very unwilling to let those crutches go when they feel insecure. And somehow during the actual shooting, little by little, he slipped back into his familiar character. And you don't notice it because you're shooting little pieces. And that's the whole game of directing. Directing takes a lot of concentration and being able to be blind to certain problems and just focus where you should be focusing. I did that in some cases. In some cases I failed. With Tommy, I wanted a different kind of performance and he eluded me.

G: *Was there more pressure on you as a young director making a big musical than there had been exerted by the studio when you made* You're a Big Boy Now *for less than $1,000,000?*
C: I have to say in all honesty that I did both films the way I wanted to do them. I had my way, within the limitations of time and money. I was very responsible. *Finian* cost as little as it did because I was very disciplined. I consider myself a very romantic human being and I really feel I was well suited to do this project. But it's not my personal kind of filmmaking, which I may never depart from again, by the way.

G: *Among your contemporaries, especially from the graduate film school at UCLA, there must have been a lot of guys who said: "He's selling out. He made a small film his way and now he's an apostate."*
C: Oh, I am the original sell-out. The day I got my first job as a screenwriter there was a big sign on the bulletin board saying: *"Sell out!"* Oh yes, I'm the famous sell-out from UCLA. Dating back to 1961, when I got my job for $300 a week to write *Reflections in a Golden Eye.* There was open resentment. I was making money. And I was sort of doing it. I was already doing what everybody was just talking about. You know, more and more I have gained the power, so to speak, to do what it is I want to do. It's like getting here by going there. It's the ancient dilemma. But I've got to be honest about *Finian's Rainbow.* I wanted to do it. I thought it was a very sweet thing. So I can't say the old thing, "Well, I didn't want to do it. The studio made me do it."

G: *Do you think that the key to the respect of young filmmakers is to bend the System to suit your personal style, as Jean-Luc Godard did when he got Carlo Ponti and Joe Levine to put up $1,000,000 and then made* Contempt *his way?*
C: Yes. But the kids at school are the most narrow-minded of any age group. There are kids at UCLA and USC who are incredible Godard addicts.

G: *Isn't it the nature of the revolutionary to be confident?*
C: Yes, but it's so narrow. I'm trying not to be narrow myself. I'm trying to bounce this whole marvelous thing of making movies off

what I am as a human being. That's why my feelings are very hurt about all of this. First of all, it's very, very difficult to make a good film. When I go to see somebody else's movie, if it was sincere in what it did, I am the best audience in the world. I really am. The only thing I can't stand is when they start getting very pretentious and dishonest. But other than that, I go in with the attitude not of "Show me what you can do," but, "Boy, isn't that nice, I'm going to see a movie." Very few people go to the movies with that attitude.

It's come to the point where I just want to get out altogether. I just want to go do my own thing. And I may do that. I'm fed up. It takes too much out of you. You don't get enough for it, in whatever commodity you're dealing in. I think a lot of people are jealous of me. Basically, my contemporaries. They say, "Well, there he is, twenty-eight, twenty-nine years old, he's got a lot of money and he's making movies."

They wouldn't want it. Not much. They want it. They just think I'm living this golden life and they don't realize that I am really straining and endeavoring to find some honest balance with myself in terms of the work of the future. I am more interested in the films that I'll make when I'm forty than I am now. I'm trying to develop myself. I'm trying not to believe all the baloney publicity written about me. There is no intermediate in this business. They either say, "Here he is, the boy wonder, the best young filmmaker . . . " or they say, "Ah, he's just a load of crap." Why doesn't someone ever say, "Well, he's a promising guy and he's somewhat intelligent and he's really trying and maybe in ten years he might be a really . . . " No one ever says that.

G: *Why did you make* The Rain People?

C: Because nobody else could have made *The Rain People.* Good or bad, it's me, it's my own. If I've got to take raps, I'd rather take raps for my own tastes. That film was a labor of love. We had a very small crew in a remodeled Dodge bus that we rebuilt ourselves and filled with the most advanced motion picture equipment available. I presented the movie to the studio as a *fait accompli.* I told them on a Friday, "Look, I'm starting to shoot on Monday and I need some money and if you don't give it to me, I'll get it from someone else." And they gave me the money. And I never showed them the script.

It's my film, from beginning to end. What it really comes down to is a pregnant woman, sitting in a car, literally walking out on all the responsibilities one associates with a young wife. And putting distance between herself and that. She has a very sympathetic husband. There's no reason she's leaving. He's not ugly, he doesn't have bad breath, he's not intolerable. For her, he is a potentially fine husband. She's a girl you might have known in college, very bright and decent, a good woman.

And she gets married and suddenly starts feeling her personality being eroded, not knowing why. What is she supposed to perform in this thing, marriage? What's her place? A lot of women have a terrible time with this. And she's pregnant. That's the final straw. So all it is, it's a trip she's taking, getting more and more pregnant and getting farther and farther away from her home.

And she picks up a guy in the car. And the guy says to her something like, "Hey, I just have to be dropped off on Union Turnpike because some people are going to take care of me and take me someplace." She drops him off and she realizes the people there who are supposed to take care of him don't want him. So she has to keep him with her in the car. So it's a story of a human being becoming more and more responsible toward another human being. It's like a woman sitting next to the kid she's going to have.

G: *What plans do you have to help George Lucas (another film school graduate) expand his fifteen-minute prize-winning student film, THX-1133-4EB, into a feature film?*

C: It's my most immediate commitment, to produce it this spring, probably for Warners. George was my assistant on *Finian. THX-1133* is a full-length story now about a futuristic society. We're going to go to Japan or somewhere and George is just going to direct it in his own way. It's all based on my strength now. Let's say *Finian's Rainbow* is a big flop. It's going to hurt George more than anybody. I'm giving him my strength. I'm saying, "If you want me, you've got to give George Lucas his break." Well, if suddenly they don't want me, then George has got a problem.

I'm in a position to make lots of money this year. If I would accept two or three of the forty films I've been offered, I could make a million. The word of mouth on *Finian* was very high the last eight months. If the picture does not get very good reviews—and I know it will get some of both—that may tarnish my reputation a lot. (The notices were mostly poor.) I have been very foolish in some people's estimations, but I think, too, very honest, in not having accepted any pictures.

I've been offered a half million dollars for a movie, to direct and write another musical. But I'm not going to do it, because I don't want to do any more. And all I got for writing, directing, and cutting *The Rain People* was $50,000, though it's going to represent a year and a half out of my life. Now what I should have done, which is what everyone else does, is to just keep accepting the big movies before the reviews of the other ones come out. So right now I'd be very securely sitting with a contract for a $500,000 picture and I'd be already committed. Well, I have no commitments.

And in a way I sort of hope it all blows up. I'm disgruntled. I could make a lot of money by just grabbing up three pictures and having writers write them and having cutters cut them, and just— zoom—go right through them. I could pile up about a million dollars, which I would surely like. Because I have no money now whatsoever. I spent it all.

I lived on what I made on *Finian.* How do you think I made *Rain People*? I bought motion picture equipment. I own the $80,000 worth of equipment in that van now. It's mine. I supported that cast and crew of almost twenty for nearly five months. I'm broke today. I am totally at liberty. I've been offered lots of big pictures. And I sort of hoped, I'll have to admit, that one would come along that I felt I could do very well. Again, it's linked to *Finian,* which is sort of dumb. But it is. So after today, I may not get the offers that I was hoping I would. In which case, it may solve some of my problems, because then I don't have to make a choice.

G: *Are you, then, disgruntled because you've somehow got yourself in a position where your reputation rests not on* The Rain People *but on* Finian's Rainbow?

C: Yeah, that's a big part of it. But let's be honest. *Finian* made *The Rain People* possible. The fact that *Finian* was made and everyone at the studio liked it meant that I could then go and do *The Rain People.* Now, I can't do another one. I need a successful picture sooner or later. Look at (Bernardo) Bertolucci, sitting over there in Italy. It takes him four years to get a film. The same thing could happen to me. My only ace in the hole was that I had a big commercial picture and I was considered flexible, which was a tremendous asset.

What I'm thinking of doing, quite honestly, is splitting. I'm thinking of pulling out and making other kinds of films. Cheaper films. Films I can make in 16mm. No one knows whether there's a viable market for that kind of film yet. All I know is that I'm tired. It's not just opening-night jitters. I've been thinking about this now for six months. I'm tired. I never knew that so many people wished you failure. I didn't realize. Let somebody else have the headaches.

G: *You once used the phrase "the Hitler syndrome" to describe how you had joined the establishment and were tunneling away at it from within.*
C: That's what I did. Here I am. But now I don't know if I'm totally satisfied with where it's all led me. I really feel I could make an important film. It may take ten years. But I feel it's possible.

G: *When* The Rain People *comes out in 1969, might it start the cycle again?*
C: *The Rain People* could be an awful picture. It's very experimental. It doesn't protect itself at all. It's not even sensational. No sex. Very sincere. And I don't even know how terrific it is. But it really tries. And I'm tired. I don't want to have to make success. You know, if it means I've got to work on $6000 films in San Francisco, then I guess that's what I have to do. (Pause.) I don't know, I'll probably do another big picture now. I really need the money.

Playboy Interview: Francis Ford Coppola

WILLIAM MURRAY / 1975

COPPOLA: This is my last interview.

PLAYBOY: *Why?*
COPPOLA: I decided recently that enough is enough. Basically, there's only one story I can tell and I've told it. I think it's time I kind of go on my way out of respect for the public.

PLAYBOY: *All right, let's start with your recent Oscar haul for* Godfather II. *How did it feel to walk away with so many awards?*
COPPOLA: Two years ago, I went to the Academy Awards ceremonies feeling blasé, not caring. I thought *Godfather I* would win most of the awards, but how important was the Oscar, anyway? Then it became clear that *Cabaret* was running away with the awards, and I suddenly started wanting to win desperately. When I didn't, I got very depressed. I figured I'd never make another film that would win an Oscar: I was going to go off and make small, personal films, the kind that rarely win awards. I had wanted to leave a winner.

This year, I thought *Chinatown* would clean up. I had two pictures nominated—*Godfather II* and *The Conversation*—and I figured that would split my vote. I was intrigued with the idea of losing twice after coming so close, which might be a record in itself. So when it all happened, I was so elated I didn't know what to do, I never expected

Best Picture. I felt *Godfather II* was too demanding, too complex. But when it won, I felt the members were telling me they appreciated the fact that we'd tried to make a film with integrity.

PLAYBOY: *What did you think when Bert Schneider, the producer of the antiwar documentary* Hearts and Minds, *read a telegram from a Viet Cong representative?*

COPPOLA: Many people voted for *Hearts and Minds* as best documentary, not because it was a great film—it wasn't, particularly—but because of what the film said. And so when Schneider accepted the award, it was certainly appropriate for him to comment on what the film was saying. It wasn't as if they were giving him an award as best tap dancer only to have him turn around and give a political speech. The academy was sanctioning that documentary, was rewarding it for the message it conveyed. So his statement was really a response to that.

PLAYBOY: *The incident caused quite an uproar. How did you personally feel about it?*

COPPOLA: Imagine, in 1975, getting a telegram from a so-called enemy extending friendship to the American people. I mean, after what we did to the Vietnamese people, you'd think they wouldn't forgive us for eight hundred years! Getting this positive human, optimistic message was such a beautiful idea to me—it was overwhelming. If the telegram had said, "You Yankee dogs have been killing us for thirty years and now we've got you, so screw you!" I wouldn't have read it. But it didn't say that.

As for the uproar caused by Frank Sinatra's reading the disclaimer expressing his and Bob Hope's reactions, well, men at that point in their lives can't understand what a message like that really means. They're not interested in the truth; they still think all Communists are bad, less than human. When people are against something, they don't even listen.

PLAYBOY: *Your career as a director has been made by the two* Godfather *movies, and most of the critics seem to have recognized what you were trying to do with them, but none has had a kind word for the novel nor for its author, Mario Puzo. The* New Yorker's *Pauline Kael, in fact, calls the book trash. Could you have made two fine movies out of trash?*

COPPOLA: When I was first offered the project. I started to read the book and I got only about fifty pages into it. I thought it was a popular, sensational novel, pretty cheap stuff. I got to the part about the singer supposedly modeled on Frank Sinatra and the girl Sonny Corleone liked so much because her vagina was enormous—remember that stuff in the book? It never showed up in the movie. Anyway, I said, "My God, what is this—*The Carpetbaggers*?" So I stopped reading it and said, "Forget it."

Four or five months later. I was again offered the opportunity to work on it and by that time I was in dire financial straits with my own company in San Francisco, so I read further. Then I got into what the book is really about—the story of the family, this father and his sons, and questions of power and succession—and I thought it was a terrific story, if you could cut out all the other stuff. I decided it could be not only a successful movie but also a *good* movie. I wanted to concentrate on the central theme; and that's what I tried to do.

So the fact is it wasn't a piece of trash. Like me, Mario went after the money at first. He's very frank about that. But if the two movies are strong, it's because of what Mario originally put in his book that was strong and valid. Mario himself, by the way, doesn't think *The Godfather* is his best book, but it's the only one of his novels that sold really well. I have great respect for Mario. He created the story, he created the characters, even in *Part II*, which I wrote more of than *Part I*. But all the key elements go back to his book.

PLAYBOY: *Did you work together on the screenplay?*
COPPOLA: Never. I would do the first draft and send it to him and he would make corrections and rewrite and change anything he wanted to and send it back to me, and then I'd rework it again, and it went back and forth. We work in totally different ways. He's much lazier than I am: which I think he'd admit. What we mainly have in common is that we both like to play baccarat and shoot dice. I like Mario very much.

PLAYBOY: *Since you weren't a famous director at the time, why did Paramount approach you about making the film?*
COPPOLA: The book hadn't yet made an impression. A lot of directors, including Richard Brooks and Costa Gavras, had already turned it down. At that time, I had an interesting reputation as a director who could

make a film economically. Also I was a writer and I was Italian, so I seemed like an intelligent shot.

PLAYBOY: *Had you heard about* The Godfather *before reading it and hating it?*

COPPOLA: Yes, and it's a strange story. One Sunday afternoon, I was sitting around my home in San Francisco, reading the *New York Times*, and I saw an ad for a new book. Couldn't tell what it was about from the book cover—it looked kind of solemn. I thought it might be an intellectual work by some new Italian author named Mario Puzo, so I clipped the ad. I was just going to inquire about it. Right then, Peter Bart, a friend of mine, came by with someone I'd never met before: Al Ruddy, who later became producer of *The Godfather* but at that time had nothing to do with the project. We started talking and Peter mentioned a book he'd just heard about: *The Godfather*, by Mario Puzo. He explained what it was about. I had no interest in filming a best seller, so I said, "No kidding— I just noticed an ad for it." At that very moment, the phone rang. It was Marlon Brando. I'd contacted him to ask if I might send by the script of *The Conversation*, which I'd written with him in mind. He was just calling to say, "Sure, send the script over."

That all happened in one afternoon. Several months later, Al Ruddy was named producer of *The Godfather*. I received my first offer to direct it and Marlon Brando would shortly have the lead. It still seems bizarre to me that the various elements came together that day in my home.

PLAYBOY: *Once you'd decided to direct the film, how did you get Brando for the title role?*

COPPOLA: I must have interviewed two thousand people. We video-taped every old Italian actor in existence. But it became apparent that the role called for an actor of such magnetism, such charisma, just walking into a room had to be an event. We concluded that if an Italian actor had gotten to be seventy years old without becoming famous on his own, he wouldn't have the air of authority we needed. Robert Evans, who was in charge of production at Paramount, wanted Carlo Ponti, which was an interesting idea: Get someone already important in life; that sort of thinking. But we finally figured that what we had to do was lure the best *actor* in the world. It was that simple. It boiled down to Laurence Olivier or Marlon Brando, who *are* the greatest actors in the world. We went back and forth on it, and I finally called Mario to ask him. He told me that, ironically enough, he'd been thinking of Brando as the God- father all along and had, in fact, written him a letter to that effect over two years before. Brando seemed too young, even to me, but sometimes when you go out on a limb and connect with someone—Mario, in this case—you say, "It's God signaling me." So we narrowed it down to Brando. He had turned down the role in *The Conversation* some months earlier, but after he'd had a chance to read *The Godfather*, he called back and said he was interested, that he thought it was a delicious part—he used that word, delicious.

PLAYBOY: *Were the studio moguls pleased?*
COPPOLA: Hell, no. Ruddy liked Brando, but he said flatly that the studio heads would never buy it. We got in touch with Evans, pitched Brando and listened to him yell at us for being fools. By now, the book was becom- ing more and more successful, and it was outstripping me in terms of my potency as a director. It was getting bigger than I was. And they were start- ing to wonder if they hadn't made a big mistake in choosing me as the director.

Time passed, the book got bigger, the budget increased and I refused to send them any new casting ideas. Besides, Brando, I already had it in my mind that I wanted Al Pacino, Jimmy Caan, Bobby Duvall, and so on. So a big meeting was scheduled with Evans. Stanley Jaffe, who was then the young president of the studio, and assorted lawyers.

Halfway into the meeting, I made another pitch for Brando. Jaffe replied, and these are his exact words, "As president of Paramount Pictures, I assure you that Marlon Brando will never appear in this motion picture and, furthermore, as president of the company, I will no longer allow you to discuss it." Boom. Final. Maybe from his point of view, at that time, it made sense. Paramount, before *Love Story*, had made a number of flops. And Brando's track record was even worse. But I insisted they hear me out, and Evans persuaded Jaffe to give me five minutes. I stood up as if I were a lawyer, pleading for someone's life and went through all the reasons I thought only Brando could play the part. After I'd fin- ished, I pretended to collapse in a heap on the floor.

So Jaffe finally relented, but he gave me certain conditions, the main one being that Brando take a screen test. I'd won. Now all I had to figure was how to get Marlon Brando to take a screen test.

PLAYBOY: *How did you?*
COPPOLA: Well, you have to realize that despite our telephone conversation I was still scared shitless of Brando. So I called him, and said I wanted to explore the role with him. At which point he jumped in and said he wasn't entirely sure he *could* play the role, and if he couldn't, he shouldn't, so why not get together and try it out? Wonderful, I said, let's videotape it. Fine, he said.

PLAYBOY: *So he never really agreed to take the screen test?*
COPPOLA: No. But he's a fantastic guy, so I'm sure if I'd been up front with him and told him the spot I was in, he'd have done it.

PLAYBOY: *How did the non-screen test go?*
COPPOLA: I got a video recorder from some friends and showed up at Brando's house the next morning with a photographer and an Italian barber I'd already picked for the role of Bonasera, the undertaker in the film. I'd dressed him in a black suit and asked him to memorize the speech at the beginning of the movie, where Bonasera asks the Godfather for a favor. But I kept him outside. Brando met us in his living room, wearing a Japanese kimono, hair tied back in a ponytail. I just started video-taping him. He began to slide into character. He took some shoe polish and put it in his hair. His speech changed: "You t'ink I need a mustache?" I was anxious to make an intelligent comment, so I said, "Oh, yeah, my Uncle Louis has a mustache." He dabbed on a phony mustache and, as I video-taped him, he reached for some Kleenex. "I want to be like a bulldog," he mumbled, and stuffed wads of it into his mouth. He kept talking to himself, mumbling, and finally said, "I just wanna improvise." I told my guys to keep quiet: I'd heard that noise bothers him. He always wears earplugs when he's working.

Then, without warning, I ushered in my barber friend, who went up to Brando and launched right into his speech. Brando didn't know what was going on for a moment, but he listened and then just started doing the scene. It was my shot. The thing worked, I had it down on tape. I'd watched forty-seven-year-old Marlon Brando turn into this aging Mafia chief. It was fantastic.

Later, when I showed the tape to Evans and Jaffe, their reaction—and this is where I give them credit—was instantaneous. They both said he was great.

PLAYBOY: *How was it, working with Brando?*

COPPOLA: Well, we all wanted to impress Brando with the fact that each of us was special in some way or other. Jimmy Caan was always trying to make him laugh; Al Pacino would be moody and try to impress him with his intensity, and when Marlon would sit down to talk about Indians or politics, Duvall would sit behind him and do Brando imitations. I got along very well with Marlon. One of the most affectionate, warm men I've ever known. He'd come in late once in a while, but he'd make up for it with his sense of humor.

PLAYBOY: *What's an example of his sense of humor?*

COPPOLA: Besides "mooning" actors on the set? Well, there's this scene in *Godfather I* where they've brought Brando home from the hospital, and the orderlies are supposed to carry him up the stairs in a stretcher. The actors couldn't manage it, so I asked a couple of muscle-bound guys on the set—real physical-fitness types—to do it. They bragged that it would be no problem for them; so while they were off being costumed and made up, Brando got the other guys to load the stretcher with a thousand pounds of lead weights. So these two guys swagger out, pick up the weighted stretcher with Brando on it—and don't let on that they can hardly lift the thing. Well, about four steps up, they both yell, "Jee-sus, does he weigh a ton!" and they drop the stretcher, which breaks up everybody on the set. That sort of thing went on all the time.

PLAYBOY: *Was it all as much fun as that?*

COPPOLA: No, that's hindsight. If you'd checked with the crew while we were filming, they'd have said *The Godfather* was going to be the biggest disaster of all time. *The French Connection* came out while we were filming, and people who'd seen the film and who saw *The Godfather* rushes implied that our film was boring by comparison. There were rumors that I was going to be fired every day. I was trying to save money during that time, sacking out on Jimmy Caan's couch. A bad period for me. I couldn't get to sleep at night. When I did, I had nightmares of seeing Elia Kazan walk onto the set, come up to me and say, "Uh, Francis, I've been asked to. . . . " But Marlon was a great help. When I mentioned the threatening noises, he told me he wouldn't continue the picture if I got fired.

PLAYBOY: *Were you given your head by the studio, were you allowed to improvise, or did you have to stick faithfully to the script?*
COPPOLA: I wasn't given my head, by any means. A lot of the energy that went into the film went into simply trying to convince the people who held the power to let me do the film my way. But there was some spontaneity. For instance, Lenny Montana, who plays Luca Brasi, the *mafioso* in the picture who calls on the Godfather to thank him for being invited to the wedding—that's before he gets his hand pinned to a bar with a knife, of course—is not a professional actor, and he was terrified of playing the scene with Brando. We shot the scene a dozen times, but he froze on every take and forgot his lines. We finally gave up. Later, I wrote a new little scene where he was at the party, before his visit to the Godfather, practicing his speech perfectly over and over. We shot that and kept one of the scenes with Brando where Brasi froze, and it made the whole thing work very well with the context of the story.

As for Brando himself, what an improviser! I told him at one point that I didn't really know how to shoot his final scene, just before he dies. What could we do to make his playing with his grandson believable? He said, "Here's how *I* play with kids," and took an orange peel, cut it into pieces that looked like fangs and slipped them into his mouth.

PLAYBOY: *Orange peel along with the Kleenex?*
COPPOLA: Right. And I thought, what a ridiculous idea. Then suddenly I saw it: Of course! The Godfather dies as a monster! And once I'd seen him with the orange-peel fangs, I knew I could never shoot it any other way.

PLAYBOY: *How about Pacino, who really had the major role in both movies? How was he cast?*
COPPOLA: We were ready to go into production before we found our Michael Corleone. The studio guys wanted Jimmy Caan to play him.

I love Jimmy, but I felt he'd be wrong for Michael—and perfect for Sonny. Other people suggested Robert Redford, Warren Beatty, Jack Nicholson, Ryan O'Neal. But all I could see was Al Pacino's face in that camera. I couldn't get him out of my head. Even when I read the book. I kept seeing him as Michael. I nearly got fired over insisting on him, but it worked out in the end.

PLAYBOY: *That's an understatement. After* The Godfather *went on to unparalleled success, what got you interested in doing a sequel?*
COPPOLA: Initially, the idea of a sequel seemed horrible to me. It sounded like a tacky spin off, and I used to joke that the only way I'd do it was if they'd let me film *Abbott and Costello Meet the Godfather*—that would have been fun. Then I entertained some Russian film executives who were visiting San Francisco and they asked me if I was going to make *The Godfather II.* That was the first time I heard the phrase used; I guess you could say I stole the title from the Russians.

In short, it seemed like such a terrible idea that I began to be intrigued by the thought of pulling it off. Simple as that. Sometimes I sit around thinking I'd like to get a job directing a TV soap opera, just to see if I could make it the most wonderful thing of its kind ever done. Or I imagine devoting myself to directing the plays of a cub-scout troop and having it be the most exciting theater in the country. You know that feeling when something seems so outrageous you just have to do it? That's what happened to me.

Then after I started thinking about the idea, when I considered that we'd have most of the same actors, the scenes we might be able to develop in depth, I started feeling it really might be something innovative.

PLAYBOY: *Do you, like some critics, think* Godfather II *is a better film than* Godfather I?
COPPOLA: The second film goes much further than the first one. It's much more ambitious and novelistic in its structure. If you get off on the wrong foot with it, I can imagine that it would be like a Chinese water torture to sit through it. But it's a more subtle movie, with its own heartbeat. And it was very tough on some of the actors, especially Al Pacino.

PLAYBOY: *Is it true that you had to stop shooting for two or three weeks when you were on location in Santo Domingo because Pacino was exhausted?*
COPPOLA: Yes. The role of Michael is a very strange and difficult one and it put a terrific strain on him. It was like being caught in a kind of vise. In the first picture, he went from being a young, slightly insecure, naive, and brilliant young college student to becoming this horrible Mafia killer. In *Godfather II* he's the same man from beginning to end— working on a much more subtle level, very rarely having a big climactic scene where an actor can unload, like blowing the spittle out of the tube of a trombone. The entire performance had to be kind of vague and so understated that, as an actor, you couldn't really be sure what you were doing. You had the tremendous . . . pressure of not knowing whether your performance would have a true, cumulative effect, whether you were creating a monster or just being terrible. The load on Al was terrific and it really ran him down physically.

PLAYBOY: *You obviously had a lot more control over* Godfather II *than* Godfather I, *didn't you?*
COPPOLA: Absolutely. I had to fight a lot of wars the first time around. In *Godfather II*, I had no interference. Paramount backed me up in every decision. The film was my baby and they left it in my hands.

PLAYBOY: *It would have been stupid of them not to, after all the money the first one made.*
COPPOLA: But Paramount was fully aware of some of the chances I was taking and went along. I guess they had to, but they did.

PLAYBOY: *One of the most important areas you explore in* Godfather II *is the connection between Mafia operations and some of our legitimate big-business interests. Are you saying that some corporations are no better and no worse than organized crime?*
COPPOLA: Right from the very beginning it became clear, as I was doing my research, that though the Mafia was a Sicilian phenomenon, there was no way it could really have flowered except in the soil of America. America was absolutely ripe for the Mafia. Everything the Mafia believed in and was set up to handle—absolute control, the carving out of territories, the rigging of prices and the elimination of competition—

everything was here. In fact, the corporate philosophy that built some of our biggest industries and great personal fortunes was a Mafia philosophy. So when those Italians arrived here, they found themselves in the perfect place.

It became clear to me that there was a wonderful parallel to be drawn, that the career of Michael Corleone was the perfect metaphor for the new land. Like America, Michael began as a clean, brilliant young man endowed with incredible resources and believing in a humanistic idealism. Like America, Michael was the child of an older system, a child of Europe. Like America, Michael was an innocent who had tried to correct the ills and injustices of his progenitors. But then he got blood on his hands. He lied to himself and to others about what he was doing and why. And so he became not only the mirror image of what he'd come from but worse. One of the reasons I wanted to make *Godfather II* is that I wanted to take Michael to what I felt was the logical conclusion. He wins every battle; his brilliance and his resources enable him to defeat all his enemies. I didn't want Michael to die. I didn't want Michael to be put into prison. I didn't want him to be assassinated by his rivals. But, in a bigger sense, I also wanted to destroy Michael. There's no doubt that by the end of this picture, Michael Corleone, having beaten everyone, is sitting there alone, a living corpse.

PLAYBOY: *Is that your metaphor for America today?*
COPPOLA: Unlike America, Michael Corleone is doomed. There's no way that man is ever going to change. I admit I considered some upbeat touch at the end, like having his son turn against him to indicate he wouldn't follow in that tradition, but honesty—and Pacino—wouldn't let me do it. Michael is doomed. But I don't at all feel that America is doomed. I thought it was healthy to make this horror-story statement— as a warning, if you like—but, as a nation, we don't have to go down that same road, and I don't think we will.

PLAYBOY: *A number of critics feel that you and others—including, perhaps,* Playboy, *with its series on organized crime—helped romanticize the Mafia in America. How do you respond to that?*
COPPOLA: Well, first of all, the Mafia was romanticized in the book. And I was filming that book. To do a film about my real opinion of the

Mafia would be another thing altogether. But it's a mistake to think I was making a film about the Mafia. *Godfather I* is a romance about a king with three sons. It is a film about power. It could have been the Kennedys. The whole idea of a family living in a compound—that was all based on Hyannisport. Remember, it wasn't a documentary about Mafia chief Vito Genovese. It was Marlon Brando with Kleenex in his mouth.

PLAYBOY: *Where do the films depart most radically from the truth?*
COPPOLA: Where you get into the mythic aspects of the Godfather, the great father who is honorable and will not do business in drugs. The character was a synthesis of Genovese and Joseph Profaci, but Genovese ordered his soldiers not to deal in drugs while he himself did just that on the side; Profaci was dishonorable at a lot of levels. The film Godfather would never double-cross anyone, but the real godfathers double-crossed people over and over.

PLAYBOY: *Still, you won't deny that, whatever your intentions,* Godfather I *had the effect of romanticizing the Mafia?*
COPPOLA: I felt I was making a harsh statement about the Mafia and power at the end of *Godfather I* when Michael murders all those people, then lies to his wife and closes the door. But obviously, many people didn't get the point I was making. And so if the statement I was trying to make was outbalanced by the charismatic aspects of the characters, I felt *Godfather II* was an opportunity to rectify that. The film is pretty rough. The essence of *Godfather I* is all Mario Puzo's creation, not mine. With *Godfather II*, which I had a greater part in writing, I emerged a bit to comment on the best film.

But the fact still may be that people *like* Marlon and Jimmy and Al too much. If you were taken inside Adolf Hitler's home, went to his parties and heard his stories, you'd probably have liked him. If I made a film of Hitler and got some charismatic actor to play him, people would say I was trying to make him a good human being. He wasn't of course, but the greatest evil on earth is done by sane human beings who are miserable in themselves. My point is that you can't make a movie about what it's like inside a Mafia family without their seeming to be quite human.

PLAYBOY: *What about those who say* not *that the Mafia is romanticized but that it simply doesn't exist?*

COPPOLA: When people say the Mafia doesn't exist, in a way they're right. When they say it does exist, they're right, too. You have to look at it with different eyes: it's not a secret Italian organization, as it's portrayed. The most powerful man in the Mafia at one time wasn't Italian—he was a Jew. Meyer Lansky became powerful, because he was the best at forging their common interests—that's just good business.

PLAYBOY: *Except that, as far as we know, AT & T hasn't killed anyone in pursuit of its business.*

COPPOLA: Who says? Who says?

PLAYBOY: *Have you got something on AT & T?*

COPPOLA: AT & T I don't know about but ATT in Chile? I wouldn't bet my life that it hadn't. And it's not just business. How about the Yablouski murders in that coal miners' union? That was just the union equivalent of a Mafia hit. How about politics? Assassination of a president is the quickest way to bring about lasting and enormous social change. What's the difference between the United States putting a guy like Trujillo in power so our companies can operate in the Dominican Republic and the Mafia's handing the Boston territory to one of its *capos*? Then, after twenty years, either guy gets a little uppity and either organization feels free to knock him off.

PLAYBOY: *Do you have any stories to tell about how the* real *Mafia reacted to the* Godfather *films?*

COPPOLA: No.

PLAYBOY: *And you wouldn't tell if you had any?*

COPPOLA: No, I *would*. But the fact is I got some terrific advice from Mario Puzo. He told me that, in his experience, Mafia guys loved the glamor of show business and that, if you let them, they'd get involved. So Mario told me that I'd probably be contacted and when I was, I should refuse to open up to them. I shouldn't let them feel they could visit me. Because if there's one thing about them, it's that they respect that attitude. If you turn them off, they won't intrude into your life. Al Ruddy, the producer, was out having dinner with a lot of them, but I wouldn't participate in any way whatsoever with them.

Funny thing is, I've never been very interested in the Mafia—even though some important guys in the Mob have the same name as I do. "Trigger Mike" Coppola was one of Vito Genovese's lieutenants, I think. Terrible man.

PLAYBOY: *Any relation?*
COPPOLA: You mean Uncle Mike? No, of course not. Coppola is a common Italian name.

PLAYBOY: *One Hollywood person who has been mentioned in connection with the Mafia is Frank Sinatra. How are your relations with him, considering that most people believe he was the model for Johnny Fontane, the singer-actor in* The Godfather?
COPPOLA: I met Sinatra several times before filming started. They were very friendly meetings, since I never liked the idea of exploiting a fictionalization of a man, any man—and I told him so. I let him know that I didn't like that part of the book and that I'd minimize it in the film. Sinatra was very appreciative. Then he turned to me and said, "I'd like to play the Godfather."

PLAYBOY: *What?*
COPPOLA: It's true. He said, "Let's you and me buy this goddamned book and make it ourselves." I said, "Well, it sounds great, but. . . ."

PLAYBOY: *Didn't Sinatra yell at Puzo once when they met in a restaurant?*
COPPOLA: That incident was caused by some guy trying to make points with Sinatra by introducing the two of them very provocatively. Puzo never meant to embarrass him in person, and he told me he thought Sinatra behaved very understandably, considering the way they were introduced. But the fact remains that Mario, who is a very fine writer, was going broke with several good novels out, so he set out to write the biggest best seller in history. He was going to do anything he had to in order to get off the merry-go-round. So he wrote the perfect commercial book. And exploiting celebrities like Sinatra was

something he felt he had to do. In the film, the Sinatra character plays a very small role. I'd have cut it out altogether if I'd had the power.

PLAYBOY: Godfather II *was supposedly cut down from almost six hours. What did we miss?*
COPPOLA: My heart was really in the Little Italy sequences, in the old streets of New York, the music, all that turn-of-the-century atmosphere. I had great scenes in the script that we couldn't include in the movie: There was one where Enrico Caruso showed up in the neighborhood and sang *Over There* to get guys to enlist for World War One. I had scenes of Italians building the subways, of young Vito courting his girl and joining his friends for music and mandolins and wine. . . . But it all got too long and too expensive.

PLAYBOY: *Have you ever considered recutting the movies into one giant film?*
COPPOLA: It's an exciting thought, and it's just what I plan to do, believe it or not. In two years, I'm going to take both pictures, look over all the outtakes and recut them any way I want to, into *one* film. You don't often do that, because there's a certain inertia: once a film is done, it's done, and you tend not to want to open things up again.

I've had an idea for a film I want to make, which I'd call *Remake*. I'd buy a film—any film—decide what I felt about it, then recut it, maybe shoot some things and make it into a whole new work.

PLAYBOY: *Some critics have charged that in cutting* Godfather II, *you gave the picture a jerky, disjointed quality.*
COPPOLA: Oh, they're full of baloney. They think a movie has to be what the last four movies were. There isn't a critic out there who knows what he's talking about. There may be three. Most are special interest critics.

PLAYBOY: *Meaning?*
COPPOLA: Meaning that there's a lot of extortion and blackmail practiced by critics. A lot of them force the film maker to participate in certain things that accrue to the critics' advantage under the implied threat of a bad review.

PLAYBOY: *Can you be more specific?*
COPPOLA: No, because of course I'm not saying they're all that way. But suffice it to say that if this sort of extortion continues, it may blow up in the biggest scandal the field of criticism has known. It's corrupt right down to the bottom. And I'm speaking as one who has enjoyed generally good favor from the critics.

PLAYBOY: *Which critics do you admire?*
COPPOLA: Pauline Kael of the *New Yorker.* When she writes about a film, she does it in depth. When I make a bad picture, I expect her to blast me higher than a kite, and I'll be grateful for that. I like *Time's* Jay Cocks, who's a friend; Steven Farber and *Playboy's* Bruce Williamson, who have liked some of my films; and Stanley Kauffmann of the *New Republic,* who often hasn't.

PLAYBOY: *Your last three films.* Godfather I *and* II *and* The Conversation, *have been negative. Does that mean you've become more of a pessimist about life?*
COPPOLA: Really, I'm not a negative person. Just the opposite. Starting now, I'm going to try to let the other side of me be more evident in my movies. It's funny, but I've noticed that very often film makers reflect things in their movies that are the opposite of what they really feel. I know some men whose films are highly sexual but who lead very tame home lives.

PLAYBOY: *Why, in both* Godfather *films, are your female characters so submissive and acquiescent?*
COPPOLA: That was how the women were represented in the original book and, from what I know, it was the role of women in the Mafia fabric. In *Godfather II,* I was interested in developing a more contemporary, political view of women in the person of his wife, Kay and in her symbolic statement of power when she had her unborn son killed.

PLAYBOY: *If Kay was such a liberated and defiant woman, why did it take her so long to leave Michael when she was no longer happy with him?*
COPPOLA: It may seem like a long time, but actually they're together only six or seven years. How many people do we know who stay together

unhappily for fifteen years or more before they finally split? Also, during the fifties, there were a lot of forces that tended to keep men and women together way beyond the point when they should have parted. Think of how many husbands have kept their wives and held their families together by promising that things would change just as soon as they became vice-presidents or had a hundred-thousand dollars in the bank or closed the big deal. I've strung my own wife along for thirteen years by telling her that as soon as I was done with this or that project, I'd stop working so hard, and we'd live a more normal life. I mean, that's the classic way husbands lie. Often the lies aren't even intentional. And it's easy to string a woman along for years by doing exactly that. Michael lies to Kay in that way and she believes him at first—because she wants to believe him.

PLAYBOY: *Why do people tend to get sucked in by their own lies? Do they just sell out to the system?*

COPPOLA: Well, people like myself, who decide that it's necessary to work within a system in order to be able either to change it or eventually to go off on their own to subsidize the kind of work they believe in, inevitably become changed by the process, if they go along with it. I know a lot of bright young writers and directors in Hollywood who are very successful—some of them I gave jobs to four or five years ago—and they're making a lot of money; but they're no longer talking about the things they used to talk about. Their conversation now is all about deals, about what's going to sell and what isn't. And they rave about their new cars and their new hundred-thousand dollar houses. They don't even see or hear the changes in themselves. They've become the very people they were criticizing three years ago. Like Michael, they've become their fathers.

PLAYBOY: *You don't think the same thing could happen to you?*

COPPOLA: Sure, it could happen to me. One of the reasons I live here and not in Los Angeles is that I'm trying to keep my bearings. I have nothing against Los Angeles: it's a terrific center of talent right now, with the finest actors and certainly the best musicians and top people in every area, but there's always been a kind of collective madness that takes place in Hollywood, and it's very attractive and seductive, but you could lose yourself in it.

PLAYBOY: *With the power and authority you wield, do you find it hard to keep a grip on your ego?*

COPPOLA: Well, I'm thirty-six now, but I directed my first play in 1956—which is nearly twenty years ago—so I haven't been overwhelmed by power overnight. But sure, everyone has that problem. Let me give you an example: Al Ruddy, who's a nice guy but who's more of a wheeler-dealer than I am, used to walk onto the *Godfather* set now and then to suggest that an actor wear a hat for such and such a scene. I'd say, "No, I already thought this scene out, thanks, anyway." And no sooner would the sentence be out of my mouth than I'd think, fuck it, he's right, the actor *should* be wearing a hat. But I wouldn't or couldn't change it. If it had been George Lucas or someone like that, I'd have accepted the suggestion. But there are some people you can't take criticism from, perhaps because you feel threatened.

PLAYBOY: *How would you feel threatened?*

COPPOLA: The artist's worst fear is that he'll be exposed as a sham. I've heard it from actors, directors, everyone. I remember hearing Peter Sellers say, "Some day they're going to uncover me and realize I'm just a fake." Deep down we're all living with the notion that our success is beyond our ability. In the last couple of years, I've grown more confident that I have ideas, that I can solve problems. That's as much as I'll give myself for now.

PLAYBOY: *Do you ever feel uneasy about the power you have to influence other people's minds through film—or in other ways?*

COPPOLA: I had a thought about that, a little fantasy that goes like this: I'm getting to be an influential person in San Francisco; what if I and five other powerful guys with cigars got together in a smoke-filled room to decide who would be the next mayor of San Francisco? We do it because we're good guys, and we really want the city to be wonderful for everybody. Then I thought, what's the difference between five good guys holding that kind of power and five bad guys? Just good intentions, and intentions can be corrupted. And it's not just, say, in the political field. Let me make a statement about power: from now on, I'm determined to give tremendous thought to the impact any project

I undertake will have on the public. It may sound wordy, it may sound obvious, but very few film makers ever really do that.

PLAYBOY: *Did you think that way about* The Godfather?

COPPOLA: No. How could I? I've spoken about the circumstances surrounding that project. But if the picture seems to some to be irresponsible because it celebrates violence, that was never my intent. In fact, there's very little actual violence in the film. It occurs very quickly. It's just that the violence happens to characters you like. If I were to roast fifty people alive in *The Towering Inferno,* it would be less horrible than shooting up a guy you've come to know and believe in. I once saw a fistfight in a New York restaurant that was modest by movie standards, but I'd never seen anything so frightening; they were real people.

PLAYBOY: *How will this determination to consider public impact effect your next film?*

COPPOLA: My next project is going to be delicate in that context. It's going to be a film about Vietnam, although it won't necessarily be political—it will be about war and the human soul. But it's dangerous, because I'll be venturing into an area that is laden with so many implications that if I select some aspects and ignore others, I may be doing something irresponsible. So I'll be thinking hard about it.

People are hungry for film now, susceptible to it because it reaches them on an emotional level. We're living in a time when things are changing quickly: Zip, there went the Catholic Church; zoom, that was the traditional family unit you just saw go by. People aren't sure of what they are feeling or what to believe in, so film can be a very influential medium now. Millions of people watched *The Godfather* around the world, each person spending three hours in a dark theater. Imagine how valuable that time with them is. It's priceless, and yet a film maker has it. I think that's an extraordinary thing.

PLAYBOY: *Do you feel that Hollywood directors in the past have been irresponsible in propagating stereotypes, in exerting the wrong kind of influence over the public?*

COPPOLA: Perhaps to some extent; but American films have followed the stereotypes, not set them. I read somewhere recently that the American film was responsible for our view of what an Indian was. But it isn't. The American film merely echoed and amplified the image that already existed in the national consciousness. It reinforced attitudes people already had about Indians when they first came here. The people who write films and the people who direct them have also been programmed. That isn't to say we shouldn't have the courage to try to break the mold, but it takes more courage and more originality than most people have.

PLAYBOY: *Isn't Hollywood much more open to new ideas, new ways of doing things than it used to be?*
COPPOLA: Yes, but it's chaotic. There's no leadership, maybe because the country itself has no leadership, either. Making movies is a great, complex, writhing crap game. No one is running anything and the only priority is the one that's become uppermost in America today: to make a profit.

PLAYBOY: *When you started out in your career, did you have to do work you were ashamed of, just to make a profit?*
COPPOLA: Well, I've done some stuff that hasn't worked out too well. But I never took on anything with the attitude that it was going to be terrible. It may have turned out that way, but I thought it was great while I was doing it. I was worried about certain films, though. I was worried while I was making them that things were going wrong and I didn't have the power to change them. During the shooting of *Finian's Rainbow* at Warner's years ago, I was brought in to direct a project that had already been cast and structured. I was also working in a big studio, in a methodology I didn't understand very well and over which I had no control. I'd express some doubts about the way things were going, and the people around me would say, "It's going great." I'll never get myself caught in that kind of situation again, because I now surround myself with people whose taste I respect and who have the right to hit all the sour notes they want. We had no sour notes on *Finian's Rainbow;* everyone kept saying how terrific everything was all the time. They were sincere; their motives were pure. But today I try to work with people who won't hestitate to say, "We're making a mistake." And if after thinking about it I agree with them, we stop and make changes—the

one good thing I'd say about the old Hollywood, however autocratic and restrictive it may have been, is that you really got opinions from people who weren't afraid to give them and you always knew where you stood.

PLAYBOY: *You mean from men such as Harry Cohn and Louis B. Mayer, the men who used to run the studios?*

COPPOLA: Yes, and Darryl Zanuck and David Selznick and all the others. People weren't afraid to back up their opinions. Today everything is very confused and people kind of float around amorphously. Nobody backs up his hunches. There are a handful of directors today who have total authority and deserve it. And then there are a lot of other directors who really ought to be working with strong producers and strong writers, but they all think they're Stanley Kubrick. The auteur theory is fine, but to exercise it you have to qualify, and the only way you can qualify is by having *earned* the right to have control, by having turned out a series of really incredibly good films. Some men have it, and some men don't. I don't feel that one or two hits or one or two beautiful films entitle any-one to that much control. A lot of very promising directors have been destroyed by it. It's a big dilemma, of course, because, unfortunately, the authority these days is almost always shared with people who have no business being producers and studio executives. With one or two exceptions, there's no one running the studios who's qualified, either; so you have a vacuum, and the director has to fill it.

PLAYBOY: *Then Hollywood today isn't as good a place to make movies as it was when it was dominated by the big studios?*

COPPOLA: There are maybe ten thousand of the finest actors in the world living in Hollywood, and there are fine writers and all kinds of talented people, but it's a sad, pent-up place. The actors are frustrated; they don't feel they have any place to work. When good actors say work, they mean work that uses the best of their talents, that uses them fully and creatively. And the truth of the matter is that there is nowhere to work that way these days. So they become petulant, they become dep-ressed, and they hate themselves for it. I feel that the film business today, with its tremendous potential to make profits, with a large new audience of people all over the world who love to go to the movies, should be providing not only a product, something it can sell, but a hospitable place for creative people to work. Now at a time when we stand on the eve of incredible profits, to think that no money, no percentage of any money, is being used to provide a really stimulating place for actors and writers and directors to work, that all the energy is going into nothing but deal making, well, that's incredible to me. L.A. ought to be the acting and theater and film capital of the world, but nothing is happening.

PLAYBOY: *Do you think you can make something happen with your own company?*
COPPOLA: What I'm talking about can't be accomplished by a little company like mine. It would take a major company to really grab this thing by the tail.

PLAYBOY: *There are rumors that you actually* were *offered control of a major studio.*
COPPOLA: Really? Where'd you hear that?

PLAYBOY: *From several people. Is it true?*
COPPOLA: Let's say that I was approached by certain people and there were discussions, but that's all. Look, I must be honest with you. I've just finished a film and I'm thirty-six. I have a good future in front of me, and I'm trying to figure out what's the most exciting, positive way to go on working in films, and taking over a studio might have been a way. But as I see things now, that would take so much energy that I'm not sure it'd be worth it. I mean, if I were running a studio, it might take me hundred B.T.U.s worth of energy to bend something a quarter inch; if I stay independent and use my own resources, those hundred B.T.U.s could bend something a foot. I think events can make the decision for you, though. If someone were to come up to me and offer me the most incredible film company in history and say, "Do what you want, we're behind you," then I'd interpret that as a cosmic indication that I should do it.

But look: the average executive of a movie studio may make one hundred and fifty thousand dollars a year, and have a corresponding power over his company. As a film artist, I make much, much more than that and, consequently, have that much more power over my company. I've already made a million dollars for directing a film.

So what do I do—ask for a million and a half? Perhaps the wisest thing to do is to use all my energies to make a film that grosses some stupendous amount, then go out and buy a major company and change it from the top. But I don't know. As soon as you become that big, you get absorbed.

PLAYBOY: *You mean absorbed into a corporate structure?*

COPPOLA: Yes, and not just in the movie business. Traditionally, our greatest heroes have been creators and inventors. A hundred years ago, what we paraded before the world was something called Yankee ingenuity. Every one of our great cartels and corporations was started by—that is the original impulse came from—an Andrew Carnegie or a Thomas Edison or a Henry Ford, guys who used their inventive genius to create something better. And we made the best products in the world! And what those men created evolved into cartels, with their rules of property and profit. By the forties, after the United States had demonstrated that the ultimate result of this ingenuity was our emergence as the most powerful nation in the world, we were being run by huge, entrenched institutions completely hostile to that kind of inventiveness. By 1941, Henry Ford couldn't have built his cheap car. We might have *had* a Henry Ford in the forties. His name was Preston Tucker.

Tucker designed a car that could be built for a fraction of the kind of money the major companies were spending on their new models. It was a safe car, a revolutionary car in terms of engineering, and it was a beautiful car. In every way, it was a much better machine than the stuff the major companies were offering, the companies created by Ford and the others. But Tucker was called a fraud, and he was destroyed. If he were alive today, he'd be hired by one of the major car companies and his inventions would be shelved or filtered out to the public as the company deemed economically prudent. Not to benefit the public but the company, and only the company. I'm going to make a film of Tucker's story someday.

PLAYBOY: *Many of the opinions you've expressed to us, including this one, reflect the antiestablishment views of the radical movement. Are you politically active?*

COPPOLA: No. Politically, no one knows what I am, including me. I have a lot of very articulate, superradical friends who criticize me for living in a big, expensive house; they apparently believe the world would be a better place if I moved into a shack. I notice, though, that, like me, they send their children to private schools. You see, I believe *everybody* should live in a nice house. I also believe in public education; until last year, I had my own kids in public schools, but I decided I wasn't going to sacrifice my children to my egalitarian ideal. The public schools in this city and all over the country are bad. I refuse to make my children guinea pigs to some social ideal, so I'm not going to send them to our crappy schools anymore. The whole school system has to be changed in this country. Just believing in certain things or giving your own money away isn't going to change anything.

PLAYBOY: *What have you done yourself to help bring about change?*
COPPOLA: In a self-sacrificing, personal way, probably nothing. Look, if someone announced next year that everyone should put all of his money in escrow and that we'd elect a board of men and women guided by the highest humantistic principles to administer the money to build homes and parks and educational centers for everyone, I'd do it in a minute. A lot of people would. But if half of the people in the world gave up their money and half didn't, the givers would be exploited by the keepers. Wealth is the only protection in a society that works which probably keeps out some people who can't afford the stakes, but it also attracts some people who can't afford it but play anyway.

Second the players do nothing. You have no option, no decision to make. You exert no control over the playing, the winning or the losing.

That simplifies the game—in the sense that somebody who has never heard of baccarat can walk in and the housemen will see that he gets the same break as a guy who's been playing for years. Fine. But I don't like games in which I can't have some opportunity to outthink the house.

Don't sneer at slot machines. They are the single most profitable form of gambling in Las Vegas. Although not for you.

Of the 684 million bucks that Vegas casinos grossed in 1974, more than $170 million came from slots. That's a hell of a lot of nickels, dimes, and quarters.

For pure entertainment, nothing beats the slots—if only because they certainly can't be considered gambling. No one knows for sure what the house percentage is, but some reasonable estimates can be offered.

It is highest at the big casinos. The casino people know that a low percentage—meaning relatively large payoffs—will attract volume, and that's the name of their game. So expect casino slots to keep between 8 and 12 percent of everything you deposit with them.

Slot players being a breed apart, many of them want to burn their dough at twice the normal rate; so they play two machines at once. In recognition of this, rumor has it that a high-paying slot will squat between two miserly machines set perhaps to keep 15 percent of what you drop in them. But that's only tumor.

It does seem to be true that the slots in gas stations and other retail places are rougher, keeping as much as 40 percent. Those at the airport aren't *that* bad, but they aren't good, either.

So, if you're going to play the slots, or if your wife is, play at the casinos. And don't sneer at them. They can be fun. For a while.

But I can't see standing in front of a machine hour after hour after hour. I mean, lots of people do it, but I don't understand it.

On the other hand, at some point during your visit invest a buck in a dollar slot or four halves in a fifty-cent slot. You might be the one to hit.

But then *stop*.

The machine doesn't owe you anything. And there is no mechanical certainty that because you see a hundred people put money into a machine, it's overdue.

When those wheels spin around, it's a fresh start every time.

Tell your wife or loved one to invest ten nickels in a slot or an equivalent unit of speculation. If the machine doesn't cough up something, she should try another one. Because, as I said, some machines do seem to pay better than others.

And at least once, throw a couple of bucks into one of the big slots. A couple of months ago, a guy did that with three silver dollars in the three-line, four-reel progressive slot at the MGM Grand. And he hit—for $62,500.

So it can happen. But don't chase it. It doesn't pay. Except, of course, as entertainment.

If you believe in miracles, head for the keno lounge. You'll be bucking a basic house edge of only 25 percent. True, there is always the chance that you may hit for the twenty-five thousand dollar jackpot. But it is remote, to put it kindly.

You get even money on a five Spot win and your chances are one in twenty. An eight Spot ticket is a 1-in-7-1,000 shot. And to hit the ten Spot; you're bucking odds of one in nine million.

Play keno because the keno runner has nice legs. Or play because the seats in the keno lounge are comfortable, the drinks are free or your favorite numerologist told you that this is your lucky day.

Don't play to win. But invest—correction, speculate—with a couple of bucks, just to see what happens.

Ever since the World Series of Poker began to be played in Las Vegas, there's been a slow but steady increase in the visibility of house-run poker games.

They are generally stud, five, six or seven cards. The stakes cover the spectrum from nickel ante, fifty cents to open, three-dollar-maximum bet, to quarter ante, two bucks to open, five-buck maximum, and on up to an occasional, and rather stratospheric game at the Tropicana at four hundred dollars and eight hundred dollars a card.

Most games are table stakes, and for the big ones, you better have five grand or more to put on the table. But, at every level, the players are probably better than the ones back home. Local people have more time to play, whether they're salesmen or professional gamblers, because the games go on and on.

The house cut is limited to a percentage of the ante or a percentage of the pot.

This may seem trivial, but it inexorably adds up to the house's profit.

Shills are usually present in the smaller games and often an off-duty dealer, or maybe a dealer who's on his break will sit in.

That's probably the ultimate tribute. You don't see stickmen from the crap tables rolling or blackjack dealers trying to beat a *compadre*. Only at poker, which says it's all about the fascination of the game.

I don't have any inside tips to offer. Poker has to be played for stakes that are significant to you without being fatal if you lose. There's no point to playing in a small game if your bank roll is a couple of grand. Purists will dispute this, claiming that the logic, the insight, the inherent excitement of poker are the same at all stakes.

Maybe so. But the bluff is basic to poker, as is the principle that you make guys pay if they chase. Both are sensitive to the willingness, and

WILLIAM MURRAY/1975   43

therefore the ability of a player to pay. And if a guy's wallet is choking on C-notes, he isn't going to run from a two-dollar raise.

Shills and local nonpro players tend to play a tight game. A table of seven players is usually cut to three, maybe four players after the first cards are dealt.

A friend recently played in a small game at the Tropicana. It was pushing four in the morning and his luck had been soso. Then came the hand. At seven-card stud, he was dealt the jack, queen, king of spades. Then came a couple of small cards and the ten of spades. His seventh was the ace of spades.

It was the first time in his life he had bought a royal straight flush. Unfortunately, nobody called his bet and there was no reason to show his hand.

With forgivable pride, he turned his cards over, pointing to his wondrous hand. Instantly, two players chorused. "Nobody paid to see!" His chagrin at the *gaffe* was relieved when the dealer said, with appropriate awe, that he had never seen a hand like it in ten years of dealing.

As it happens, I am nuts about poker. But about the only times I get to play are those four, five or six times a year when my wife and I have an argument. In the wake of a domestic squabble, some guys go out and get drunk, some go on the prowl for other women. I play poker, in the biggest game I can find. Sometimes I come home excited and sometimes I come home chagrined. That's poker.

Again, unless you are an excellent poker player, don't try the game in Vegas. And never, never play in a game you can't afford, because, of all the casino games, poker will exhaust the undercapitalized player by far the fastest.

There's just no way around the disadvantage of valuing the money you bet more than the other players do. You'll start scared and end skinned.

Gambling is a part of the soul of Vegas. But gambling is only part of the entertainment, of the total appeal of Vegas. Enjoy the golf, the tennis, the great food and plush hotels. Enjoy your stay.

Gamble—but just for the fun of it.

Coppola's Cinematic *Apocalypse* Is Finally at Hand

TONY CHIU/1979

In the weeks leading up to the Wednesday premiere of Francis Coppola's over-budget, overdue and, some say, over-previewed film about the Vietnam war, many close associates of the project, as well as their families and friends, have taken to wearing olive-drab baseball caps inscribed "Apocalypse Now: Release with Honor."

The filmmaker himself refuses to; Mr. Coppola sees no reason to whistle in the dark even though his repeated screenings of *Apocalypse Now* as a "work-in-progress," most notably at the Cannes Film Festival, where it shared the award for Best Film, resulted in some unfavorable preliminary reviews. "People don't understand—I'm very pleased with it," he says. "It's taken a long, long time, but I feel I've staged a real piece of work about an important American era. I think it's a monument."

These days, monuments come dear. Of the film's $30.5-million final budget, Mr. Coppola was forced to personally cover some $16 million, in the end offering as collateral all that his *Godfather* successes had purchased. But the forty-year-old filmmaker insists, "I'm not worried about the money. I know it could go either way, but it's not like I might lose my kids. Even if I were wiped out, I could get a job to direct a picture tomorrow for a million dollars. Does this mean I'm going to have to do Goldie Hawn movies? Maybe that'd be exciting—really. So I am not brooding at all.

From the *New York Times*, 12 August 1979, Sec. 2, p. 1+. Reprinted by permission.

"I just hope people will give *Apocalypse* a chance, will know that they're going to see a heavier picture, and won't sit there with their girlfriend saying, 'Aw, this is asking too much of me, let's go catch *Animal House* again.' "

In a society that pays at least lip service to the virtue of modesty, such bravado can provoke hostility—as well as sarcastic nicknames like the current "Ayatollah Coppola."

The stately three-storied gabled Georgian house, flanked on three sides by a fifteen-foot-deep porch, sits north of San Francisco in the sunny Napa Valley. The hum of traffic from the road a half-mile away is sponged up by intervening vineyards; it is so still the metal windchime hanging from the magnolia tree twenty-five yards distant can be heard inside.

Downstairs, the large rooms with chest-high hardwood wainscoting are hung with Japanese prints, as well as Chagall and Picasso lithographs. The furniture is pricey but subdued; here, the lord of the manor's five gilded Oscar statuettes would stick out like hot dogs at a four-star restaurant. Yet, this is a country retreat (there is another residence in San Francisco, near his offices), and any air of formality is dispelled by little touches: notes for family and guests casually taped to the wide-open front door, issues of *Popular Science* in the living room and, in the airy kitchen, a vintage Wurlitzer jukebox housing two dozen eclectic 78s—press button No. 4 and Enrico Caruso croons "O Sole Mio."

Upstairs, half the master bedroom has for the last few weeks been usurped by a rented hospital bed. In it is Francis Coppola. "I've heard that I'm recovering from a heroin problem," he says with a grin, adjusting the traction weight he straps on for several hours a day. "But it's just my back—whenever I finish a film, my back goes out."

Mr. Coppola (pronounced *Cope*-uh-lah) is a born showman. In conversation, his mood ranges from defiant pride tinged with insecurity ("A picture like *Apocalypse*, the only critics that count are the audiences") to off-the-wall whimsy ("I bet Goethe would have made films if he lived today, because he loved the theater. He was fascinated by light and physics and gadgetry, and he loved cute girls"). Compelling on almost any subject, he is never more passionate than when he discusses his work.

Apocalypse Now is about a military hit-man named Willard (Martin Sheen) dispatched from Vietnam into Cambodia to "terminate" a rogue soldier. His target: Kurtz (Marlon Brando), a much-decorated Green Beret colonel who has fashioned a private army out of fellow deserters and area tribesmen. Three-fourths of the film is devoted to Willard's journey up-river; the last quarter is staged at the renegade's Angkor Wat-like compound. There, Willard hears of the horrors that drove Kurtz beyond the pale—and finds himself incapable of completing his mission.

The resolution of Willard's dilemma long stymied Mr. Coppola. And the climax he finally showed, in rough-draft form last spring at the White House, in Los Angeles and at Cannes, proved controversial. In that ending, Willard at last performs what is simultaneously an execution and a mercy killing—only to realize, as he stands frozen on the temple steps, that Kurtz's bloody mantle is now his for the taking.

Mr. Coppola explains, "I was trying to say that morality is an issue we have to take as it comes. One day you lie to your wife, another day you don't. And when morality gets up onto its higher levels, so that it's not just a matter of a lie, it comes into that realm of madness where it's life or death. I wanted to push for something almost mythic—recognizing, of course, when you even mention the word 'myth,' you're considered a total phony."

Most critics attending the public screenings applauded the film's first three-fourths, an almost hallucinatory vision of life in the combat zone, but not a few found fault with the claustrophobic last quarter; several even urged Mr. Coppola in print to switch to an alternate climax, known to exist, in which Willard calls in an air strike to bomb Kurtz's compound into pebbles.

Mr. Coppola says of the big-bang finale, "The guys putting up the money thought there was a battle at the end, so I figured since we built this set, we'll blow it up and I'll get a big scene I can play with. But I just couldn't do it; explosions are no substitute for human beings and ideas."

"I really like what we went into Cannes with," he continues. "We also showed a slightly different version that doesn't fade out with Willard still on the steps. So many people preferred it, because it gives some sense of finality, that I'm using it. . . . I mean, I'm making this for people, so the hell with it."

Apocalypse Now will open in New York (at the Ziegfeld Theater), Los Angeles and Toronto with a twelve-week, reserved-performance engagement using a 70-mm print. This 146-minute version carries not a single credit (a program will be distributed). But when the conventional 35-mm prints go into release in October, and four-and-a-half minutes of credits are tagged onto the end, those hankering for an apocalyptic finale can have it—sort of.

"The distributors from Japan and Germany got together with the distributor from Italy—the Axis powers, I call them—and they all wanted the picture to end with explosions." Mr. Coppola sighs. There are a lot of practical concerns when you make a movie, so I said, 'Show the 35s, I'll put the explosions under the titles.' "

It would take but a subtle editing change to integrate the explosion footage into the version that will be reviewed, but Mr. Coppola insists he isn't tempted: "The explosions are purely a graphic device, not a story point."

The long journey of *Apocalypse Now* to the screen started in 1967, when, under Mr. Coppola's sponsorship, John Milius loosely adapted Joseph Conrad's *Heart of Darkness* into a screenplay in which the character Kurtz was envisioned, in Mr. Coppola's words, as "a battle-mad commander wearing two bandoliers of machine-gun bullets." Mr. Milius's film school classmate, George Lucas, was to direct it cheaply, on 16-mm film. But by the time the budget of $1.5 million was finally secured, Mr. Lucas, with *American Graffiti* behind him, was already deep in preparation for *Star Wars*. So Mr. Coppola, fresh from the triumph of *The Godfather: Part II* took on *Apocalypse Now* as his own, raising the budget to $12 million.

"I had this idea," he recalls, "that if I took this war film, and put some terrific stars together with me as a director, I could make a picture and own it, too. I'd been around a long time, done a lot of good work, but I still had to go hat in hand to the movie companies. However, if this picture made a lot of money, I could use that money to build my own movie studio. I thought it would go like this. . . ." Mr. Coppola snaps his fingers twice, then drops his hand and shrugs.

When he failed in his well-recorded wooing of stars like Steve McQueen, Robert Redford, Al Pacino, Jack Nicholson, Gene Hackman and James Caan—and still decided to start shooting in the Philippines, his surrogate Vietnam, in March, 1976—the filmmaker waded in hip-deep. Once on location, he almost sank.

"Everyone was alienated by the place itself," Mr. Coppola says of the equatorial islands. The single greatest setback was Typhoon Olga, which he remembers rather benignly: "A storm came in off the South China Sea, split, and one part hit one obscure town, the other part hit another obscure town two hundred miles away—and both were our main sets. How can you take it seriously?" On top of inhospitable climate, isolated locations and improbable logistics, there were problems with the stars— Harvey Keitel, the original Willard, was fired and his replacement, Martin Sheen, suffered a heart attack; Mr. Brando reported for work an estimated ninety pounds overweight. There were also rumors of corpses disinterred to dress sets (denied by Mr. Coppola); of bribes paid to Filipino officials (not denied); of prodigal amounts of footage being shot ("Mostly on the big battles," says Mr. Coppola) and, most damaging, of $60,000 shooting days squandered while the script was being torn apart.

"I had gotten totally sucked into the problems of setting up the big scenes," Mr. Coppola admits. "But in movies, people are not interested in just seeing helicopters fly by, or seeing explosions. They want a story and character interaction. I finally realized that the script wasn't really engaging, that it didn't weave the characters and themes together to some high point which then resolved itself. I had left a flank totally open—I should have been working more as a writer."

Willard's picaresque journey up-river was never a problem. "Scenes like the helicopter battle [led by Robert Duvall] are just a lot of work," he says. "If shot and edited halfway well, I knew they would be high points."

But the climax proved elusive indeed, with much of the problem stemming from the film's source. Over the years, Joseph Conrad's intro-spective, atmospheric works have resisted successful translation to the screen. Mr. Coppola agrees in part. "Most people who tackle Conrad get lost in the jungle, and *Apocalypse* is derivative of Conrad. But the Lucas-Milius script simply took the metaphor of the boat going up the river and the name Kurtz; and though I put in several scenes which made more use of *Heart of Darkness*, it was never my intention to do a literal adaptation of the book."

Instead, Mr. Coppola feels his problems lay in the motivational differ-ences between the novel's protagonists and the characters in the film; the roots of Kurtz's madness are not quite the same, nor was Conrad's narrator an assassin. Given these new plot dynamics, Mr. Coppola found himself searching for "an ending that truly addressed the themes I thought were coming into play. This meant no purely mechanical or dramaturgical ending."

Ultimately, he maintains, it was not Conrad but another noted author who pointed him away from the apocalypse: "One of the books Kurtz quotes is *The Wasteland*. Something from T. S. Eliot kept teasing at me, almost advising me about the ending. . . . 'Not with a bang, but with a whimper.' "

In June 1977, after sixteen months of on-again, off-again location photography, the crew of *Apocalypse Now* at last decamped from the Philippines. As Richard Marks supervised the editing of some 1.1 million feet of film—eight times the norm—and Walter Murch started creating the complex soundtrack, Mr. Coppola pushed back the scheduled Easter 1978, release date.

Finally in May 1978, he exhibited a rough cut to theater owners. But the versions shown in New York and San Francisco ended differently; suddenly, seven months before its new Christmas premiere, *Apocalypse Now* was plunged into the heart of controversy. Mr. Coppola fanned the furor by staging a string of unannounced screenings, inviting audiences, via a three-page questionnaire, to help him shape the final film. Such trial runs may be an entertainment industry tradition—many Broadway-bound shows play out-of-town engagements and most films have sneak previews—but when the premiere was again postponed, to August 1979, Hollywood sniggered; it was a reaction that has lingered.

His recuperation from a post-Cannes hernia operation and his time in traction have afforded Mr. Coppola a rare chance to reflect: "Sometimes I think, why don't I just make my wine, do some dumbbell movie every two years, and take trips to Europe with my wife and kids [the Coppolas have two sons and a daughter]. I've had it in terms of going to incredible extremes, half-blowing my personal life, just to make a movie. I'm always going to bed in a cold sweat—will that star do the picture, how am I going to film this scene, will they like it. I know that feeling translates itself into your insides; I know I'm losing years of my life."

In fact, since starting *Apocalypse Now*, Mr. Coppola has also made time to supervise the editing of the *Godfathers* for NBC-TV; helped launch the film *The Black Stallion*; geared up such projects as *Hammett* for the director Wim Wenders, a comedy for the actress Cindy Williams and, with George Lucas, a samurai epic being directed by the Japanese master Akira Kurosawa; re-edited his college pal James Caan's *Hide in Plain Sight*; become distributor of Hans-Jürgen Syberberg's seven-hour film, *Hitler*; started his long-planned script about Preston Tucker, the flamboyant car maker, and made notes for *Elective Affinities*, a complex work based on a novel by Goethe ("I see my work in the future as becoming more personal, more theatrical, and probably having smaller audiences.").

Also complicating the filmmaker's life, according to his wife Eleanor Coppola's published diary, *Notes*, was a long-term relationship with another woman. Today, murmurs Mr. Coppola as he uncharacteristically drops his eyes. "There is no other woman."

"I've been almost asking for a real shakedown," he continues softly. "This is a period of strange turning points for me. I used to be sort of a goofy kid—oh boy, I have a new sportscar; gee, I'm directing a movie; wow, that girl likes me. Well, it's not like that after forty. I'd like to build a harmonious relationship between my personal life and my work—I'd like to be happy, to feel good."

"I dream of being part of a really scintillating world cinema; it would be nice for movies to again become special events," continues Mr. Coppola, who once considered booking *Apocalypse Now* into Radio City Music Hall. "So quickly, the forms we work with ossify. If I ever got the bucks that, say, George Lucas got from *Star Wars*, I'd put every penny into changing the rules. Those people in Hollywood respect my ability, but they think I'm a little crazy. They would like me to be taught a lesson; you know, play ball. But with half a break, people like myself and George, who's building his own production facility, are going to turn the studios into dinosaurs. I believe within ten years half of them will be gone, and there'll be new companies."

Including, Mr. Coppola hopes, a restructured version of his own company, American Zoetrope which in the late '60s and early '70s attracted young filmmakers who are today some of the leading under-forty producers, directors, writers, editors, and technicians.

The new Zoetrope, he says, will be "in a little factory, like a Republic or an RKO, making one movie a month in the old style and at an intel-ligent price. But I believe we'll be the first all-electronic movie studio in the world. We'll use the full magic of technology; we won't shoot on film or even on tape, it'll be on some other memory—call it electronic memory. And then there's the possibility of sythesizing images on computers, of having an electronic facsimile of Napoleon playing the life of Napoleon. It's almost doable right now; it just takes the wisdom and the guts to invest in the future."

Mr. Coppola is rechristening his studio Omni Zoetrope ("We don't push the 'OZ' connotation") and is negotiating for the Hollywood General production lot in Los Angeles. This pending deal, involving an estimated $1-million down payment, shows a certain confidence in light of his hefty debt from *Apocalypse Now.*

There is widespread doubt the epic will break even. Mr. Coppola himself concedes, "Here's a work that gives audiences all the goodies of an action-adventure movie, then comes to a place that just deals with ideas. And the big moment, the big scene, is not another helicopter battle, but it's a guy, a face, alone in a dark room, telling the truth."

By the industry's yardstick, *Apocalypse Now* needs worldwide rentals (the fees remitted by the theaters, as opposed to ticket sales) of some $70 million to merely recoup its $30.5-million cost. This is because the final budget does not reflect such other costs as distribution, advertising, making multiple prints and, in this case, sizable long-term interest on the various loans.

A factor in Mr. Coppola's favor is his ownership of the film, which means, for instance, that all TV revenues go to him (he has already rejected one network's offer of $12 million). Calculating foreign sales conservatively, *Apocalypse Now* needs domestic rentals of some $40 million, a sum on a par with, say, *The Goodbye Girl*. Mr. Coppola himself thinks "if it did $25 to $30 million domestic [in the range of a film like *The Trial of Billy Jack*] it would pay for itself down the line. Maybe it would take five years, but my investment would be clean.

"And I can't say I'm losing sleep. As long as this picture's not an artistic disgrace, I'm sure I could start all over again; I'm a well-known film director at a very affluent time. On the other hand, if *Apocalypse* became a film that people sort of had to see, then we would do real well."

By January, the film will be in full international release—and Mr. Coppola should know whether he can afford to start on a personal project, or if he ought consider one with Goldie Hawn.

Flashback: Several weeks ago, at the dinner table in Mr. Coppola's house in Napa. It is late at night. As the espresso is served, he is relaxed; but even relaxed, his mind is never far from his trade. After soliciting casting suggestions for a key role in *Hammett*, he is reminded that Paramount has asked again about his directing *The Godfather: Part III*, which Mario Puzo has written with John Travolta in mind.

He shakes his head wryly and says, "What I'd really like to do is *Laverne and Shirley Meet the Godfather*." A pause, so as not to step on the chuckles. "Or how about *Abbott and Costello Meet the Godfather*? With John Belushi as the Godfather?" The laughter builds. Francis Coppola puffs out his cheeks, furrows his brows and pops his eyes in a dead-on Belushi imitation; then, in Lou Costello's rising wail, he hollers, "*Heyyy, Aaaabbbboott!*"

Francis Coppola's Biggest Gamble: *One from the Heart*

SCOTT HALLER / 1981

Underneath the flashing neon signs, next to the cumbersome camera equipment, Gene Kelly is offering advice. "Cut the legs out of that bit," he says. "The public will never know it's gone." Dressed in a navy blue sweater, checkered slacks, and a sporting cap, Kelly looks as if someone has plucked him off the putting green and dropped him onto the set of a movie musical. While cast and crew wait for scene 106, take 22 of *One from the Heart* to commence, Kelly confers on a dance combination with choreographer Kenny Ortega. Ortega is four decades Kelly's junior and wearing black leather pants, a high-fashion black T-shirt with wrap-around zipper, and bright red socks. Past these unlikely collaborators walks a high-heeled showgirl with a button pinned to her scant, sequin-speckled costume. It reads: "I Believe in Francis C."

Welcome to Zoetrope Studios—or Hollywood, Francis Coppola style. Elsewhere in the city, production companies are closing down as the movie industry copes with shrinking audiences, rising costs, and smaller-than-anticipated ancillary markets. But Coppola, a constant maverick, has envisioned a different future, and he has engineered a brave new world at Zoetrope. Established sixteen months ago by the award-winning writer-director of *The Godfather* (1972), *The Conversation* (1974), *The Godfather: Part II* (1974), and *Apocalypse Now* (1979), this studio is, as its production head Lucy Fisher notes, "a concept as well as a geographic location." The concept is this: an updated version of the old studio system, complete with contract players, contract writers, senior

From *Saturday Review*, July 1981.

filmmakers on hand such as Gene Kelly, and a distinctive studio signature on each film it makes. With Zoetrope, that imprint should stand for projects believed to be too uncommercial, too expensive, or too unusual by the major studios. (In its earlier incarnation as a mere production company—with no Hollywood lot or moviemaking facilities of its own—Zoetrope was responsible for *American Graffiti* and *The Black Stallion* as well as the Coppola films.)

In an era when Paramount or Universal constitutes a single company in a vast conglomerate, Zoetrope is the project, pride, and property of one man, forty-two-year-old Francis Coppola. It has been his long-simmering, ambition to mate the old Hollywood of solid craftsmanship, company loyalty, and sound-stage productions with the new Hollywood of computer wizardry, film-school graduates, and sophisticated storytelling. As governor of this ramshackle, ten-acre, would-be Shangri-La, Coppola has added movie mogul to his impressive list of roles. He is already established as a screenwriter, director, producer, advocate of technological advances, self-appointed American ambassador to the European filmmaking community, and patron saint of the movie-brat generation.

Imposing and impulsive, Coppola has a natural affinity for anything out-sized, even his beard is bushy and his waist wide. "Francis likes living on the brink," says Paramount Pictures chairman Barry Diller. Indeed, his last film, *Apocalypse Now*, nearly drove him over the brink. On that controversial Vietnam epic, the director gambled sixteen months of shooting on location in the Philippines, a budget that ballooned from $12 million to $31 million, and the near-dissolution of his nineteen-year marriage to wife Eleanor. (She, in turn, got her revenge. She chronicled her husband's manic extravagances, inconsistencies, and infidelities of that period in a published, equally controversial memoir, *Notes*).

Zoetrope ranks as the most ambitious undertaking yet from a man who has consciously escalated the challenges in each of his successive endeavors. Instead of a $31 million war film that must return $70 million in world-wide rentals just to break even, this time Coppola's challenge involves prime Hollywood real estate, full staff, and a plethora of projects that he is overseeing. A few months before he acquired Hollywood General Studios for $6.7 million in March 1980, Coppola told a reporter: "There's no one like Zanuck around anymore. And there are no studios like there used to be. I can envision Zoetrope being that way, with a great restaurant where we can all sit around, . . . The way it was, what I missed out on." Zoetrope still does not have a restaurant, although it does offer a screenwriting seminar twice a week for interested staff members. It sponsors an apprenticeship program, and it schedules a regular Friday afternoon party at which star and stagehand can fraternize. "In its best moments," says screenwriter B. Armyan Bernstein, who wrote *One from the Heart*, "it's like the small college we all wanted to go to."

But like the hero of his favorite movie, Michael Powell's *The Thief of Baghdad*—which was shot years ago on this same lot—Coppola is particularly susceptible to do-or-die situations. And already, Zoetrope has turned into one of those situations. Although it originally announced plans of six to eight films a year, the studio is only preparing two movies for imminent release—Coppola's *One from the Heart* and Caleb Deschanel's *The Escape Artist*—after sixteen months of operation. A third movie, German director Wim Wenders's *Hammett*, remains unfinished a year after shooting was completed. Caught between great expectations and fiscal facts, the mogul has been forced to close down his story department. All further projects are on hold. And once again, Coppola appears to have underestimated the cost of his vision.

"It's like I'm at a poker table with five guys," Coppola says. "And they're all betting two or three thousand dollars a hand, and I've got about eighty-seven cents in front of me. So I'm always having to take off my shirt and bet my pants. Because I want to be in the game. I want to play."

Or as Coppola's longtime associate Fred Roos puts it, "We're always out there on the thin edge."

Born in 1939 in Detroit, Coppola grew up in New York, where his father, Carmine, played flute for Toscanini in the NBC orchestra. Coppola studied theater arts at Hofstra College on Long Island, graduating in 1959. He then parlayed campus fame at UCLA's film school into a staff position at Seven Arts. As a *Wunderkind* in Wonderland, he directed his first film for a major studio at age twenty-seven, turning his master's thesis into *You're a Big Boy Now* (1966), a coming-of-age comedy. After a big-budget studio flop, the musical *Finian's Rainbow*, and a small-budget "personal" flop, the drama *The Rain People* (1969), he won his first Oscar the next year as co-author of the screenplay for *Patton*. In 1972 *The Godfather* was released, and suddenly Coppola could afford to refuse any offer Hollywood might make. He became the senior member and father figure of the film-school generation (George Lucas, Steven Spielberg, Martin Scorsese) that was rising to power in the city of their dreams.

Those dreams seem to have been nurtured by old-fashioned studio movies watched at Saturday matinees. Even the name that Coppola selected for his operation reflects a respect for a venerable tradition: the original Zoetrope was an 1834 version of a rotating drum that had slits in its side. Through these slits one looked at a band of drawings lining the inside of the drum. When the drum revolved, these appeared to move like an animated cartoon, producing the earliest *motion* picture.

Unfortunately, the studio system Coppola admires began to fray during the late forties—for several reasons. To begin with, a series of anti-trust suits banned the studios from ownership of the theater chains that provided guaranteed outlets for their products. At the same time, as America moved to the suburbs and television began its slow but steady infiltration of those homes, movie attendance plummeted. By 1951, U.S. theaters were selling thirty-four million fewer tickets *each week* than they had just three years earlier. No longer guaranteed an audience or an outlet, the studios changed production policies. They stopped making large numbers of B-movies and concentrated on big-budget films that might propel television watchers out of suburban living rooms. And as Hollywood unions muscled increasingly more lucrative contracts for their members, it became cheaper to shoot films on location with foreign crews. Accompanying these developments was the dismissal of contract players and writers. As a result, just as the legendary moguls of the era were passing away, their production facilities fell into disuse. In this evolution from factory to distribution center, the studio became less of a home for loyalists who made movies and more of a haven for agents, lawyers, accountants, and bottom-line businessmen who made deals.

Zoetrope, in addition to its contract policy and distinctive ambience, resembles the old-time studios in another way: It is dominated by one personality who sets policy and tone for the studio. Harry Cohn at Columbia, Darryl Zanuck at 20th Century-Fox, Jack Warner at Warner Bros. ruled their respective dominions with an autocratic hand that contributes as much to the lasting legend of their empires as do the classic films they made. Hollywood still treasures the line reportedly spoken by Bette Davis, explaining that she was attending Harry Cohn's funeral only "to make sure the son of a bitch is really dead." Around

Zoetrope, one hears faint echoes of such comments: "There's a real need to keep Francis happy," says one executive. "After all, we're all here on his money." Lucy Fisher adds: "There's not much point in hiring the imagination and then harnessing it."

Nonetheless, Coppola's philosophical forefathers rose to power under different circumstances. Paramount Pictures was created by one-time furrier, Adolph Zukor, whose film background was not making movies, but exhibiting them. William Fox, the founder of 20th Century-Fox, began his career in the garment business. Before Harry Cohn started Columbia Pictures, he had worked on the business side of movie production. Even when Mary Pickford, Charles Chaplin, D. W. Griffith, and Douglas Fairbanks banded together in 1919 to create United Artists—a studio, like Zoetrope, bent on making movies outside the conventional system and sensibility—they did not deign to run the operation themselves. Instead, they hired a businessman—in fact, a former assistant to the Secretary of the Treasury—to serve as the company's first president.

By contrast, Coppola has no formal business background. "I've been putting on shows since I was a little kid," he says. "And I always hoped people would like what they saw when they came. That's enough about business that anyone should have to consider."

None of the executives Coppola has appointed at Zoetrope can boast extensive experience on the business side of moviemaking, either. President Robert Spiotta (also a Hofstra grad) spent sixteen years in the oil industry; his most recent position before arriving at Zoetrope was marketing manager for Mobil Oil. Bernard Gersten, the executive vice-president, does have extensive production credits—but in New York theater, not Hollywood films. Lucy Fisher, the head of production, is a Harvard graduate who trained under the Alan Ladd, Jr., regime at Fox—but, at the age of thirty-one, she's no long-term veteran. "The industry is called show *business* for a reason," says a producer at a rival studio. "And Francis doesn't really know about business. He doesn't want to, and he doesn't want anyone else around to question what he does know."

In a notorious office memo circulated during the *Apocalypse Now* days, Coppola explained, "I am cavalier with money because I have to be, in order not to be terrified every time I make an artistic decision." Consequently, art and money have been dueling constantly at Zoetrope.

Currently, the kingpin project of Zoetrope is *One from the Heart,* a $23 million romantic fantasy musical set in Las Vegas over a fourth of July weekend. The first film . . . Coppola has directed since *Apocalypse Now,* it is labeled "a simple little love story" by the director. Outside the city limits of the neon Nevada metropolis, a live-together, middle-class couple (Frederic Forrest and Teri Garr) have a fight, split up, and venture into Vegas, where each finds a fantasy lover. Travel agent Garr meets Raul Julia, a lounge waiter and piano player. Gas station attendant Forrest encounters Nastassia Kinski (the star of *Tess*), a high-wire artist who has run away from the circus. As in the mixed-couples musicals of an earlier era, there are several lavish production numbers, hundreds of extras, and a happy ending.

Instead of shooting the film on location, however, Coppola has opted for what he calls "a theatrical reality," recreating Las Vegas on the Zoetrope lot. Here in the heart of Hollywood stand the Vegas airport terminal, a desert motel, and a spectacular re-creation of the Vegas strip. Zoetrope's strip encompasses two sound stages and includes 125,000 light bulbs, ten miles of neon, and a paved intersection. "I wanted to take a fable-like story and treat it almost the way Disney would approach a story in his animated films," says Coppola. "Treat it with very expressive sets and lighting and music that heighten the story. If we had made the movie in Las Vegas, it would have been just another relationship movie set on a real location with people jumping in and out of cabs, talking about their love affairs. I wanted to do something people hadn't seen before."

The decision to transform what was originally a modern-romance comedy set in Chicago into a studio-lot Las Vegas musical boosted the film's $15 million budget to $23 million. Tax-shelter investors were found to cover the additional amount, but just as the movie entered production, those investors pulled out. Coppola was required to offer his real-estate holdings as collateral for the necessary bank loans. Staff employees accepted half-pay during the cash-flow crisis. And in a melodramatic moment that moved Coppola to tears and prompted memories of Frank Capra movies, crew members voted against the wishes of their powerful unions and did not walk off the set, even though the week's payroll was not met. About this time, the "I Believe in Francis C." buttons first appeared.

What prompts that belief? For one thing, *The Godfather*, which has accumulated worldwide grosses approaching $300 million. As Coppola once begrudgingly observed, "You see, I could make five failures, five pictures that nobody liked, and I'd still be the guy who directed *The Godfather*." Since that film, Coppola has displayed a consistent talent for turning dark horses into winners. "There's something very Dostoyevskian about Francis," says the head of one production company, enunciating the industry consensus. "He works best when he's in trouble and in debt." Coppola didn't decide upon the narrative structure and ending of *The Godfather: Part II* until several weeks before the film's release. It then went on to snare six Academy Awards and an eight-figure gross (of which the director reportedly received 15 percent). Although making *Apocalypse Now* brought him to near bankruptcy, he will probably break even on the film after a network television sale.

Last January, while *One from the Heart* was in jeopardy, Zoetrope presented in New York a restored 1927 silent French epic *Napoleon* at Radio City Music Hall with a live orchestra playing a score composed by Coppola's father. The movie grossed $800,000 in a mere eight showings. Admittedly, with a live orchestra at each performance, *Napoleon* is an expensive project to mount, and it yields only a small profit. But the film will eventually tour the country with the orchestra on a soundtrack, and Zoetrope executives predict that it will become the largest grossing foreign film ever released in this country.

Besides his bewildering but charmed track record, Coppola garners his associates' confidence through a mercurial mixture of infectious enthusiasm, devil-may-care flamboyance, pioneer spirit, and perseverance. Director George Lucas (*Star Wars*) has said of his friend, "Francis could sell ice to the Eskimos."

Coppola vigorously defends himself against charges of excess and extravagance. "I feel very sure that the audience wants something that is unusual. As a moviegoer, I really am bored by the large amount of films. The storytelling technique is all the same. When the public gets wind of another kind of approach, it responds. I think that had a lot to do with the success of *Napoleon*, aside from the fact that it's a wonderful movie. It smelled like a different kind of event." He is likewise convinced that, set in a surreal Las Vegas, *One from the Heart* will constitute a different kind of moviegoing experience. "With its polarity of fantasy, glitter, reality, disappointment, and everything turning on the notion of chance, Vegas is the perfect place to set a love story," says Coppola. "The city is a metaphor for the state of love itself. I want the film to *be* the emotions of these people, just like in *Apocalypse Now*, I wanted the film to *be* the war. I wanted you to have a direct experience with the film, which was as though you were having a direct experience with the war. I'm interested in films that *are* what they're *about*."

These days, in what he calls "the middle-aged period of my work," Coppola doesn't resemble the ranting and raving director who dominated reports from the set of *Apocalypse Now*. On this set, the legendary logistical problems of *Apocalypse Now* are a running joke. "I need a helicopter right outside in five minutes!" he shouts to the crew. "To the Philippines!" For *One from the Heart*, Coppola shows up for work in coat and tie—the only suit on the set—and stands around the rehearsal piano with Gene Kelly, the sixty-eight-year-old hoofer emeritus of *Singin' in the Rain*, who is overseeing the dance sequences. (Coppola has also installed Michael Powell, the seventy-two-year-old director of *The Thief of Baghdad*, as another senior artist in residence.)

On the set, Coppola's presence is now largely benevolent: Waiting for a camera set-up, he points across the set to a smiling stagehand huddled with a blonde walk-on, dressed as a cocktail waitress. "Who's the guy with the girl on his lap?" Coppola asks a crew supervisor.

"If he's an electrician, he's going to get his pink slip," says the peeved production manager.

"Nah."

"I'm taking care of your money, Francis. You don't want him doing that on your time."

"Leave the guy alone," answers Coppola, and that is what happens.

During the actual filming, Coppola isn't a presence at all. He sits in a silver trailer a hundred feet outside the sound stage, watching the scene on video monitors. Under these conditions, he can adjust and edit each sequence as it is shot—a procedure that he foresees as the future of all filmmaking. On this movie, Coppola is also using a process of "pre-visualization" that allows for action, dialogue, and music to be designed, recorded, and previewed on videotapes before shooting begins. It's Zoetrope's equivalent of the theater's dress rehearsal, designed to eliminate the last-minute complications that plagued *Apocalypse Now*.

"During *Apocalypse,* Francis was out there with the typhoons, waiting all day for the light to get right," says Lucy Fisher. "He was literally at the mercy of the elements. So this time he decided he wanted the safety and security of a studio."

From his trailer, Coppola also issues directorial suggestions that are relayed via a loudspeaker for everyone to hear on the casino set. "Try not to anticipate the kiss," he tells Teri Garr as the extras eavesdrop. "And try to appear more happy that he's kissed you, Teri. I know you wish it was me, but *try.*"

As Zoetrope awaits the autumn releases of *One from the Heart* and *The Escape Artist,* the studio exists in a self-inflicted state of suspended animation. "You know that T. S. Eliot quote?" asks screenwriter Bernstein. " 'Between the idea and the reality, between the motion and the act falls the shadow.' Well, at the moment, we're in the shadow." At least one of its two movies must turn out to be a major hit if the studio, as currently conceived, is to continue.

Elsewhere, though, there are indications that aspects of the old-fashioned studio concept are receiving consideration as a result of Zoetrope's presence. Paramount Pictures is planning to establish a new department of contract writers, and several other companies may do likewise. As the cost of filmmaking has spiraled, the financial advantages of dependable talent-at-hand have increased. Pooling creative resources is an increasingly popular notion. Several years ago, Paramount moved its feature-film office from Beverly Hills back onto the studio lot, and chairman Barry Diller believes the effects of such gestures "are not direct, but powerful nonetheless. It has to do with feelings of pride and proximity." It was Coppola who urged Diller to make that move. "You can learn a lot from Zoetrope. I certainly have," he says. Indeed, Paramount has built a new commissary on its lot.

Whether or not Zoetrope can continue as a new-fangled edition of the old-fashioned studio will depend, as does everything on the premises, on Francis Coppola. As chairman of the board *and* chief creative talent, he is the company's principal asset and its principal problem. He is the Godfather of the lot, mobilizing trusting employees and longtime associates to suit his changeable nature—all in the name of the family of art. And he is the Good Father of the lot, shepherding talented minds under one roof—all in the name of the future of art. If Zoetrope survives,

it will be because Coppola the director has shared his controlling interest with Coppola the executive. "If Zoetrope doesn't make it, Francis can
work at any studio anytime he wants," says one studio head. On the
chance that day may come, Francis the administrator has shrewdly paid
Francis the artist $3 million to direct *One from the Heart*—a fee that the
major studios would have to exceed for his services.

It's particularly appropriate that a compulsive gambler like Coppola
should risk the future of his dream by erecting a miniature Vegas on
his own property. As he strolls onto the set, among the milling masses—
technicians, actors, extras dressed as show-girls, and Shriners—he stands
unnoticed for a minute in the center of an intersection. Above him, in
twinkling lights, is a huge sign that says: "Lady Luck." Over that sign,
outlined in neon, is the lady herself, continuously kicking a vengeful
leg. In any direction he looks, the glittering signs—Chance, Craps,
Double Odds—recall his massive bet. "If we ever had a lot of money,"
he says, "we could be a very dangerous company." Expert storyteller
that he is, Coppola has turned his own career into the best cliffhanger
in Hollywood.

Some Figures on a Fantasy: Francis Coppola

LILLIAN ROSS / 1982

Francis Coppola, the talented, original, volatile forty-three-year-old moviemaker, who is a movie writer (*Patton, The Conversation,* and other pictures), a movie producer (*American Graffiti, The Black Stallion,* and others), a movie director (*The Godfather, Apocalypse Now,* and others), a movie impresario and distributor (Abel Gance's 1927 epic *Napoleon* and others), and a fan of other people's movies (Michael Powell's *The Thief of Baghdad,* Alexander Korda's *Things to Come,* Andrzej Wajda's *Ashes and Diamonds,* Akira Kurosawa's *Yojimbo,* Stanley Kubrick's *Dr. Strangelove,* and about five hundred others), started working on his movie *One from the Heart* in 1980. The year before, Mr. Coppola had bought Hollywood General Studios, built in 1919—one of the oldest movie studios in town. Harold Lloyd started making *his* movies there in 1922. The studio occupies almost nine acres of land in the heart of Hollywood, one mile from the Goldwyn studios and two miles from Paramount. Mr. Coppola paid seven million two hundred thousand dollars (some cash, many mortgages) for the studio and renamed it Zoetrope Studios—after his production company, American Zoetrope, which he had founded in 1969, in San Francisco, as a center for young filmmakers. "The Zoetrope was an early device to create the illusion of a motion picture," Mr. Coppola explained recently to a visitor at his studio. "In the 1860s, it was a popular toy—a revolving cylindrical box with slits in it, making pictures appear to move—but I'm sure it was used much earlier. In Greek, *zoe* means 'life,' and *trope* means 'turn,' or 'movement,' so the word really means 'life movement.' " Two of American Zoetrope's early movies were *THX 1138* (1970), co-written by George Lucas, with Walter Murch, and directed by George Lucas, and *American Graffiti* (1973), written and directed by Lucas, who then went out on his own to make *Star Wars* and its sequels. At Zoetrope in Hollywood, Mr. Coppola had nine sound stages; several one-story and two-story buildings; four bungalows, including one that was used by Harold Lloyd and is still named for him; and plenty of wardrobe space and rehearsal space. He borrowed an additional three million dollars and spent it repairing and renovating the place, with new roofing, new air-conditioning, new lighting, new carpeting, and a large assortment of the latest kinds of electronic equipment (some of it designed by him), for making movies in a new way, which he called "the electronic cinema." He gave the studio streets and parking area new names, among them Federico Fellini Lane, Akira Kurosawa Avenue, Buster Keaton Boulevard, Raoul Walsh Alley, and Sergei Eisenstein Park. He hired a hundred and eighty-four people, including a number of electronics technicians and experts, to work with him at Zoetrope Studios. One of the most dramatic components of Mr. Coppola's technology was a custom-designed twenty-eight-foot-long image-and-sound-control van, complete with kitchen and bath. "The concept behind this unit is that movies are like music and should be composed along the same lines," Mr. Coppola said when he introduced his van to people at Zoetrope Studios. The van was filled with a good deal of unusual electronic equipment. "Much the same as a twenty-four-track music-recording studio booth," Mr. Coppola said. "But here we include image as well as sound, and we can use it in the way that best suits each production. I'm rarely in the van during an actual take, but in the van afterward I can review each shot, make immediate cuts, and know right away whether I want to shoot additional material or make a change in a scene." The system enabled Mr. Coppola to edit *One from the Heart* while it was being shot.

Before, during, and after the making of *One from the Heart*, Mr. Coppola did considerable talking to everyone involved in the movie and to others, interested in moviemaking in general, about the meaning as well as the practical uses of his new technology. A notably unpretentious man, who, like most artists, follows his feelings together with his ideas in creating his work, he found himself from time to time sounding oddly philosophical. He is burly, untrim, overweight—two hundred and thirty-five pounds at five feet eleven inches—and he has none of the health-conscious, life-preserving habits, disciplines, or self-indulgences of many of his Beverly Hills, Pacific Palisades, or Malibu peers, who diet, exercise, get plenty of sleep, and have an obligatory daily massage between work and dinner. Mr. Coppola eats too much and is always short on sleep. He has a three-inch-long curly black beard and long, wavy black hair, and he wears horn-rimmed glasses for nearsightedness. His clothes invariably look rumpled and slightly out of season. He has remained untouched by most of Hollywood's social patterns, including the need to go to A parties, to sit in special seats in certain restaurants, and to get there in the most expensive cars. On the infrequent occasions when he has free time, he likes to stay home and practice on one or the other of two musical instruments he plays: the tuba and the string bass. He also likes to cook; his veal Marsala and his spaghetti with his own marinara sauce have a great reputation among his friends. In cooking Japanese food, he prides himself on his ability to fillet a tuna and then make tuna sashimi. He does not measure his words. He is not cautious in expressing his ideas or his uncertainties about them. He likes to throw out his ideas—to try them out on people who he thinks might share his deep interest in motion pictures. Using a tape recorder, he often makes oral notes to himself in the middle of the night, after his co-workers are asleep. Occasionally, on request, he has offered transcripts of his rough notes to magazines concerned with movie technology; to the press; and to colleagues. "I worry about content," he said in one of his messages to himself. "I worry about story. . . . The talent for writing a good tune is especially admirable when we think how long composers have been arranging and rearranging those few notes into something that sticks as a melody. A story must be like that—a specific talent to come up with the sequence of events, the unfolding of information that captures us and has us eagerly awaiting the outcome, as though we were children. And even if we already know the story, we enjoy going through it again." In another of these messages, he said, "There is and can be content in technology. New tunes that we've never heard before, because they've never been possible before."

Ray Stark, the producer of *Annie* and many other expensive Hollywood movies, who describes himself as "one of the *oldest* working movie producers in the business," feels that technology is of less importance than some other elements of moviemaking. "Francis Coppola is one of the unique talents in this business," he said to a recent visitor in his office at Columbia Studios, in Burbank. "But the only things that matter in the movie business are: one, a good story; two, interesting casting; three, a good director. A computer and all the technology in the world can't create a story, can't feel as an actor, can't think as a director. It's the human element that makes a motion picture. The basic problem in the movie business is still the expense of lighting and of camerawork, all the time it takes to set up a shot. Technology has not changed that—at least, so far."

"Ray is correct about the expense," Mr. Coppola says. "My point is, with a new technology we're going to make that cost much lower."

One night recently, Mr. Coppola stated to himself, "I am more interested in technology than I am in content. Technology is one aspect of today that is truly fresh, brimming with new tunes and story turns. Ones that we have never heard or thought about before. But my interest in technology is a temporary phase, a vehicle taking us from the old world . . . into still another new era of art and thinking."

Not long ago, in the Harold Lloyd bungalow at Zoetrope Studios, sitting alongside a newly purchased bass that he had not yet had time to practice on, Mr. Coppola said, "The adventure of *One from the Heart* was simply my trying to own the rights to my movies." By then, *One from the Heart* had come and gone on public screens. Mr. Coppola was in Hollywood for a few hours, to see a screening of his new movie, *The Outsiders*, and was about to leave for Tulsa, Oklahoma, where the image-and-sound-control van—along with much of the other technological equipment and some of the personnel of his company—was waiting for him. He had made *The Outsiders* there and was about to put the finishing touches—including music composed by him, with rhythm tracks worked out by Stewart Copeland, the drummer in The Police—on another movie, *Rumble Fish*. He had made both pictures after the release, early this year, of *One from the Heart*. "I think it's wise to separate the earning of money from the making of a movie, but I wanted to own the *rights* to my own movies—to be the one to decide what to do with what I make," Mr. Coppola said, giving his bass a wistful look. "At the same time, I was trying to use new methods. Everyone seems to be encouraging you to be ordinary, to tell the same old story the same old way, package it this way, package it that way. Just get the money. All that doesn't interest me. I like to experiment—to push the techniques of moviemaking forward and simultaneously find the most economical methods of making a film. I tried to make *The Outsiders* as I imagined fifteen-year-olds and sixteen-year-olds would like it to be. In making *One from the Heart*, I was trying for something different. I wanted the scenery, the music, and the lighting, for example, to be *part* of the film, not just a background for the action."

One from the Heart took about twenty-two months to make, including time that Mr. Coppola spent working on the screenplay with Armyan Bernstein, the original writer of the story, and working with the actors and dancers in rehearsals of one kind or another as well as the time he spent shooting the picture. Development of the music and art concepts began in September 1980. The actual filming began on February 2, 1981, stopped on March 31, 1981, resumed after three weeks, and finished on June 29, 1981. The movie was released about seven months later, on February 11, 1982. Its cost came to twenty-seven million dollars. At the start, M-G-M was slated to distribute the movie domestically, but M-G-M had provided none of the money for making it, and in February 1981, because Zoetrope had differences with M-G-M over the question of "completion" responsibilities, Zoetrope made a distribution deal with Paramount. The completion agreement, one of the elements in some distribution deals, is like an insurance policy covering all concerned to guarantee completion. With a completion agreement in hand, a movie-maker can obtain financing—the financing in this case being a loan from the Chase Manhattan Bank. "Still no money up front," Mr. Coppola recalled recently of the Paramount deal. "But a very favorable distribution commitment. A four-million-dollar advertising budget, a low distribution fee—better than the average, which is generally thirty percent—and six hundred prints out to theatres across the country on February 10, 1982." On January 15, 1982, Mr. Coppola announced that he had ter-minated the agreement with Paramount, mainly because Paramount, he claimed, refused to live up to its completion agreement, and also because of what he felt was poor handling of a screening for exhibitors. On January 29, Columbia Pictures became the distributor of *One from the Heart*. On February 11, the movie opened in San Francisco, Los Angeles,

Denver, Chicago, Washington, Boston, New York, and Toronto. By April 1, the only theatre it was playing in was the Guild, on West Fiftieth Street, in New York. At that point, Columbia was willing to release several hundred prints of the movie in a hundred markets around the country. Mr. Coppola said no—he wanted to withdraw the picture entirely. Columbia agreed to the withdrawal. For the next seven months, *One from the Heart* couldn't be found in any theatre in the United States.

Before *One from the Heart* was withdrawn from distribution in this country, it had generated a disappointing one million two hundred thousand dollars in gross box-office revenue. Zoetrope's share of the gross revenue was almost negligible. In theatrical motion-picture distribution, the amount of money that a distributor receives from the theatre owners is called "net rentals." Net rentals—in movie-business jargon, "the remittance from film exhibitors to film distributors"—are a percentage of box-office receipts (it is usually negotiable but generally begins at ninety percent for the distributor and ten percent for the theatre owner, the percentage changing as a movie plays out) calculated after subtraction of the "house nut." The house nut is the amount of money that theatre owners claim it costs them just to open the doors of their theatres. When people in the movie business use the term "house nut" or "house expenses," they usually give it a somewhat melodramatic reading, occasionally accompanied by a bit of a leer. Distributors reluctantly tolerate this deduction. After the theatre owner's house nut and his percentage and the distributor's lion's share of the gross have been taken into consideration, the split between distributor and theatre owner is likely to be about fifty-fifty. The producer's percentage comes out of the distributor's fifty percent. Film distributors take a "distributor's fee," the norm for which is generally acknowledged to be thirty percent of the net rentals; and mention of this is often accompanied—especially when the mention is made by the few highly talented filmmakers who have written, directed, and produced movies and then handed them over to distributors—by a considerable show of agitation. In addition to the distributor's fee, distribution deals usually allow the distributor to recover, on a dollar-for-dollar basis, all money spent on prints and advertising, and may also allow the distributor to handle negotiations for other rights, such as cable-television, network-television,

television-syndication, video-cassette and video-disc, publishing, sound-track, music, and merchandising.

"The exhibitors' share and the distributor's fee come off the top, and then, depending on how much is spent on prints and advertising, what's left is used for recoupment," Mr. Coppola has explained. "If there's anything left after you break even, it's usually a small pool, and it's divided up among the people who own shares of the movie. *One from the Heart* will have to earn from two and a half to three times its cost, or—according to a broad rule of thumb—about sixty-eight million dollars, before we break even."

One from the Heart runs for a hundred minutes. As Mr. Coppola describes it, it is "a fable about love and show business." As Columbia Pictures describes it, it is "a romantic comedy, a musical fantasy, and an erotic love story." It takes place in Las Vegas. Because Mr. Coppola wanted to get away from realism, and achieve certain effects of fantasy, he decided to make the entire movie at Zoetrope Studios—a procedure counter to the pattern that most movies have followed for the past thirty years or so, of being shot on location, and more like the moviemaking pattern of the nineteen-thirties and forties. *One from the Heart* stars Frederic Forrest, Teri Garr, Raul Julia, and Nastassia Kinski, and features Lainie Kazan and Harry Dean Stanton. The cinematography is by Vittorio Storaro. Among the other credits: songs and music by Tom Waits, sung by Crystal Gayle and Tom Waits; costume designer, Ruth Morley; production designer, Dean Tavoularis; executive producer, Bernard Gersten; co-producer, Armyan Bernstein; producers, Gray Frederickson and Fred Roos; screenplay by Armyan Bernstein and Francis Coppola; directed by Francis Coppola. Technical credits are given to a hundred and eighty-four people, including set decorators, sound editors, re-recording mixers, camera operators, grips, lead-men, a visual-effects editor, a miniatures supervisor, casting directors, a script supervisor, choreographers, costumers, still photographers, electronic-cinema technicians, publicity people, a production coordinator, special-effects coordinators, transportation coordinators, title designers, color technicians, and numerous assistants. Credits are also given to the Sony Corporation; to Colossal Pictures (title designs); to Dreamquest, Inc. (motion-control photography and matte paintings); to The Optical House, Modern Film Effects, and

Zoetrope Images (opticals); to Technicolor, Metrocolor, and Dolby
Stereo; and to Columbia Records (original-soundtrack album).

Francis Coppola was born in Detroit, Michigan, on April 7, 1939, and he
grew up and went to school in Queens, New York. His father, Carmine
Coppola, is a composer and conductor, who once played flute under
Arturo Toscanini in the NBC Symphony Orchestra, and who since early
1981 has been the conductor of the sixty-piece symphony orchestra
providing live music at the screenings of *Napoleon*. Francis Coppola's
maternal grandfather, Francesco Pennino, was one of Enrico Caruso's
accompanists; he came over from Naples and settled in Brooklyn. Detroit
was Francis's birthplace because Carmine Coppola had taken the family
there from New York when he got a job as flutist, arranger, and assistant conductor of the orchestra for the *Ford Sunday Evening Hour* on
radio. Francis Coppola was originally known as Francis Ford Coppola,
having been named after the *Hour* and his father's boss. A few years
ago, Mr. Coppola decided that he liked his name better without the
Ford. Distributors, however, are still attached to it, and use it in his
name most of the time.

When Francis was nine, he was stricken with polio, and the disease
left him paralyzed for a year in his left leg, arm, and side and in his entire
back. He was unable to walk during that year, and he spent most of the
time in bed, cut off from other children except for an older brother and
a younger sister. "My greatest pleasure during that year was to watch
Horn & Hardart's *Children's Hour* on television every Sunday morning,"
he recalled recently. "I loved little children very much then, as I do now,
and I dreamed of being involved with them someday in theatrical activities. I had a Jerry Mahoney puppet that I could make talk and sing, and
I had a tape recorder, a record player, and other equipment that I could
use to make up shows with. I am sure that from those shows came the
idea of my studio—a place where we could work together like children,
with music, puppets, scenery, lights, dramatic action, whatever we wanted
to do." At the age of fifteen, because of some proficiency in playing the
tuba, Francis was awarded a band scholarship at the New York Military
Academy, at Cornwall-on-Hudson. He was there for a year and a half.
Then, while his parents were on the road with the musical *Kismet*, for
which his father conducted the orchestra, Francis ran away, made his

way to the family's home, in Great Neck, and enrolled in Great Neck High School. He graduated in 1956.

In collaboration with Francis, Carmine Coppola composed the music for *Apocalypse Now*, in 1978, and for *The Outsiders*. Talia Shire, Francis's sister, who is an actress, played in *Rocky* (the part of Sylvester Stallone's girlfriend) and in *The Godfather* (Al Pacino's sister). Francis's brother, August, runs an educational and apprenticeship program for Zoetrope Studios. Gian-Carlo Coppola, Francis Coppola's eldest child, who is nineteen, has been working with his father as an assistant for a couple of years and is an associate producer of *The Outsiders*. Roman Coppola, Mr. Coppola's second child, who is seventeen, worked as an assistant sound mixer in the making of *The Return of the Black Stallion*, a Zoetrope production, which was filmed in Morocco last winter. Sofia Coppola, Mr. Coppola's youngest child, who is eleven, sings, dances, and acts (non-professionally) with a group called the Dingbats, which she founded a year and a half ago with Jilian and Jenny Gersten, twelve and thirteen, respectively—the daughters of Bernard Gersten. The girls have also published a summer newspaper, the *Dingbat News*, which has been more or less the official Zoetrope newspaper. Eleanor Coppola, Francis's wife, who is a designer in various media, works outside the movie industry. She helps out unofficially in many capacities in Mr. Coppola's productions, however, and she supervises the logistics of taking the Coppola family along on locations where Coppola movies are being made. "Francis wants his family with him," Mrs. Coppola says. "We travel together like a circus family, with Francis on the tightrope and the rest of us holding the ropes."

In 1956, Francis Coppola enrolled in Hofstra University, where he majored in theatre arts. Two of his classmates were Ronald Colby, a cherubic, good-natured man, who is now a Zoetrope producer, and Robert Spiotta, now the president of Zoetrope Studios. Mr. Spiotta, who is forty-five, is an athletic-looking six-footer and, unlike Mr. Coppola, is very well groomed, with a neatly trimmed beard, and, unlike many Hollywood executives, is addicted to Eastern, almost preppy clothes. He played end on the Hofstra football team and acted the part of Stanley Kowalski in a school production of *A Streetcar Named Desire*, which was directed by Mr. Coppola. Also at Hofstra, Colby directed an original musical by Mr. Coppola called *The Delicate Touch*, about a school for pickpockets. Lainie Kazan, who plays Maggie in *One from the*

Heart, was another classmate who participated in Mr. Coppola's Hofstra productions. In 1960, after graduating from Hofstra, Mr. Coppola enrolled in the film school of the University of California at Los Angeles. While he was still attending the film school, he worked as an associate producer, sound man, and writer for Roger Corman, a producer-director of low-budget, money-making horror films with such titles as *The Masque of the Red Death, Attack of the Crab Monsters,* and *The Terror,* and also of a kind of classic, *The Day the World Ended.* Mr. Coppola worked on movies called *The Premature Burial, Tower of London,* and *Battle Beyond the Sun,* and then, in 1963, he wrote and directed his own horror film, *Dementia 13,* for Mr. Corman. In 1967, he won considerable critical praise for his first important directorial effort, *You're a Big Boy Now,* which was shot entirely on location in New York City. After that, he directed *Finian's Rainbow* and *The Rain People,* and was co-author (with Edmund North) of the screenplay for *Patton* (directed by Franklin Schaffner and starring George C. Scott). In 1971, being under considerable financial pressure as the owner of American Zoetrope, which he had established two years earlier, he somewhat reluctantly worked for Paramount Pictures as the co-author (with Mario Puzo) of the screenplay for *The Godfather* and director of the movie based on it. As co-author and director, Mr. Coppola was paid a fee of seven hundred thousand dollars and was given a six percent profit participation in the movie, which was released in 1972, and which has set box-office records that are among the highest in movie history. As of last month, the movie had grossed almost two hundred million dollars in the United States and throughout the world. In 1974, also for Paramount, Mr. Coppola directed *The Godfather, Part II,* which, like Part I, earned a great deal of money. Mr. Coppola's share of the profits of *The Godfather*—both parts—has been about seven million dollars so far.

Between making *The Godfather* and *The Godfather, Part II,* Mr. Coppola, among other things, wrote, directed, and, with Fred Roos, produced *The Conversation,* starring Gene Hackman. The movie, which was about a professional eavesdropper, cost a million eight hundred thousand dollars to make. It was financed by Paramount in an agreement with Mr. Coppola, together with two other directors, William Friedkin and Peter Bogdanovich, who had joined forces as the Directors' Company, an experimental effort that turned out to be short-lived. *The Conversation* has still not earned back its cost, but it has earned much acclaim and several awards, including the Palme d'Or, for best picture, at the 1974 Cannes Film Festival.

In 1972, Mr. Coppola undertook to produce *American Graffiti*, a small film to be directed by George Lucas, who had been unable to get any major company to finance it. Mr. Coppola wanted to invest his own money in the movie and own it himself. "Everybody advised me *not* to invest my own money," Mr. Coppola has recalled. "So I turned the film over to Universal and lost the chance to earn enough money to set up my own studio. That movie could have brought me over twenty million dollars. After that, I decided that I would try to finance all Zoetrope films myself."

In 1976, Mr. Coppola started making *Apocalypse Now*, about the Vietnam War (screenplay by John Milius and Francis Coppola). He produced and directed the movie, which starred Marlon Brando, Robert Duvall, and Martin Sheen. For *Apocalypse Now*, as for *One from the Heart*, Mr. Coppola's cinematographer was Vittorio Storaro, and his production designer was Dean Tavoularis. *Apocalypse Now* took sixteen months and cost thirty-two million dollars to make. The movie has grossed just over a hundred million dollars to date. *Apocalypse Now* won the Palme d'Or award (shared by *The Tin Drum*), for best picture, at the 1979 Cannes Film Festival. Thus, Mr. Coppola became the only director to win the award twice. "It takes years and years for the value of a movie to be revealed," Mr. Coppola explained recently. "My guess is that *Apocalypse Now* is worth between ten and fifteen million dollars to me. We got four million nine hundred thousand dollars in 1980 for the cable-television rights. It was shown only once in Japan on television, and for that we got a million one hundred thousand dollars. It is still to be sold to the television networks here for major release, and to the affiliates, and then for television syndication. There are many important values not yet exploited. We owe United Artists, the distributor, only three million dollars of the twenty-seven million we originally owed them. That movie will bring in a lot of money over a long period."

In the late seventies, Mr. Coppola and Steven Spielberg gave each other one "point"—one percent ownership of net profits—for the help each had given the other in their respective movies: *Apocalypse Now* and *Close Encounters of the Third Kind*. Because the profits of *Apocalypse Now* are still in the future, while those of Mr. Spielberg's movie are in the past, present, *and* future, Mr. Spiotta often kids Mr. Coppola about the deal, describing it as "the *best* deal you ever made." Mr. Coppola's one point has so far brought him $365,072.

One from the Heart was rated "R" by the Motion Picture Association of America. It is the story of an unmarried couple, Frannie and Hank, who have been living together in a small house in Las Vegas for five years and are dissatisfied with each other. Frannie works for a travel agency, and daydreams about going to Bora Bora and finding a man to go there with her. Hank runs an automobile-repair shop and junk yard, and daydreams about having a romantic alliance with a glamorous girl. They have brief alliances with other partners, Frannie with a singing waiter who does indeed want to go to Bora Bora with her, and Hank with a seductive young tightrope walker from a circus family. Hank then wants to get together with Frannie again. After some resistance and turmoil, she returns to him, and that's that.

Because Mr. Coppola wanted the movie to be what he called "theatrical" instead of "naturalistic," he decided against making it on location in Las Vegas. Instead, he created his own, stylized version of Las Vegas at Zoetrope Studios. "The real Las Vegas is like Burbank," Mr. Coppola said at the time. "We're going to tell this simple story in a fantasy way, so we'll make our own fantasy of Las Vegas, which for me is a metaphor for America itself, and like the 'Mahagonny' of the world."

It took more than two hundred carpenters and other craftsmen to build the studio Las Vegas, which consisted of six paved streets, seven houses, a motel, a travel agency, a department store, the Strip, an automobile-repair shop and junk yard, and a replica of McCarran Airport. "I want to do something that people haven't seen before," Mr. Coppola said. "I'm so happy we're all acting out this fantasy. A company like this can make twelve movies a year like this one, each better than the last." He set his electronic-cinema methods in motion to that end, and, in addition, found new ways of bringing the optical effects, the dancing, and the songs together with the acting so as to realize his particular vision on the screen. The electronic-cinema method, which Mr. Coppola says he has developed and improved further in the making of *The Outsiders*, included what Mr. Coppola calls the "pre-visualization" of the movie. The pre-visualization was accomplished by means of tapes of the actors reading their parts, videotaped rehearsals, Polaroid stills, artists' sketches, and a filmed walk-through of the story in the real Las Vegas— all of which enabled Mr. Coppola to rewrite and edit the script while the movie was still being shaped and before the actual filming started.

All the music for *One from the Heart*, including twelve songs and their lyrics, was composed by Tom Waits, a jazz-style singer well known for his records *Blue Valentine* and *Foreign Affairs*, and for his songs about transients hanging around in seedy bars and motels. Waits and Crystal Gayle, a country-and-western star, did all the singing in *One from the Heart*, which was recorded during the making of the movie. The record was just brought out by Columbia Records a few weeks ago. Mr. Coppola's idea was to have the record make a kind of detached comment on what was happening to the characters in the movie, and to have it give a truer sense of the soundtrack. "The record didn't work out that way by the time the movie was released, so I stopped it until it sounded right to me," Mr. Coppola said the other day. "It's really nice now, even though Columbia insisted on making the cover look like a Tom Waits–Crystal Gayle record instead of one from the movie." Gene Kelly, the actor, dancer, and choreographer, whom Mr. Coppola had engaged as "executive for musical production and development" for Zoetrope Studios, worked as a kind of over-all consultant on the dances for *One from the Heart*; Mr. Kelly starred in *An American in Paris* (1951), which was directed by Vincente Minnelli, and *Singin' in the Rain* (1952), which he co-directed with Stanley Donen. "We're going to use color the way *An American in Paris* did," Mr. Kelly said at the start. "We're going to *paint* the picture." Vittorio Storaro, the cinematographer for *One from the Heart*, who was born, in Rome, the year after Mr. Coppola, was also the cinematographer for Warren Beatty's *Reds* and for several movies directed by Bernardo Bertolucci, including *The Conformist* and *Last Tango in Paris*. "Storaro's use of color and form is always imaginative, always sensual," Mr. Coppola said. "Just what we want for this picture."

Among the major trips that Mr. Coppola took in connection with the making of *One from the Heart* were five from Los Angeles to New York, four from Los Angeles to Las Vegas, and two from Los Angeles to Rome; he was accompanied on a few of them by his cast and crew. The making of the movie took seventy-nine rehearsal days and seventy-two shooting days. There were several "wrap" parties for everybody involved in making the picture. Usually, in moviemaking, the wrap party is held after the shooting has been completed. For *One from the Heart*, Mr. Coppola said, they might as well have a party at the end of each week's shooting, because there was perpetual doubt whether there would be enough money to continue shooting the following week.

Right before starting production of the movie, Mr. Coppola, who lives in the Napa Valley, just north of San Francisco, gave a big party at his home, which occupies some seventeen hundred acres, including two hundred acres of vineyards. The party was a barbecue, with about three hundred and fifty guests, among them everybody working for Zoetrope and everybody working on *One from the Heart*. At the party, everybody talked eagerly about the making of the movie. Late in the afternoon, while toasting marshmallows, Mr. Coppola said exuberantly, "Something incredibly great is about to happen." The executive producer, Bernard Gersten, said, "You just begin to smell the movie around the corner." Before joining Mr. Coppola, Mr. Gersten had been, among other things, an associate producer of the Shakespeare Festival in New York. Because his wife—the Eliot Feld company's dance manager, Cora Cahan—and their two children stayed behind at their home in New York, Mr. Gersten made thirty-two commutation trips between Los Angeles and New York during work on the movie.

When the movie was finished, Mr. Coppola said, with satisfaction, "The entire film has so many long takes—one goes on for ten minutes. The average hundred-minute film has hundreds of cuts, and the takes are much shorter."

For these long takes, two hundred thousand feet of film was shot, of which ten thousand feet was used in the movie. For the entire movie, twelve hundred and thirty-one video cassettes were used, three hundred and eleven storyboards were made, and thirteen hundred photographic stills were taken—many in the pre-visualization stage. Eight wind-making machines and eight rain-making machines were used, and nobody counted the gallons of water spilled for the scenes in the rain. "After making *Apocalypse Now* in the Philippines, I felt this was a better way of making movies than slogging through the jungles," Mr. Coppola says now. "We did everything in relatively small spaces right in the studio."

Technically, Mr. Coppola owns *One from the Heart*. (*The Godfather*—both parts—is owned by Paramount. Mr. Coppola is a profit participant in *The Godfather*, receiving six percent of the net profits of Part I and a larger percentage of the gross profits of Part II, but he has no say in what Paramount does with the movie. To own a movie is to own the negative, the copyright, and the right to show it or arrange for a distributor to show it.) From the start, he was intent upon arranging financing and distribution deals that would enable him to retain ownership rights. Although he kept informed about proposals for deals, the job of day-to-day negotiations for them fell to Robert Spiotta, Zoetrope's president. Mr. Spiotta, a patient, calm, good-natured man, is adept at following the rhythms and speech patterns of corporate executives, including the practice of turning almost any noun or adjective into a verb (in the movie business one "strategizes" what one is doing for a movie, "finalizes" it, and then "platforms" it), while trying simultaneously to tune in sympathetically to Mr. Coppola's artistic intentions and resolutions. Mr. Spiotta graduated from Hofstra the year after Mr. Coppola, and worked for Mobil Oil for the next sixteen years, winding up as an international marketing manager in Europe. In 1978, he quit that job to join Zoetrope. Mr. Spiotta recently explained to a strictly non-business type *how* a movie must earn two and a half times its negative cost to make a profit, and he proceeded to review as simply as possible the very complicated and somewhat elusive history of the financing and distribution arrangements he made for *One from the Heart*.

"The twenty-seven-million-dollar cost will ultimately be provided from several sources," Mr. Spiotta said, having explained that he was using the future tense because of yet-to-be-collected guaranties from foreign distributors. "To start with, the Chase Manhattan Bank lent eight million; it later expanded that loan by four million, and lent an additional seven million against foreign contracts. Then, we borrowed three million from Jack Singer, a Canadian investor, who is primarily in the real-estate business, and we put up the studio as collateral. But though we also got some smaller loans, from other sources, including Paramount, Security Pacific National Bank, and Norman Lear, we wound up two million dollars short of the twenty-seven. We still owe two million in outstanding bills to various creditors. The preliminary budget for *One from the Heart* was for fifteen million dollars, but in September 1980, when Francis decided to make the whole movie on the lot, we had to budget the movie at twenty-three million one hundred thousand dollars. In early March of 1981, after M-G-M dropped out, we made our distribution agreement with Paramount. The agreement stated that the film would complete photography by mid-April, according to the original shooting schedule, and provided for an unspecified completion amount, if that was needed, after the budget had been exhausted. But Francis found that additional shooting was required. Instead of going to Paramount for money at that point, we went ahead to finish the film. We didn't know in April what the over-budget would be, and we thought that Paramount would be more likely to give us some completion money once the figure became definite. Francis shot an additional thirty-two days, and after that the film went into what is called post-production. The titles were more expensive than we had figured on, and so were the special effects. By October, we were over budget by four million dollars, so we deducted the cost of the extra shooting days from the four million, and asked Paramount for less than two million dollars— less than half of the over-budget. That's when communication with Paramount broke down. Paramount felt there was no obligation for it to put up *any* money, because we had exceeded the shooting days allowed in the contract. We felt strongly, and still do, that, despite the extra shooting days, Paramount had an obligation to provide completion funds. As a consequence, Chase Manhattan Bank had to provide further funds in the form of personal loans guaranteed by Mr. Coppola and his wife and utilizing as collateral just about everything they have, including his seventeen-hundred-acre estate in Napa Valley and once again, of course, Zoetrope Studios."

"You need a lot of capital to start with in order to get close to the box office," Mr. Coppola said in his studio bungalow recently, with one hand on his new bass, which so far he had still not played. "It's like the oil business. George Lucas, for example, now has incredible wealth, in cash. I'm in a different position. My home telephone has been shut off all this past year, because I haven't been able to pay my telephone bill. I wanted to own all my own pictures. I once owned the *Black Stallion* film rights. The film will probably make a profit of three million dollars, but I had to turn over my rights to United Artists in order to hang on to *Apocalypse Now*. United Artists was the distributor of both pictures, but I was guaranteeing their cost. I didn't have the financial equity to provide for *The Black Stallion*, because I was still making *Apocalypse Now*, which was going over budget. I believe that an artist has a right to own what he creates, but I can't get my hands on the capital that I need to do the creating. I was running a movie studio that had no money. The day I started shooting *One from the Heart*, I had no money. Every week, I had to start out by wondering, Where can I get the five hundred thousand dollars we need for this week's shooting? As we went along in shooting *One from the Heart*, we were always short of money. Before we started shooting the film, everybody at Zoetrope took a big pay cut for a period of six months. They were wonderful. Assistants to assistants came to me with ideas for raising money. All these people were paid back in full eventually, by the way, but all along the line they were really great. At one point in February 1981, the bank stopped advancing us money and sent people to California to review our case. We considered stopping production of the picture. If we'd stopped, though, a lot of people would have been hurt. So in April I had to make myself personally liable for any loans beyond that point. The bank by then had advanced us ten million as a loan—actually, two million more than it had wanted to be in for. A good part of my personal finances are never separate from those of my company. I just put the money where it needs to go. So three million dollars could be in the budget for me as director of *One from the Heart*, but I'd put the money right back into what was needed to go on making the movie. Whether it's your own or someone else's money you make the movie with, you're under pressure. I find that it's worse, however, when you use someone else's money. Then you always have someone looking over your shoulder."

In August of 1981, the Paramount distribution office in San Francisco, in order to satisfy complicated state theatrical-exhibition laws, held a screening for exhibitors of the rough cut of *One from the Heart*—a version that lacked, among other things, most of the movie's twelve songs. One of the exhibitors at this screening lost no time in sharing his opinion, which was unfavorable, with a film critic on a San Francisco newspaper—an erratic development that was regarded by everybody concerned as a highly unprofessional violation of privilege. The film critic then reported the irregular and premature comments in the news-paper, and they were read and resented by Mr. Coppola. He objected to what seemed to him to be the casual way the distribution office had held the screening. He said to a friend, a novelist, in San Francisco, "How would you feel if you were in the middle of writing a novel, and your publisher

showed a rough version of your novel to the manager of the Barnes &
Noble bookshops? And then this manager called up an influential book
critic and made disparaging remarks about your manuscript, and you
learned about the incident by reading those remarks in the press?"

As 1981 drew to a close, details of the distribution deal with Paramount
were still up in the air. On New Year's Eve, Mr. Coppola, who was working
in the Technicolor lab in Rome with Vittorio Storaro on the final touches
on *One from the Heart*, suddenly decided that he wanted to hold a screening of his movie in New York City. He telephoned Bernard Gersten and
asked him to try to get the Radio City Music Hall for the screening.
Mr. Gersten got it, for one day and evening, at a cost of twenty-four
thousand dollars. In the *Times* of Sunday, January 10, 1982, at a cost
of twenty-seven thousand dollars, Mr. Coppola placed a full-page ad:
"On Friday, January 15, at Radio City Music Hall, Francis Coppola presents the final preview of his new movie." The ad showed a large picture
of the faces of Teri Garr and Frederic Forrest. The title "One from the
Heart" was written in script across the picture, which had tiny stars
sprinkled over its background. Under the title were the words "A new
kind of old-fashioned romance." Two screenings were announced:
7:30 P.M. and 10 P.M. General-admission tickets would cost five dollars.
First-mezzanine reserved seats would cost ten dollars.

On the day of the screening, people started lining up for general
admission early in the morning. The outside temperature was about
twenty degrees Fahrenheit. Because of the lineup, reminiscent of what
one used to see during Christmas or Easter Weeks in the Music Hall's
movie-cum-stage-show period, Mr. Coppola ordered free soup—split-pea
soup with sausage slices—delivered to the waiting audience in the
afternoon. Cost: three thousand three hundred and fifteen dollars.
Accoutrements of the evening included programs, posters, and buttons
reading "I was at *One from the Heart* Radio City Music Hall," which
together cost fifteen thousand dollars and brought the cost of the preview to almost seventy thousand dollars. The Radio City Music Hall
box office that night took in slightly over fifty-one thousand dollars
in gross receipts for the two performances, which were sold out, with
eleven thousand people paying to see the movie. In addition, five
hundred people came as Mr. Coppola's guests: any film critics who

asked for free tickets; movie stars in the movie; movie stars in general; producers, directors, and writers of other movies; stage actors; relatives; friends; friends' doctors—representatives of every kind of show-business activity. Zoetrope employees flew in from California, mostly at their own expense. Film critics flew in from Los Angeles, Chicago, Boston, and Toronto. The program for the evening included a press conference and a big party for the guests—the latter held, at a cost of nineteen thousand four hundred and ten dollars, in the Tower Suite at the top of the Time-Life Building. An eight-piece dance orchestra played at the party, and the celebrators were offered a buffet with shellfish, cabbage soup, three kinds of pasta, cold cuts, and desserts, along with drinks.

Backstage at the Music Hall around seven o'clock, Mr. Coppola, dressed in a heavy khaki-colored down parka, light-brown pants, a brown jacket, a maroon-and-white checked shirt, a pink tie, and worn-looking brown loafers, was surrounded by family, friends, colleagues, and other supporters. Off to one side, the Dingbats—Sofia Coppola and Jilian and Jenny Gersten—wearing rented tails and top hats and clutching canes, were practicing a tap-dancing routine. Mr. Coppola was greeting one well-wisher after another. He was elated. "We finished mixing the sound for the movie at 6 A.M. today," he said. "Final changes on the negative were made in Rome last night, and the master print just got here. I was all over the Music Hall this afternoon. Finding out how the house lights work. Everything. It's the most beautiful theatre you've ever seen. Not one of these multiplex shoeboxes. And we've got this perfect big, big screen. In the Academy aspect ratio, one point three three to one—one and a third times as wide as it is high. The original ratio for movies. We made the movie, and now we're going to lay it on the audience. I feel as though I were back in college. In fact—" He called to all those around him, instructing them to form a large circle, to hold hands, to lift their held hands up and down three times, in a ritual, while calling out "Pa-wa-ba!" each time. "It dates from my days at Hofstra, when we put on plays. It exorcises the evil spirits and invokes the good spirits. I still do the 'pa-wa-ba' before we do the first shot of all my movies."

The house lights were dimming. Mr. Coppola hustled out, toward the back of the house, clasping hands on the way, calling out reminders that he would see the hands' owners at the party later on. "Francis invites everybody," Bernard Gersten said, hurrying to catch up with Mr. Coppola and make a path for him. "There are no Hollywood-type A, B, and C lists for parties with him. Everybody's an A."

People in the audience, mostly under forty, and enthusiastic, also held out their hands for good-will shakes, saying, "Thanks for the evening," or "Thanks for making it," or "I love your work."

"This movie is different," Mr. Coppola said a couple of times.

"Different?" some of the well-wishers repeated, looking put off.

The movie started. Mr. Coppola removed his parka and tossed it into a corner of the lobby floor. He paced back and forth in the lobby, occasionally opening an aisle door to listen to laughter, to murmurs, to applause for some of the striking cinematic effects; to note the silence during romantic scenes.

At one point, he was stopped in his pacing by a man holding a microphone and a man with a portable camera on his shoulder. "I'm Josh Howell, 'Eyewitness News,'" the first man said. "Could we just photograph you walking around?"

"I'd rather not," Mr. Coppola said. "I'd rather be free just to hang around the house."

Soon after that, Mr. Coppola settled down on the floor at the back of the center aisle. On the screen, Teri Garr and Raul Julia were dancing a tango. "It's very romantic," Mr. Coppola said to a companion next to him on the floor, pushing his glasses up on the bridge of his nose.

When the movie ended, Hank and Frannie were together again on the screen. The audience applauded. Not a shattering ovation—just appreciative applause. Then, for five minutes or so, almost everybody in the audience stood up and stayed put, staring at the white, still screen, apparently reluctant to leave. Slowly, people began filing out. Mr. Coppola picked up his parka and quickly headed for a large rehearsal studio backstage, where the press conference was to be held.

About seventy-five people were at the press conference, including many photographers and television-news cameramen as well as people who write about movies. Most of their questions carried with them heavily inside information.

No. 1 was "How do you feel, now that everyone dislikes the picture?"

No. 2: "Doing this the way you have done it, what is your purpose, and have you, in your opinion, accomplished your purpose?"

No. 3: "But will this film be commercially successful?"

No. 4: "How important is the success of this movie to your future ventures—to your future movie productions and movie ventures?"

No. 5: "Is this film your homage to Fellini?"

No. 6: "Is there an agreement with Paramount on this film as to its distribution?"

No. 7: "Mr. Coppola, do you feel you love this movie as much as Hank liked Frannie?"

No. 8: "Mr. Coppola, why do you take these kinds of chances?"

No. 9: "Mr. Coppola, you helped create George Lucas. Why hasn't he helped you?"

Visibly trying to remain calm, Mr. Coppola replied.

To No. 1: "A lot of people in there looked as though they *did* like the movie. They seemed to laugh throughout the picture; they stayed pretty motionless and intent throughout the picture; there weren't many walk-outs. At the end, there was a play of emotion and enthusiastic applause that lingered throughout the titles and even after the titles. That's what I saw. If someone saw it a different way, then maybe that's so."

To No. 2: "A lot of people who spoke to me told me it was a very unusual and beautiful picture. When I make a film, I take a jump into something I am interested in. In this case, in the film, I was interested in show business, in gambling, I was interested in love, and I was interested in fantasy, and I was interested in music. Those are the things I worked with in my film. I am very proud of it, and I imagine that years from now, just as in my other films, people will see something of these elements and see it as an original work. It's not a copy of anything. It entertains people, and it is innocent."

To No. 3: "How the hell do I know?"

To No. 4: "I know very specifically what I want to do and where I am going. It's just two different roads I can travel to get there. The result of the success of this film determines maybe an easier road."

To No. 5: "No."

To No. 6: "About a week ago, I saw the film in Rome and then in Paris. I showed it to a few friends, filmmakers, directors, people, kids. I felt real good about their reaction, and, more important, I felt real good about my own reaction to it, which is all that really matters, I guess. At that time, because of a series of business discussions going on with Paramount, I became frustrated, and I decided that I didn't care whether Paramount released the picture or not. At that point, I terminated Paramount's release of the film. But Barry Diller, the chairman of Paramount, asked us not to announce the termination until we had a chance to discuss it further. I had to finish the film. I had to bring it to a stop, because we were involved with the bank and these various things that had to come to a close. I was very concerned about the sloppy way the film was shown to the exhibitors when it wasn't finished, and I was concerned about the way the film was being prejudged. And I just wanted a chance to show it clean to an audience. The thing with Paramount is a tricky situation, because I terminated them. I had hoped that that would bring us around to make an agreement. Whether that happens or not depends on the reaction of people to the film, so I don't really know what's going to happen."

To No. 7: "I love this movie, because I like to watch it, and I like the music, and I think it is beautiful."

To No. 8: "I'm a guy who's been around for twenty years. I've made a lot of films, and you know them. I've also produced a lot of films. You know them, too. I've written a lot of films and I've discovered a lot of new talent. I was the one responsible for making Part IIs, if you want to consider *that* something. Every time I want to make a movie, every time I want to make a film, every time I want to sponsor a filmmaker, I have to go, hat in hand, to a series of studio executives who don't have my background and my experience. So I find that frustrating. So, since I don't have any money really, to speak of, I use what little I have to try to get to the point where we can have our own studio, where we can make films like the films we've made over the last twelve years—all of the quality that this film has. I will stand by this film, because I know what went into the making of it. That's what I want. But I can't do that if I have to be controlled by people who say what film you can make and who's going to supervise what. So if I have my own studio, to keep the control and supervision to myself, it is taking a risk. Taking risks like this one creates some excitement. You may not have been excited, but others were. I don't know, but it was something."

To No. 9: "I don't need to be bailed out. My friendship with George Lucas is such that I know that's not his style of doing things. He would help me in other ways. George is a good friend, not in a money-lending way but more in the way of giving me a lift to the airport if I needed it." Without missing much of a beat, he went on, "I'm a guy who feels,

Let's get out and take some chances. What I really don't understand is why you guys don't seem to like that. Why don't we all cheer the moviemakers *on?*"

A bit later, Mr. Coppola went back into the theatre, where the second screening of *One from the Heart* had started, and he moseyed around, observing both his movie and the audience reaction to it. Then, along with six hundred and forty-seven guests, he went to the party celebrating the event in the Tower Suite of the Time-Life Building. Over their drinks, shellfish, cabbage soup, pasta, cold cuts, and desserts, the guests told Mr. Coppola that they had enjoyed his movie very much. Norman Mailer told him it was "an extraordinary film." Joseph Papp told him it was "a pioneering film, as big in its way as *Star Wars.*" Robert Duvall told him it was "a lot of fun and technically dazzling." Thomas Hoving told him, "I liked it. I liked it very much." Andy Warhol told him, "It's really lovely." Carly Simon, Richard Gere, Susan Sarandon, Christopher Walken, Robert De Niro, and Martin Scorsese all told Mr. Coppola they enjoyed and admired the movie.

Mr. Coppola did a lot more kissing and gave a lot more hugs. The orchestra played "One," from *A Chorus Line,* about fifty times, and the Dingbats did their dance routine to it a couple of dozen times; many of the guests rewarded their efforts with generous applause. Everybody seemed to have a good time at the party, and most of the guests, when they left, kept their "I was at *One from the Heart* Radio City Music Hall" buttons on.

Before the evening was over, some television stations included reports on the *One from the Heart* preview in their news programs. One station reported on the preview by interviewing four people who walked out on the movie before it was over, and who, like most early walkouts, made negative pronouncements on what they had walked out on. The United Press issued a report that was published in newspapers around the country. One of the papers headlined that story 'ANGRY COPPOLA DROPS PARAMOUNT AS DISTRIBUTOR FOR MUSICAL."

The next morning, Mr. Coppola held a meeting with about a dozen of his associates at his New York apartment, which is at the Sherry Netherland—four rooms with a kitchen. It has Art Deco furniture in the rooms and French theatrical posters on the walls, and that morning a vase filled with large red tulips occupied a non-working fireplace in the living room. Mr. Coppola, who had just awakened, sat barefoot on a sofa wearing a green silk dressing gown and his horn-rimmed glasses; sipped a cup of espresso; and listened to reports indicating that *One from the Heart* might not be greeted by the kind of enthusiasm that had been expressed the night before by many of those in the audience, including Robert De Niro, Joseph Papp, Robert Duvall, Martin Scorsese, and Thomas Hoving.

"It looks as though the press is lining up against the movie," said the publicity woman for the New York area. "But Jonathan Cott, of *Rolling Stone*, loved it. Rex Reed hated it. *Variety* will do a long interview with you any time you say, and you will have a platform for what you want to say."

"I don't want a *platform*," Mr. Coppola said. "From what I saw last night, the audience was interested in this picture. They could see that this picture is different. I think this picture will be like *Apocalypse*, *One from the Heart* will change the way people look at movies. Just as *Apocalypse* eventually did. In my opinion, the people who liked the movie the least were the critics—the people who want to tell you how you should work, what you should do. It seems to me that journalists who write about the entertainment business have a tough row to hoe. They need to stay on top, to set the tone and rules for what *they* say is or is not a good film. When a good film comes along, one that they think will work out with the public, they act a little bit like Danton, who when the rabble rushed by his house to make a revolution ran out behind them to lead them. When a film is successful, many journalists seem to feel as though they had made the filmmaker. Then, in the future, if that same filmmaker does not seem to be respectful of these journalists they seem to want to unmake what they think they have made."

"The Paramount thing keeps getting in the way," a publicity man said. "Every time you come out with a picture, people want to talk about all your financial troubles instead of just looking at the picture. Maybe it was a mistake to hold the preview."

"I *had* to show the picture," Mr. Coppola said. "I was trying to say to the public, 'Endorse this picture as collateral, so that the banks will allow me to go on.'"

"I'll work on the distribution, and in two weeks you'll have a distributor," said the president of Zoetrope Studios.

"What we've got to decide now is when to hold a preview in Los Angeles and where," said a vice-president.

"Los Angeles is a real cow town," said an older Zoetrope executive working in the realms of publicity and advertising. "Monday through Thursday, Los Angeles is asleep, so we ought to hold it on a Friday, Saturday, or Sunday."

"The best thing with this movie might be to make it impossible for people to see it, and let people imagine what it is," Mr. Coppola said. "Maybe I'll just withdraw the picture. Five years from now, I'll show it."

"If we give too much notice for the preview, the movie companies will buy up all the tickets," said Zoetrope's director of special projects. "We don't want an audience full of people in the business."

"These things only work when you spring them," Mr. Coppola said, without great interest.

"How about having the preview on Wednesday?" said the company president. "The next day, we can have a deal in place."

"They don't come out on Wednesday. They come out on Friday," said the older executive working in the realms of publicity and advertising.

"It doesn't matter when you have the preview," said the company president. "They're going to come out no matter what."

"I'm tired of making films so that people can come out and try to shoot them down," Mr. Coppola said. "I don't know whether I want people to see this picture. Why can't I just put the studio up for sale? Liquidate everything. Can't a guy opt out? Can't I just liquidate? All I have to do is give the bank back twenty million bucks. Right?" There were some uneasy laughs all around, but Mr. Coppola looked serious. "I think the artist still has a right to show his work or not to show it," he said.

"You have risked everything to make this picture," the New York publicity woman said. "You wanted to make what you wanted to make."

"I like the idea of pulling the movie," Mr. Coppola said. "And then maybe showing it thirty years from now."

The executive producer said, "Please, Francis, don't decide what the entire press is going to say about the picture. Let's think about the previews. Can we do two cities? I would not do central U.S.A.—I'd do Toronto after Los Angeles. We'll see what happens. *Then* we'll decide."

Mr. Coppola said, "Right at the point when the movie industry, by its own admission, is falling apart, you try to do something different, something to bring it away from the television mentality—the quick cuts, the hyped-up action, the cut to her, the cut to him, the warmed-over stories, everything done in the editing room instead of by the maker of the movie. And people ridicule you for making the effort. That's what gets me upset."

There was a brief silence.

"*Treasure of the Sierra Madre*, directed by John Huston, was a big flop at the previews," the older executive said. "I was there. I remember. It was 1948. If Warner Brothers hadn't owned their theatres themselves at that time, the picture never would have been shown. Then it went on to win three Academy Awards."

"*Traviata*, the first time out bombed," the executive producer said. "They tried to murder Stravinsky's *Sacre du Printemps*."

"At the press conference, the first question they asked me was 'How do you feel now that everyone dislikes the picture?' " Mr. Coppola said. "Why do I have to put up with that? I feel dirtied by it."

"You let that guy get to you," said the Zoetrope president.

"From the start of this movie, I felt I was a cat on the griddle," Mr. Coppola said. "It's not the way I felt when I was a kid and we put on plays. The show would open. People liked it. Then we would all go to the dance. I like the idea of telling the bank, 'Take the studio. Take everything. I'll just keep one little can of film.' "

Mr. Coppola's associates gave weak smiles.

"It's probably the most interesting movie I've ever made," Mr. Coppola said. "I feel the movie will be studied thirty years from now. Maybe I just ought to transfer it to a cassette and release it as just that."

Again, there were weak smiles from the associates.

"Why can't I just pay all the money back?" Mr. Coppola asked.

"Because it's not twenty million only," the Zoetrope president said. "It's seven million more on the foreign contracts. Just because some ass asks you a dumb question . . ."

"The best way I can use my energy is in trying to make a beautiful film," Mr. Coppola said. "Instead, if you want to make a film you are thrown into merchandising. If the truth were known about distribution methods, the distributor wants and gets cable, network sale, cassettes. Distributors have delayed bookkeeping. They are marketing executives. And they all have lawyers. Hollywood is infested with lawyers. With big egos. They don't know about making pictures."

"When the picture starts making money, all those guys will slip back into the mud," the co-producer said.

"I can't try to make movies the way they do for television, which is the bargain-basement way," Mr. Coppola said. "I'm not going to do all that. My father always told me it's tough to get people to try something new. They're like kids resisting a new kind of food. Once they try it, he told me, they'll get to like it. But you have to *give* it to them to try. The things you come to love best are the things you didn't love at first. I've got to make the films my own way."

"You make them, and I'll worry about the distributors," the Zoetrope president said.

"I'm in no rush," Mr. Coppola said. "The distributor is merely what bus you're going to get on."

The West Coast preview was to be held on the following Wednesday, January 20. In the meantime, Mr. Coppola read some additional press comments on the New York preview. Rex Reed's piece, in the *News*, was headlined "HERE'S ONE FROM THE HEART: HOGWASH!" and Stephen Grover's, in the *Wall Street Journal*, "COPPOLA OFFERS UP 'ONE FROM THE HEART' TO WARM RESPONSE." Janet Maslin wrote in the *Times*, "At the film's end, it was greeted with measured, if not wildly enthusiastic, applause. So the evening, with its two sold-out previews, could in no way be viewed as a fiasco. But neither was it the triumphant debut Mr. Coppola had doubtless hoped for two weeks ago, when he hurriedly planned this unorthodox unveiling of his ambitious new musical movie."

In Los Angeles, full-page ads were placed in the January 20 Los Angeles *Times* and U.C.L.A. *Daily Bruin* announcing two screenings for that night, to be held at the Village Theatre, in Westwood, an upper-middle-class neighborhood near the university. The theatre's capacity was fourteen hundred and seventy-seven, and the tickets were sold out. The response of the audiences was enthusiastic—much *more* enthusiastic, Mr. Coppola and his Zoetrope colleagues thought, than that of the audiences at the Music Hall. "How can you figure these things? Maybe the difference was, at the Music Hall there was no popcorn," Mr. Gersten said, with a grin, to a reporter. "At Westwood, there was popcorn. So the response was very, very good."

Then, on January 22, came what the Zoetrope people called "a breakthrough review." Sheila Benson, the film critic for the Los Angeles *Times*, wrote a review that began, "It's so easy to love *One from the Heart*; you just let yourself relax and float away with it. A work of constant astonishment, Francis Coppola's new film is so daring it takes away your breath while staggering you visually." Mrs. Benson also wrote, "The picture comes from the same artistic impulses that inspire airbrush art, three-dimensional pop-up greeting cards, and the delicately beautiful new neon that illuminates L.A. shops. It is post-Warhol, where everything is 'pretty,' all slickness and sleekness, and it cherishes its surfaces even more because of the hollowness they cover. . . . Coppola's leap into years-ahead technology is sure and dazzling. 'It's artificial,' he seems to say. 'Isn't it gorgeous?' Indeed it is—sumptuous, sensuous, stunning. . . . Two kinds of audiences will accept *One from the Heart* easily, *naifs* and sophisticates. Those in the middle will worry too much about the silhouette-thinness of the characters. They shouldn't. Musicals have been far emptier than this in terms of real emotion, and very few have dared this greatly."

By now, Robert Spiotta, Zoetrope's president, was working day and night to make distribution arrangements for *One from the Heart*. Mr. Coppola was in hiding, working on the screenplay for *The Outsiders*, which he was scheduled to start directing in three weeks. For the next eight days, Mr. Spiotta met with executives and lawyers of motion-picture companies that put up or obtain money to make movies and then distribute them or else just make the deals to distribute movies whose financing has been arranged by others. Lawyers and marketing experts on both sides had their own meetings with each other. With valiant attempts to be matter-of-fact, Mr. Spiotta described his negotiating efforts to a reporter. "In this industry, the greater your need, the worse your deal," he said. "Money is very powerful, and power is used to the hilt. These people are corporate animals. We have three viable alternatives. One, we can make a two-picture deal with Warner Brothers for *One from the Heart* and Francis's next picture, *The Outsiders*. We're reluctant to make the two-picture deal with Warners, because they are more interested in *The Outsiders* than in *One from the Heart*. Two, we can make a deal for *One from the Heart* with Columbia and a separate deal for *The Outsiders* with Warner Brothers. Three, we can make a separate deal for *The Outsiders* with either Warner Brothers or Columbia and distribute *One from the Heart* ourselves. We want to develop a good relationship with Warner

Brothers, because they will distribute *The Escape Artist* and *Hammett*—two pictures produced but not directed by Francis. The situation at Columbia is also favorable, thanks to their recent successes. On a lesser scale, there's Filmways, which is being acquired by Orion, whose key people liked *One from the Heart* very much. Filmways has become a much more serious consideration, because of the Orion involvement. But that would be a back-end deal, which means no money up front. There would, however, be a low distribution fee and tremendous input by us in the marketing campaign. What we'd like to get is a negative-pickup deal, with a low distribution fee—lower than twenty-five percent—and a substantial advance up front. All deals are different. Some deals have distribution fees tied in to box-office grosses. The better the business at the box office, the lower the fee for the distributor. If a picture does badly, the fee is higher. Deals should be made quickly. It's important to pick the optimum time."

A couple of days later, Mr. Spiotta, sounding wearier, reported, "Columbia is very eager to have *The Outsiders*, but it has less than the required enthusiasm for *One from the Heart*. We want to deal with a company that is enthusiastic. The trouble is, distributors are greedy. They want everything. For example, Universal has shown a late interest in *One from the Heart* and has offered us a deal that would give us six million dollars up front, but it wanted too much in return. It wanted all domestic rights—cable-television, network-television, cassette, and disc— but we want to retain as many rights as we can. We want to keep *something*. Most producers don't have the stature or the audacity to keep many rights. For example, Francis controlled the rights to *Apocalypse Now*, which was distributed by United Artists. That picture has already brought in a hundred million dollars. The cost was thirty-two million dollars. We still owe three million dollars, but the value of unsold rights will far exceed that amount. We may have terminated our distribution deal with Paramount for *One from the Heart*, but nobody in this business stays on the outs with anybody else. Eventually, we all need each other. Warner Brothers are still high on our priority list. I believe we can agree on a distribution fee. The more serious issue with Warner Brothers is the license terms. They would like to have the distribution rights in perpetuity, and we're attempting to restrict them to ten years and the guarantee on the number of prints and the amount of money spent on advertising. We want very much to duplicate the guarantee we had from Paramount, which was for six hundred prints and four million dollars guaranteed in advertising."

The next day, Mr. Spiotta, sounding still wearier, said, "I saw Francis and explained the level of interest of each studio and the problems with each deal. He said, 'Let's distribute it ourselves.' At this point, there's a great deal of risk and uncertainty in doing that, and Francis is not pig-headed when it comes to business. We want three things. One, we want the best long-term distribution deal in respect to economics. Two, we want restriction of distribution rights to domestic theatrical—no cable, no cassettes, no foreign deals. Three, we want to be comfortable with the distribution. Attitude is a very critical area. The number of prints, what theatres, the advertising budget—all reveal attitude."

The next day: "The Warner Brothers deal fell apart. Warners would not back down on the issue of perpetuity, and although we were close on the distribution fee, it was not as low as we wanted. At this point, time is working against us. We're very eager to get the film released according to the original schedule. We decided to engage Irwin Yablans, the independent film producer who made *Halloween*, and who worked as a consultant for us on the distribution of *Apocalypse Now*. Yablans has an exceptional knowledge of the theatrical-distribution business, and he also has great esteem for Francis. He quickly started getting in touch with theatre owners directly to explore the possibility of opening *One from the Heart* ourselves, without a distributor. Within one hour, Henry Plitt, of the Plitt chain, in Los Angeles, offered us the Century Plaza Theatre, and Bernie Myerson, of the Loews chain, in New York, offered us the Tower East and Loews Paramount. During the next twenty-four hours, we also secured key theatres in Denver, Las Vegas, Boston, Chicago, Washington, northern New Jersey, and Long Island. At this point, we don't necessarily intend to *distribute* the film ourselves, but we do intend to release the film *without* a distributor, to demonstrate our ability to get playing time directly from exhibitors. Francis would love to distribute the film himself. But, from a practical point of view, distributing this film beyond an initial limited release without a distribution organization would be madness—and we could never attempt it on a film that cost twenty-seven million."

"They know that a Coppola movie is out of the ordinary," Mr. Gersten said a few days later, when he arrived in New York to work on advertising for *One from the Heart* with the advertising agency that was already hand-ling the *Napoleon* ads. Mr. Gersten also started working with Howard Deutch, who had been engaged by Paramount to make a trailer and commercials for *One from the Heart* back in the days when Paramount was going to distribute the film. Other Zoetrope executives stepped up plans for the première of the movie. Mr. Spiotta, however, continued talks about distribution with Columbia, Universal, and Filmways. Mr. Coppola made some final changes in the negative of the film and, on January 26, sent it, along with the soundtrack, by courier to Rome for final processing. Twenty-five prints, at a cost of two thousand dollars each, were ordered. Two days later, Mr. Spiotta had some news to report. "At first, Columbia had less than the required enthusiasm," he said to a reporter. "But the people there looked at the film again, and this time they were more encouraged. Columbia is potentially our best bet."

The night of Friday, January 29, Mr. Spiotta had news of an agreement with Columbia. "We agreed on the deal at 5 P.M.," he said. "I'm sure all the arrangements we've made for bookings will be taken over by Columbia. We want to open on schedule, for starters, with forty-one screens in eight cities. The deal does not involve a great deal of up-front money. None, in fact. We've decided to gamble on the back end—to go with a lower distri-bution fee and retain control of all rights, rather than take the Universal deal, which provided six million dollars up front but meant losing control of all rights."

"We turned down Universal's six million dollars up front because we wanted to retain the rights for ourselves," Mr. Coppola said. "Now it's up to Columbia."

In New York, Mr. Gersten was still working with the advertising agency on the ad that showed the faces of Teri Garr and Frederic Forrest coming together in a kiss, and they had been struggling with the line "Francis Coppola takes a very special look at love" versus the line "Francis Coppola takes a chance on love" for the advertising copy, and also with "A new kind of old-fashioned romance" versus "A new kind of valentine."

The next day, Mr. Gersten and the ad agency were told to stop strug-gling, because Columbia was taking over.

"The die is cast," said Mr. Gersten. "Columbia's advertising people are coming in with a whole new concept of what we should do. They're planning to show Raul Julia lying on top of Teri Garr, and over it they want to say, 'Francis Ford Coppola, the man who brought you *The Godfather* and *Apocalypse Now*, takes a light look at love in a spectacular way.' And they want to put *One from the Heart* not in script but in Deco type, something like *Pennies from Heaven*. And under the title they want to say, 'Sometimes you have to break apart to come together.' I don't like what they're doing, and I told them so. I told them that Francis himself has wanted to leave out the Ford in his name, because he himself has said, 'Never trust anyone who uses three names.' " Others at Zoetrope were pleased with Columbia's approach, and said they were impressed by Columbia's ability to create a completely new campaign overnight.

Having been relieved of responsibility for the ads, Mr. Gersten now devoted himself to arranging, and then accompanying Mr. Coppola on, a whirlwind pre-opening promotional tour across the country, starting with an appearance on the Merv Griffin television show in Los Angeles on February 4: One hour with Merv Griffin in his own Merv Griffin Theatre, in Hollywood, answering Merv Griffin questions like "Why did you spend all that money?" Plane to Las Vegas that night. Next morning at nine, in a Caesar's Palace conference room, a press conference with a dozen representatives of television, radio, and newspapers, answering questions about electronic-cinema procedures, about why Paramount did not come across with the *One from the Heart* completion money, and was it *after* that that Mr. Coppola decided to drop Paramount as the distributor for the movie? Plane that afternoon to Chicago, limousine to the Ambassador East, for what are known as one-on-one interviews—in this case, two interviews with Gene Siskel, of the Chicago *Tribune*. Mr. Siskel first did an interview for his public television program, with a television crew that was interested in Mr. Coppola's remarks and hung around listening to the second interview, for the newspaper. In reporting on his questions to Mr. Coppola, Mr. Siskel wrote in the *Tribune*, "Why couldn't we just see *One from the Heart* without having to worry about who was going to distribute it? . . . Why didn't he [Mr. Coppola] act more like his co-equal as the greatest of American filmmakers, Martin Scorsese, who manages to release his extraordinary movies with a measure of dignity and without going nuts in public?" Mr. Coppola's apparently calm answer was "Why does one weigh two hundred and forty pounds and the other weigh something like ninety-six pounds? Obviously, it has to do with a difference in personality. . . . I finance my own pictures, and Marty doesn't. So I'm usually in a financial situation that he isn't." On the same day, Mr. Siskel's review was headed "COPPOLA'S LATEST FILM IS MORE FROM THE LENS THAN THE 'HEART.' "

Next day: Press conference at 9 A.M. at the hotel with about forty people, arranged by Columbia Pictures field representatives. Mr. Coppola and Mr. Gersten and also Gian-Carlo Coppola, who was accompanying them on the tour, said they were impressed by Columbia's efficiency. That afternoon, plane to Toronto, with Mr. Coppola carrying three frozen pizzas (gift from Columbia) from Chicago's famous Pizzeria Uno. In Toronto, Columbia field representatives had set up a press conference with fifty people at the Sheraton Centre Hotel and one-on-one interviews with Jay Scott, of the *Globe & Mail*; Bruce Kirkland, of the *Sun*; and Ron Base, of the *Star*. Late that night, still carrying the three Uno pizzas, Mr. Coppola returned home to his apartment at the Sherry Netherland, heated up one of the pizzas, ate some, and went to sleep. He worked all the next day, Sunday, on casting for *The Outsiders*, taking time out only to look at some newly developed high-definition video systems that the Sony Corporation wanted to show him.

On Monday morning, the Columbia people had Mr. Coppola scheduled to appear on *Good Morning America* with David Hartman, and they wanted to show some clips from *One from the Heart* during the interview. Mr. Coppola said he didn't want the clips shown. "To put a little fragment of the movie on television is stupid," Mr. Coppola said. "Commercials and trailers are different. I'd prefer not to show *any* clips on *any* talk shows. I'd rather just talk about the movie. You sit there, and then you're supposed to look up at where the clips are shown. You feel like a jerk. Besides, this movie is not a conventional movie, and showing fragments is misleading." The clips were not shown. On *Good Morning America*, Mr. Coppola followed Olivia Newton-John singing "Let's get physical . . ." and Erma Bombeck giving a humorous report entitled "The Cost of Wives." "We are a very small company," Mr. Coppola said to an endlessly smiling Mr. Hartman on the program. "We don't have wealth or power. I'm facing the question now of whether Zoetrope can win the right to exist."

Back to the Sherry Netherland. A breakfast there at eleven-thirty with twelve people who write or talk about movies for a living. Immediately afterward, another breakfast there, with twelve more people who write or talk about movies for a living. Some more casting work on *The Outsiders*. Appearance on another television talk show. Back to work on *The Outsiders*.

Plane to Washington, D.C., the next morning. Appearance as a guest at the Washington Press Club in connection with the opening of *Napoleon* at the Kennedy Center, where the orchestra was to be led by Carmine Coppola. Several one-on-one interviews. Then the black-tie opening of *Napoleon*. Afterward, a midnight party in the foyer of the theatre.

Next morning: Plane directly to Los Angeles, where Mr. Coppola, Mr. Gersten, and Gian-Carlo landed in pouring rain. "We were charged up," Mr. Gersten said over the telephone to a friend in New York. "We were finding positive signs wherever we went, in everything."

The première of *One from the Heart* was held that night—Wednesday, February 10—at Plitt's Century Plaza Theatre, in a complex of shops across the street from the Century Plaza Hotel. It was still raining. Present were two klieg lights, executives from Columbia Pictures, all the stars and other members of the cast of *One from the Heart*, and some other celebrities. The theatre capacity was fourteen hundred seats, and the house was full. Afterward, there was a party in a nearby Chinese restaurant. Celebrities who attended told Zoetrope people that they had liked the movie. "It's lovely. It's charming. He made a hell of a movie," Peter Falk said. And Steven Spielberg said, "I thought it was a great achievement, a complete conceptual design. You know, from the beginning to the end, it's a wonderful dream. It's a dream about reality relationships, but it's very, very entertaining. And all the things I'd heard about it—I didn't expect it to be this entertaining. It really sort of took my breath away. All those dissolves and people appearing behind scrims. It was as if Francis went to Broadway and made a movie about it. It's just wonderful."

The movie opened officially the next day, in forty-one theatres in eight cities—San Francisco, Los Angeles, Denver, Chicago, Washington, Boston, New York, and Toronto. The reviews were uneven. Many critics had already reviewed the movie, after seeing one or another of the previews. The day of the opening, the *Times* review, by Vincent Canby, was unfavorable. Mr. Canby wrote, "Nothing had quite prepared me for the staggering number of wrong choices—made by one of our most talented and adventurous film makers—that are contained in the version of *One from the Heart* that I finally saw." Mr. Canby criticized the story, the action, the screenplay, the casting, the acting, the dialogue, the music, and the style, and wound up calling the movie "unfunny, unjoyous, unsexy, and unromantic."

Mr. Coppola did not appear bothered by the bad reviews or by other negative comments on his movie. "It's like the first reaction to *Apocalypse Now*," he said on hearing about the reviews. "Everybody talked against that one at first, too. At first, they didn't like what I had done. A lot of them wanted me to go on making *The Godfather, Part III*, or something. Then everybody came around."

The amount of business a movie does after its first week determines whether it has what is known in the trade as "legs," and the legs are carefully evaluated. After *One from the Heart* had appeared on the forty-one screens in the eight cities, it was regarded as practically legless.

"It's worse than we expected," Mr. Gersten said. "It's disappointing."

The legs situation did not improve during the next few weeks.

Mr. Spiotta said to a reporter, "In San Francisco, Los Angeles, New York, and Toronto, it did well at first, but it was disappointing in Denver, Chicago, Washington, and Boston. Columbia made what is called an exit survey—interviewing at random people as they leave at the end of a screening. Their survey told us that people who went to the movie with some awareness of what to expect liked it, and people who had thought it was something else had a negative reaction. Fifty percent of those who saw it liked it. The other fifty percent knew little about the picture beforehand—they didn't even know it was directed by *Francis*. At that point, we decided to get Patrick Caddell, of Cambridge Survey Research—the guy who did polls for President Carter—to do a survey to provide more data on the reasons people liked or disliked the film, thereby enabling us to design a new campaign aimed at the target audience. All of which, of course, should have been done months earlier."

By then, Mr. Coppola was deeply involved in preparations for shooting *The Outsiders*. "*The Outsiders* has been set up as a separate company, and it's in Tulsa," Mr. Coppola said to a reporter. "We brought most of our electronic setup to Tulsa. Our whole methodology is with us. I like to work on a lot of things at the same time. This is going to be the busiest year of my life. I'll be directing at least three more films. I treasure *One from the Heart*. It's an unusual film, and it can be proved only by time. Maybe it's something only *I* cherish. Maybe the film doesn't make itself understood. All I know is that I got twenty-seven million dollars' worth out of making the film, because it represents everything I will want in the next thirty years. There's plenty to learn from that movie. When I decided to preview the movie at the Music Hall, it was a romantic gesture. I wanted to demonstrate to Paramount that it should help me. For me, it was a beautiful evening. It was like being in the theatre again. I was running around deciding how to have the house lights. I didn't anticipate the Paramount controversy. All I wanted was to get the money, so that I could finish the film. I don't have any bad feelings toward Paramount. The Columbia people are real professionals. They jumped in with both feet. When the record of *One from the Heart* comes out, a new campaign will be stimulated, because I think the songs, the lyrics, and the singing performances are wonderful and got little attention. Fundamentally, I think what can be blamed for what happened to this film is the way, for a year prior to its release, it was associated with conflict, money problems, the threat of bankruptcy. Right away, it was bad, even before the reviews. The public shied away. The trick now is to encourage good word of mouth. As for me, I have to work in the only way I know how. Some people are quick to tell you how to function, and when you don't do what they want you to do they become angry. I don't know why some of the reaction to what I do is so cynical. I know that I'm for intelligence, creativity, and friendliness, as opposed to greed, power, and hostility. Whether you're the director or the producer or the owner of a movie, as soon as you form an organization to make a picture you're a businessman. The problem is to be in all that and still to be free."

"We made a lot of mistakes," Mr. Spiotta said. "We should have had trailers in the theatres at least two months before release. We did not. The publicity was not right. We had no time for research. We should have had the attention of the public on the *film*, not on Zoetrope, not on Francis and the financial problems. We didn't bring the music out as an album before the picture was released. In retrospect, the ad campaign was all wrong. After the Music Hall previews, we went on the wrong assumption that we had to get the picture out in a hurry. We should have waited."

One week after the opening—at a cost of about twenty thousand dollars—Zoetrope Studios officially engaged the Cambridge Survey Research organization to make a study of people's views on *One from the Heart*, whether they had attended the movie or not. Cambridge interviewed four hundred and fifty-one moviegoers at theatres in Chestnut Hill, Massachusetts; Paramus, New Jersey; Denver; and Los Angeles. Half the people interviewed had attended *One from the Heart*; the others had seen other movies. The survey found:

(1) "Half of those attending *One from the Heart* considered it a good or excellent film."

(2) "Most people attending the other movies had at least some awareness of *One from the Heart*," because of negative publicity pertaining to the Coppola studio's distribution problems or to negative reviews, or both.

(3) "Coppola commands a strong personal following." Half of those who did not see the film but had heard of it were unaware that Coppola had directed it. Filmgoers who were disappointed in the movie had expected a more realistic treatment of the romantic theme.

(4) Negative reviews and negative publicity dominated the responses of those not attending *One from the Heart*.

(5) People who disliked the film had not expected to see the kind of movie they saw.

(6) "Many of those who attended the film, particularly women, were disappointed with the film's dreamy or surreal aspects." They had expected a more typical love story.

The survey recommended a "marketing strategy" based on its finding that those who liked the movie were sixty-three percent male; sixty-nine percent single; forty-four percent between the ages of twenty-six and thirty-five, with thirty-nine percent twenty-five or under; fifty-nine percent once-every-two-weeks filmgoers; and seventy-three percent college-educated. Cambridge Survey Research recommended:

A marketing strategy which can maximize the box office of this core support group and its word-of-mouth potential must incorporate the following:

(1) Coppola.

(2) An innovative film which only he can do; which he always does.

(3) A love story or romance captured by an extraordinary atmosphere of fantasy-photography, scenery, lighting, and music.

If in the process of communicating these chief messages the audience infers that the film contains an upbeat message or that a blend of normal, frustrating daily lives and dreams of exotic places and lovers is reached, so much the better. Those themes must be subordinate to the three main messages, however—their impact is not as strong and their cumulative effect will be to mislead people if no other accompaniment exists.

Among further recommendations, the report warned, *"Beware of misleading women,"* and advised using radio to link the film's background music with a message about the film's Coppola-innovative romantic story of realism *and* fantasy, and having Mr. Coppola make a personal appeal on radio and television, explaining how he had tried to do something different in his new movie. The report concluded, "If people understand better than they have so far just what precisely they might go to see, *One from the Heart* can generate interest, better word-of-mouth, and break through the vicious cycle of bad publicity, mixed reviews, and poor box-office which is now threatening it so severely."

Cambridge also recommended that Mr. Coppola show segments of *One from the Heart* in television commercials.

At Zoetrope, the report was read and studied by Mr. Coppola, Mr. Spiotta, and Fred Roos, one of the producers of *One from the Heart.*

At Columbia, James Spitz, the president of domestic distribution, still had confidence in *One from the Heart.* "Box-office grosses for the picture are so far disappointing, but we're tenacious individuals, and we think there's a following for the picture," Mr. Spitz told a reporter. "We'll create a groundswell for the picture. Give it a quote class presentation unquote. That's what we did with *Tess.* Gave it a successful image. One of the great strengths of Columbia is, we believe in the team concept. We all saw the film at the Westwood preview. We all thought it was a unique piece of work. We all thought commercially it had potential. We've probably got the most innovative, most contemporary marketing methods. We brought in new marketing concepts for the picture. We prescribed new ads. We gave the picture a different look advise. We're proceeding to launch this picture like *Tess.* On the basis of that parameter, we're going for the really big presentation in class theatres—New York's Tower East; Mann's Chinese Theatre, in Hollywood; and Century Plaza, the Chicago Water Tower, and ten suburban theatres in affluent, middle-class areas. We'll then pull back to eight theatres in eight cities and try to maintain the run as long as possible in New York, Los Angeles, San Francisco, Cincinnati, Seattle, Toronto, and Dallas. We're going at it with renewed vigor. Nothing is written in stone in the film business. We'll profit not only in the film business. We'll profit not only in the film but in the relationship with Francis Ford Coppola."

Others on the Columbia team echoed Mr. Spitz's views on marketing *One from the Heart* with renewed vigor, in the customary noun-into-verb idiom. "We'll platform the picture from eight cities," said Peter Benoit, Columbia's national publicity manager. "We did that with *Absence of Malice*. By the time that picture broke wide, there was an awareness of the picture's content. By the time that picture opened, there was already a groundswell. With *Neighbors*, we knew we had to capitalize on the immediacy of the picture. So we opened it in fourteen hundred theatres. That's called get-the-money. With a special-handling picture, we give it a special-handling release. Like *Tess*. Here we've got something special—our relationship with Francis Ford Coppola."

At Zoetrope, Fred Roos said, "We want to pull back to cities we're comfortable in. A movie's life is years and years. Our concern is that the picture's reputation is solidified for the future."

By April 1, seven weeks after the opening, when the only theatre showing *One from the Heart* was the Guild, in New York, there were forty-three people in the theatre at the last showing. The next day, the movie was gone.

"Columbia was willing to release four hundred prints in a hundred markets," Mr. Spiotta recently told a reporter. "But we decided to remove it from release. We didn't want to go through those kinds of motions. Columbia was very cooperative. A few weeks ago, Francis had a chance to make a few changes in the movie, to polish it here and there. And now he feels it's even better. This fall, we're releasing it in three test markets—in Dallas–Fort Worth, in Minneapolis–St. Paul, and in Vancouver—and with a new advertising campaign. The final chapter is not yet written."

In April, Mr. Coppola announced that Zoetrope Studios—the actual real estate—was up for sale. At about the same time, the big business news about Columbia Pictures was that the Coca-Cola Company stockholders had voted overwhelmingly in favor of acquiring the movie company, thus making Columbia a wholly owned subsidiary of Coca-Cola. "Within the structure of Coca-Cola, Columbia will be tantamount to one can in the overall corporate six-pack," *Variety* wrote in its report of the merger. "That is, Col's annual gross of $700 million will be swallowed up by Coke's annual $5.9 billion gross."

In Tulsa, Mr. Coppola was immersed in working on his two new movies, but he kept posted on developments concerning his past debts. "Chase has been insisting that we sell the studio in order to pay it back," he said, fairly unemotionally, to a friend. "If we sell the studio and other assets in order to repay Chase the thirty-one million they are owed on *One from the Heart, Escape Artist,* and *Hammett,* they are willing to cooperate and not foreclose on the collateral. When a bank loan is in trouble, the bank turns it over to 'work-out' people, and they are very, very, *very* tough. We may get them to understand, however, that the best thing I can do to repay them is to go on working. One thing about me, I sure put in the hours."

A few weeks later, Mr. Coppola said, "Whatever happens with *One from the Heart* now may have an effect on how easy or difficult it will be for me to go on making movies, but I know for certain now that making that film the way I wanted to make it has already given me a lot. I've already learned so much from the experience in two major ways: first, about the filmmaking process itself, what I feel a film *is*; and, second, various practical realizations having to do with the things that make it possible to make a film—the raising of the money, relations with the press, and so on. The *most* important single thing I've learned, actually, is to play everything closer to the vest from now on. I enjoy the work I do, and, because I enjoy people, I tend to try my ideas out on them. I always find myself talking, and showing people things and ideas, much the way a playwright wants to get an audience reaction to his play. Bouncing off their reaction, you get a whole new bunch of ideas. So I would find myself telling everyone everything—even things that haven't yet been proved, or things that are only hopes or ideas. In the past, I often found myself in all kinds of trouble that I wouldn't have been in if I had kept my ideas to myself. There are all sorts of storms and turbulences out there in the world, and, because I tend not to be concerned with protecting myself, even though I thought I was only putting a toe in I'd be sucked way out in the storm. People on the outside have their arguments and different positions they're in tumult over, and if they hear a peep out of me I've let myself be sucked into the middle of *their* storms, thus making it very difficult for me to pursue my own business. I therefore jeopardize myself—make my job much tougher than it needs to be. The issues I found myself immersed in during the making of *One from the Heart*—all the trouble about the financing—have always been the thing of least interest to me. Money has never been the most important part of my life, and, of course, that is why I was able to take some risks in order to do my work. Quite ironically, I think that *One from the Heart* was overshadowed in the minds of the public by the money troubles. Few people seemed to look at the movie in just its own light, as a personal film a filmmaker had made in which he was maybe trying to find a new vocabulary for himself. What is important to me about the movie is the way I felt about it and the way I thought film might someday be used.

"Ever since I started making films, I've tried to use the theatre director's approach—imagining this enormous production as an event that I want to create—and then I've gone with the camera and sound and tried my very best to record it as I imagined it. There is another point of view—the illustrator-director's approach—which I think is the opposite of my own. That starts with a series of pictures, moving pictures, which you produce, and which, when the pictures are displayed, *becomes* a production."

In May, Mr. Coppola made an arrangement with the Chase Manhattan Bank that required him to increase his personal liability in exchange for an extended repayment schedule; the agreement allowed both Mr. Coppola and Zoetrope the opportunity to liquidate real property, including the Hollywood studio, and various motion-picture rights for the repayment of the Chase loan. Under the circumstances, Mr. Spiotta was satisfied with the agreement. "Banks don't win by suing clients," he explained to a business novice. "Had the agreement not been reached, it would certainly have required a bankruptcy action by Zoetrope and possibly personally by Francis. Now Francis can do the one thing that can turn his financial fortunes around, and that one thing is going on to make other films."

Last month, Mr. Coppola took a quick trip to Europe in connection with the openings of *One from the Heart* in France, Germany, and Sweden.

"At the French pre-opening screenings for critics and others, the response to the movie was so much more alive than it was here," Mr. Coppola told a strongly pro-*One from the Heart* friend on his return

to this country. "The reviewers were really *interested* in what I was trying to do. Business there has been good—as good as the business for *Blade
Runner*, anyway," he said. "But in Sweden the movie is doing very, *very*
good business. In Sweden, they really seem to *like* the movie."

Mr. Coppola was quiet for a moment, looking somewhat puzzled.
"I'm bothered by the nagging idea that I failed in what I was trying to
do," he went on. "*One from the Heart* had its roots in so many of the
aspects of my life that to have had it rejected here with such indigna-
tion causes me to wonder about all my preoccupations and ideas. First,
there was theatre, and theatre for me was technology: lighting boards
and fly systems and trapdoors. There was remote control, as demonstrated for me by my Lionel train set when I was a little kid—the way
I controlled the milk car and the cattle car, the switch tracks, and, best
of all, the direction of the locomotive. Then, there were the songs. The
first time I heard songs in a story I cared about was when my family
went to see Sigmund Romberg's *The Desert Song* on the occasion of my
brother's birthday. I will never forget it, though I could have been only
five or six years old. This, along with the experience ten or twelve years
later of watching my father as he conducted the orchestra for the road
company of *Kismet*, fixed in me the desire to create fantasy with music
and songs. Then, when I was paralyzed, although I loved my brother
and sister with a kind of fairy-tale devotion and intensity, I was always
hungry to be with other children. When I put on my shows alone in my
room, I dreamed about the day when I would put on shows with others
and people would come to see them. I was dreaming, I'm sure, about
having a place like my studio, where we could learn, and teach what
we learned to others."

Mr. Coppola paused, and then he said, "I doubt whether many people
understood the depth of my feelings on this subject. I have no doubt
that I have the energy and the resourcefulness to keep going with the
studio. But sometimes I wonder whether it's worth it in such a cynical
and frightened world." He paused again and pushed his glasses up on the
bridge of his nose. "I love *One from the Heart* not only for what it is but
for where it was going," he said. "I love Zoetrope Studios for the same
reason. We were doing all sorts of things for the first time. I'm sure that
we have profoundly influenced other moviemakers, and we deserve the
opportunity to go on. Every once in a while, I start feeling a bit down,

but I'm really enthusiastic about the future. My head is percolating with new ideas about everything. You know, some of those Chase bankers told me they liked the movie. I told the bank I'll make the first payment with the money we get from the sale of the studio and the money owed us for the foreign distribution of *One from the Heart*. For the second payment, I'll use the money we get from the cable sale of *One from the Heart, Hammett,* and *The Escape Artist.* In the meantime, I'll be finishing everything on *The Outsiders* and *Rumble Fish.* So what if my telephone is turned off again at home? Or my electricity is shut off? Or my credit cards cancelled? If you don't bet, you don't have a chance to win. It's so silly in life not to pursue the highest possible thing you can imagine, even if you run the risk of losing it all, because if you don't pursue it you've lost it anyway. You can't be an artist and be safe."

Idols of the King: *The Outsiders* and *Rumble Fish*

DAVID THOMSON AND
LUCY GRAY/1983

We had seen Francis Coppola several times over the last year and a
half—at Napa, on the weekend he realized *One From the Heart* had
failed; at Napa, a year later, as the editing of *Rumble Fish* was going on
above the winery; at the Tosca one night, in San Francisco, as he took a
breather from the two-week task of rewriting *The Cotton Club*. It has
been a time of turmoil, ending and beginning again, as Zoetrope
lingered in the balance and its founder got on with making movies.

Amid all that thunder and darkness, *Rumble Fish* is his best film, the
most emotional, the most revolutionary and the most clearly in love
with 1940s movies. It has a mood from Camus and the French
Existentialists, but it looks and feels like Welles and Cocteau. The
Tolandesque fusion of Tulsa heat wave and the fever dreams of adoles-
cence is a rhapsody to fraternity, in particular to the triangle of two
brothers and their broken father—Matt Dillon, Mickey Rourke, and
Dennis Hopper. It is deliberately an American art film—as full of the
heart's creaking sounds as *Kane*—and a legend of love, aspiration, and
loss in a remote province of a world that looks to L.A. as the light. So
open in person, Francis Coppola is also a closed-off, guarded man,
afraid to divulge all his experience, a Michael Corleone trying to be like
Sonny, as well as a Matt Dillon longing to be as cool as Mickey Rourke.

From *Film Comment*, vol. 19, no. 5 (September–October) 1983. © 1983 by *Film Comment*.
Reprinted by permission of the authors.

Rumble Fish is a myth as beautiful as *Orphée,* but it is also a confession on the maker's own early life and abiding psychology.

The happiest years in his forty-five were at the ages of five and six. They gave rise to his intense admiration for his older brother, Augie, to whom *Rumble Fish* is dedicated. And as we met Francis Coppola again, in his Sherry-Netherlands apartment, it took several minutes to recognize his child-like nature beneath the exhaustion of round-the-clock rewriting and rehearsals on *The Cotton Club* (which began shooting in late August). He had been up all night writing with his newest signing, William Kennedy (*Legs, Billie Phelan's Greatest Game, Ironweed*). He pierced his beleaguered greeting with an excited story about having fired a group of secretaries, that afternoon at the Astoria Studios, because they had been short-tempered with his daughter, Sofia, and her friends who were trying to help round the place. "I simply can't abide that nine-to-five attitude. It's not conducive to the kind of filmmaking I believe in."

Having sent off another guest and completed a short meeting in the next room, Francis settled into conversation with us. He never found a comfortable sitting position; he vibrated with desperate energy. But as the conversation picked up momentum, so he found passion, unexpected insight and associations too quick or instinctive for sentence structure. We sipped wine from his own Napa Valley grapes as he made dinner plans with his son. That arranged, he demonstrated some new sound equipment for an advanced video player. He chose a Shostakovich symphony, and the booming, crystal-clear sound drew his daughter and friends, now back from the studio, to gather for a listen. We could imagine Coppola convincing teenagers of the merits in the sophisticated *Rumble Fish,* so long as he could do it in person. They may feel that he has created, as an adult, what everyone hopes to create as a child: a huge playroom full of equipment and people willing to devote themselves to any scheme he might invent. *Rumble Fish* is a Xanadu of a picture, and Coppola is just like Charlie Kane, too busy, too creative, too happy spending money to grow old. He may never make his Media Dome in Belize, but its romance goes everywhere with him. Zoetrope, among other things, still owns the rights to *On the Road* and *Peter Pan*. Francis Coppola is the one man who could make those two books in one movie. —**D.T., L.G.**

Q: Rumble Fish *is so completely different a film from* The Outsiders, *not just in black and white and color, but in the tone. And everybody said, "Well, he's off in Tulsa, making two films," rather in a way that, once, people would go up to the desert and make two westerns at the same time.* Rumble Fish *makes* The Outsiders *seem an odder film than I thought it was when I first saw it.* The Outsiders *almost felt like a film in which you weren't quite there all the time.*

A: No, I don't think so. *The Outsiders* was the type of film that I personally liked, a melodrama with a romantic tone. I liked the book a lot when I read it; I thought it was sweet and youthful and had something in its little, simple theme that was of value, and I wanted to make the picture very much as the book was. Maybe that's what you're interpreting as my not always being there, except that I *did* make the decision to make it exactly like the book.

The key to *The Outsiders* is the score; the fact that it's this schmaltzy classical movie score indicates that I wanted a movie told in sumptuous terms, very honestly or carefully taken from the book without changing it a lot, with young actors—putting the emphasis more on that kind of *Gone with the Wind* lyricism which was so important to the young girl [Susie Hinton] when she wrote it.

I liked the film on that basis. It's how I made it and why I made it. But if you think about my career, I've never made two films that were alike . . . maybe the two *Godfathers.* But every one of my films is very different from one another and I was feeling that I was in kind of a journeyman period of my life, approaching a future style of work as a more serious, older man which would be based on a tremendous amount of exploration while I had the chance to do that.

To me it's nothing to say, well, I'm going to make that film and it's going to be that kind of film. Like *The Outsiders*—it's not that I couldn't make that sixteen other ways. People suggested, "Well, are we really going to make this book like that?" "Well," I said, "little kids wrote me a letter and wanted me to make it that way." Of all the letters I get from movies, *The Outsiders* is the one where all of these cute little fourteen-year-olds . . . so I'm in it for *them.* I feel I must have gained something, although it wasn't as challenging, cinematically or even on the level of acting and other things as, say, the one that came afterwards. But I always had this idea that I wanted to make one film that was romantic and schmaltzy, like *The Godfather,* and one film that was more of an art film, more in the direction of *Apocalypse.*

Q: *Can you tell us when it was that the idea for* Rumble Fish *came up?*
A: When I was working on *Outsiders,* I had heard about another book from some of the kids who had read it, called *Rumble Fish,* and it reminded me of "The Banana Fish," a short story of Salinger's. What was it? "Wonderful Day for Banana Fish" ["A Perfect Day for Banana Fish"]? And it just stuck in my ear, the odd word, rumble fish. Also, when I saw a copy of it, it was very short and I like short novels. I just started to pick it up and read it. It was written when Susie Hinton was older— and drunk, I think. It had tremendous, really impressive vision and dialogue and characters and complicated ideas, the kind of ideas you don't totally understand in your head but you feel that you understand them. It's the fact that you keep thinking about it that makes it enticing. And it affected me that way along with the fact that we had seen Mickey Rourke at one of the auditions for *Outsiders* and were very impressed with him, yet there was no real part for him to play.

So we teamed Mickey and Matt, which had a lot to do with Fred Roos saying, "Well, that would be great," because I was even wondering whether I should do it younger. The story is written about a fourteen-year-old. Somehow, because of the mention of the color blindness, I just imagined it in black and white. It was suggested from the novel, I didn't impose that. And then the idea that if we want to show that someone goes color blind, then maybe we would have to have color in it and then take the color away again to give the feeling of color blindness. And that's where the idea of having some color elements in the piece and then the more that got moved around, we thought maybe only the fish themselves—the metaphor of the story—would be great if they were in color.

Q: *We're talking about a time during the shooting of* The Outsiders?
A: Yes. While we were shooting *The Outsiders,* I was writing the screenplay of *Rumble Fish.* And thinking about it and what have you, and the idea certainly came that we could go right from one to the other, and although it would have the same cast, the films would be totally different. For one thing, not only were they both in black and

white and color, but *Outsiders* was in wide screen and *Rumble Fish* is in 1:1.85, which is the closest we could get to 1:1.33 which is more for filmmakers—the lenses are better. And I really started to use *Rumble Fish* as my carrot for what I promised myself when I finished *Outsiders*.

Also, quite honestly, as you can figure out, I threw *Outsiders* into production immediately after the failure in the United States of *One from the Heart*. Rather than go through six months of being whipped for having committed this sin of making a film that I wanted to make, I escaped with a lot of young people to Tulsa and didn't have to deal with the sophisticates. I had been a camp counselor when I was younger, and I always got along very well with kids. I like being with kids rather than adults, so it turned into a way for me to soothe my heartache over the terrible rejection at that point. Also, *The Outsiders* had a certain financial promise to it, and I knew right then and there that even though the *One from the Heart* reception happened on one particular day, three months later I was going to be in the heaviest financial trouble I had ever been in. So rather than worry about it, I just started working, figuring that the thing that could save me the most was if I stepped up production. Also, a lot of the electronic experimentation that we had been doing was beginning to bear fruit, and I felt confident that we could make the films for modest sums, very well controlled. And in fact that's what happened. *The Outsiders* threw up just enough money to help me at a time when I needed some big bucks.

Q: *When you proposed doing the second film, virtually without an interval between the two, was raising the money easy . . . ?*
A: Well, no one took me seriously at all. We were working on *Outsiders*, and I knew we had this abyss coming up, because those kinds of financial problems don't hit for a while. Like, you're in trouble, and everyone knows you're in trouble. But by the time all the wheels turn the rest of their revolution, you're three or four months down the ride. So I figured as much production as I could get would be good. Most people looked at me, "Oh, sure, sure, *Rumble Fish*, but pay attention to *The Outsiders*." And they just sort of ignored it. But when the tint film was over I got very serious and said I'm really going to make it. Warner Brothers turned us down, some people say because they felt that we would compete with *The Outsiders*. I feel that *The Outsiders* suffered from a

little bit of the chaos of everybody turning yellow when they saw the rough cut of it, and that influenced it being cut shorter and shorter.

I actually have to go look at the movie again, because I didn't understand why so many people disliked it when I didn't think there was anything all that important to dislike. I thought it was very much like the book.

I believe directors should direct—they *are* directors. If I get a job to direct *A Streetcar Named Desire* in a play, the theatre, I'm going to do my best to do *Streetcar Named Desire*, I'm not going to try to imprint it with my own bizarre imagination, although I could. That was the attitude. I took it to do that, and I was very proud of the fact that I was able to do that. Go take something, assess what it is and make it like it is. But, nonetheless, maybe it's true—my interest in it was of a certain . . . it was a lot of work. You do a film like that—take the fight scene in *The Outsiders*, that was as hard as anything I've ever done. It's hard as anything in *Godfather*. It was also more unusual in concept. So we were working very hard. I guess maybe it really comes down to the fact that I *might* have written a script that took *The Outsiders* and interpreted it in a way different than the way she told the story, but then it wouldn't have been *The Outsiders*. So what do you do? And with *Rumble Fish,* I guess we were starting to get a real means of production. We had a very good production team, we were full of energy and enthusiastic and everybody was up for making the film again. And I would talk with the photographer during the end of *The Outsiders* and we decided, oh, we're going to use all short lenses and it's going to look like this. . . .

I used to kid around and say it was an art film for kids or that it was Camus for kids, or it looked to me like the way I imagine those kinds of writings of the Existentialists. And it appealed to me that kids could see *Outsiders* as a lavish, big feeling epic about kids without any English on it. Those kids have gargantuan romantic feelings if they're anything like we were, so I wanted to do that, but the other one I wanted to be like *Peter and the Wolf* for kids, where you were making a film and you say, "Aha, films also can be made in black and white with 14 mm lenses, and the soundtrack and the music can be part of the movie. The acting can be of this very convincing although somewhat stylized nature, etc., etc., etc. And let young people see that." Anyway, give it to them, and even if they don't like it at first, when they're two years older they might.

Q: *You dedicated the film to your brother, and it makes one suspect that,*
although The Godfathers *are both films about brothers, the way in which*
Rumble Fish *is about brothers may be much more personal and important*
for you.

A: It is. It's very personal. *Rumble Fish* does come out of a certain period
of my life when I was about seven, eight, nine, in an area not too far
from here, near Astoria Studios, in a place called Woodside. I was in a
wonderful kindergarten in another neighborhood by the beach, and my
memory of being five years old is really wonderful—it's still the best five
or six years of my life—and then we moved to this other neighborhood
and suddenly it was alleyways, which is what *Rumble Fish* looks like in
that movie. And I had a brother five years older—I *have* a brother five
years older than me who was my idol, who was very, very good to me.
Just took me everywhere and taught me everything. You know, when
he went out with the guys, because he was the leader of the gang and
he was tremendously handsome, still is. . . . He could easily have shaken
me, said I don't want to take him. I slept in a room always with him
up until I was ten or eleven. Until he moved to the attic and just got
depressed and stared at maps of Tahiti.

He was a very advanced kid. He was a great older brother to me and
always looked out for me, but in addition, he did very well in school and
received many awards for writing and other things, and he was like the
star of the family and I did most of what I did to imitate him. Tried to
look like him, tried to be like him. I even took his short stories and
handed them in under my name when I went to the writing class in
high school myself. My whole beginning in writing started in copying
him, thinking that if I did those things, then I could be like he was. He
had always liked big dreams and read books. He was reading André Gide,
Jean-Paul Sartre, telling me about James Joyce when I was fourteen. I
didn't understand it much. And he always included me.

When I was in military school one year I was sent to live with him in
California; he was a UCLA student and he lived in some little dinky
house in Westwood and we had three other guys living there, and there
were a couple of girls living there and it was this wonderful summer . . .
and it was all this intellectual stuff, reading books. That's when I started
to write to be included in that crowd that I was five years too young for.
And when I went back to military school after that, I could never get

with it again, the level of what was going on there, and I ran away ulti-mately because of that—went to Great Neck High School, which was more along the lines of this experience with my brother.

At any rate, this relationship with him during those years was a pow-erful part of my life. I had a dream once as a kid that scared me to death. I was in one of those kinds of streets and there was an enormous manhole, big manhole cover, and these tough kids were getting my brother and putting him in there and were going to cover him in this manhole. And I ran to the different houses to get a phone to call the cops. I never forgot that dream. And somehow, all of the feelings of what I'm telling you about . . . the jacket in the movie that his son wears, you know, Nicholas Cage, that wild goose jacket? That was *his* jacket, my brother's; it was a copy of his real one.

And he had such a magical allure in that way that when I read the book it recalled that. So I made the character look like Camus, and that was the initial handle that Mickey used with the cigarette. I would say that my love for my older brother formed the majority of aspects of what I am, and the other part was formed by my father in terms of my atti-tude towards music. My father played the flute and you can imagine how that felt to a little kid. So I think that a lot of what I'm like is from the fact that I was the audience of the most remarkable family. And I took it all as magic—I believed everything. My mother, who was a kind of childlike woman, pushed a lot of magic. I believed in Santa Claus until I was nine or ten.

Q: *It is one of the most pulled-together, precise films I have ever seen.*
A: Well, it went well. It went smoothly.

Q: *Sound, picture, color . . . everything . . . the shading in light and dark, everything.*
A: The music came out of another thing. I have this idea of what kinds of films I want to be making in a couple of years, which are quite differ-ent than what I'm doing now, or that anyone's doing now, I suppose. And one of the things I'd like to be able to do is write my own music.

I also promised myself that on *Rumble Fish* I could write my own music, and I had a very, very precise concept of how it was going to work. In fact, I had done a lot of it in a kind of mock-up by getting my kids and their friends and my nephew to read the script while we were in a recording studio and I was beating out different metric ideas to express time. One of the central concepts was the idea of time running out, and young people not understanding that time is running out. So we cooked up this whole score with all percussion and solo bass, which I played myself. Well, one idea came along that the drummer to do the times be Stewart Copeland, who is such a good drummer and he had that precision in some of the Police things. So I met him and he was a terrific guy and I enjoyed meeting him, and he came after rehearsal to provide these rhythms. We had these rehearsals with the drummer who turned out to be a composer actually there. In other words, the project was sort of born in that kind of theatrical happening. What happened with the music was that more and more I thought what he was doing was so good that I just kind of faded back and then I said, "Look, I think what he's doing is great." And he's a pretty interesting fellow. Then, of course, the other component was to try to express the time running out by time lapse, so that I had this thing of streets, and the shadows just go down the hill like that. . . .

Q: *Is it hard for you now, deep down, to believe that you have become easily the best known and the most remarkable member of the family?*
A: Well, I can understand that I'm more famous than any of them. I think it's a little bit like Napoleon's family. You know, when we were kids and we went to say our prayers at night at four and five years old, the beginning of memory, we always included in our prayers, "And let Daddy get his break." It was a major theme of my family.

We were told by my mother to pray for it. I can remember as a kid of fifteen working in a Western Union office and making up a phony telegram which said, "From so and so at Paramount Pictures, Dear Mr. Coppola, you've been made the composer of *Jet Star*, please come to Hollywood immediately. . . . " And we went and delivered the telegram, and then we had to tell him that it was fake.

What inspired my father's career was his vanity and his desire to be appreciated. He did everything, he had little samples of radio programs—in other words, he had his fifteen-minute radio program back in the '40s and I remember those tapes. Since I was the only kid

who could sing, the only good graces I got in my family was when
I sang my father's songs for company, because no one else could do it.

Q: *When you asked him to compose some of the music for some of your*
films, was that a continuation of that?
A: I always felt that my father was a . . . There are few musicians
around, except for that generation, who are master orchestrators and
conductors. But aside from that, he also had, I thought, a really terrific melodic imagination, and as he got older he always fought being
schmaltzy. Some of his serious compositions are quite impressive. Somehow it was always a dirty trick that he never got the break that he seemed
to want so much. I didn't want it as much. My brother was always very
concerned with being the biggest guy and the most powerful guy and to
win the awards. I was not ambitious as a kid.

Q: *I'm surprised you didn't want to sing.*
A: I did a little bit. That was one of the few things that got me some
pluses, and I don't know why I never went and really studied. Everyone
always used to say, "You know, you ought to study, Francis," but they
never did anything about it, and then I guess when I got more into high
school, my whole schooling was so kind of meshugenah. I never went
to any school longer than a few months and so I never got into a glee
club or anything. I went to twenty-four schools before college, so I never
really took in any of them. My major passion in those days was science.
I was reading about scientists and I could have been a physicist if I had
had the math. I remember things I sketched out that I see have happened.

Q: *If you do compose music for your own films, how will your father feel*
about it?
A: Well, first of all, I'm going to make two pictures now, *Cotton Club*
and *Interface,* and then I intend to take, who knows, maybe three years
off. Not so much because I have other stuff I want to do, that I would
really like to do, but I'm becoming bored with the movie business. It
doesn't entice me anymore; it's kind of a nowhere situation for a guy like
me. So the projects that I would work on, starting in three years, would
go on to a time that wouldn't be relevant in terms of my father's lifetime.
Also, he knows that I have these aspirations. He's not encouraging me

at all, but he knew that I wanted to do the music on *Rumble Fish*, and when he heard a little tape—some of it had been recorded—he commented how a section of it sounded just like something he had written. I neglected to tell him that that same section also sounded like something some guy a hundred years ago had written. But my father has never been a very encouraging man.

Q: *Have you helped his career, do you feel? Do you feel proud of him?*
A: I made his career. I feel the guy deserved whatever success he got for himself. I didn't put the notes on the paper. He can take a big sheet of paper and write out a score for a sixty-piece orchestra. How many people can do that? I'm very proud of that. His knowledge of music is tremendous. It's like Leonard Bernstein or these masters who just know it. I have a lot of respect for him. He has a brother, by the way, too—a very big musician—there's a big, competitive story there. He lives right here in Central. . . . He's a very well-known conductor, more successful than my father is. He's a big deal in the family.

Q: *You were saying that you had a row at the studio today with people over an incident provoked by your daughter. Some of the kids just came into this room and it makes me think, just from seeing you at home a few times like this, that you love to have them around you.*
A: Well, as a child, I always loved other children. And one of my great frustrations, as with many children, was that I didn't have friends, or that I didn't get to be in school long enough or wasn't able to keep my early friends from kindergarten where I was very happy. Kindergarten was really—and I'm not exaggerating—was five times as good as the rest of this life. It's never gotten back to that. For me it was a magical time, building stuff and telling stories and playing with girls— it was just all it should be. And, if anything, I tried to create that again.

Zoetrope was nothing more, and is nothing more, than a college drama department rolling over into adult life, and even the incident you're talking about today isn't really the incident about Sofia, it's the point of view that a movie studio and the movie business is some- thing for youth and for experimentation and for life and for fun and for all those qualities. I loathe the other force that wants to bulldoze it into something of accounting and bureaucracy and nine-to-five and, "What do you mean, there's children in this studio?"—I hate that. I will kill that. Because that to me is what has destroyed a big part of our movie heritage in the country already. It's as though someone tore down the Chrysler Building, which is what has happened to Warner Brothers, or knocked down the Brooklyn Bridge, which is what happened to MGM. And not only did the edifices or the systems go, but the tradition of the youth coming in, the young people.

I find as I'm now pushing forty-five, all the more precious to me is to make sure that the young people inherit the cinema. Because the middleman and the merchandising men and the marketing men will close the youth out of it, and the traditional old leaders out of it—the so-called valued, former filmmakers who still want to work and participate. See, my whole idea was to *keep* those two extremes. To me, it's a war, that I don't imagine I would try to win, but it's the same thing that happened to automobiles when the designers stopped designing cars, and the kids didn't run to the newspaper because the 19XX Pontiac was coming out . . . we ran, we would walk miles to see a new car. And that problem spread all over every level of our lives and our world and it's going so quickly that I need almost a couple of years to think about it, to understand whether I should give up or I should . . . or maybe I'm doing it in a wrong way.

I never thought of myself as a younger person as being particularly special or particularly talented. I just knew that I work harder than anyone and I had a lot of good ideas, fresh imagination. But I couldn't make anything where people'd say, "Ah, isn't that beautiful." Even now I can't do it. I've never made a film that has been received like that. A lot of my films in retrospect have been that, but the pleasure of making it and putting out like you serve a meal and everyone says, "Oh boy, was that good!" I've never really had that.

I always used to feel as a kid that maybe there were people who had a lot more talent than I had; that I just had a little ribbon of it, a little thread of it—but then if I could follow it long enough that I could find the real deposit later. And then maybe a lot of those people who had such impressive flash-in-the-pans of talent would fade away, and they have. So that I'm now, more than anything, interested in getting to go my own way. And I don't think that the regular movie business is going to tolerate me.

I think that my kind of unfortunate thing with the newspapers is just based on a misunderstanding, really. A misunderstanding that can't be undone. But they didn't count on one thing: how a lot of the stuff I did was really sincere. I didn't show *One from the Heart* to do a publicity scam; I showed it to try to save it. And I didn't show them the studio to be a wise ass; I was proud of it. I thought it was a good idea. And they're so cynical today that they assume that anyone who does that kind of stuff must be getting Park Place and Broadway in a Monopoly game, is going to make them pay. So I always have been too candid, I always tell people everything that I feel and I'm aware that I have seriously endangered, if not half-finished, my ability to go on doing my own things. Because of a couple of misunderstandings.

Q: *If somebody swooped down and said "All right, we'll give you billions of dollars," would you have a field day or would you still quit or would you wait three years and think about it?*
A: First thing I would do is take the bulk of it, and I would try to unite, not in fact but in spirit and economics, Canada, all of North America, Mexico, Central America, South America. I would make this continent so economically protected that it would form some kind of common market. Because I would guess that if you could pull that off, then it would be something so formidable that there's no one else on earth that could want to give that any trouble, because it would be too stable, it would be too rich.

Q: *No one ever makes the connection between your thoughts of going to Belize and its proximity to the area over which America is most troubled and where it needs an American to speak to people.*
A: There are many other aspects to this issue. You can imagine that I have been talked to by people in Washington, and people say, "Well, why do you want to possibly do anything in a place like that, in a troubled area. . . .?" What they don't stop to think is that troubled areas always get the money, because Belize is necessary to the area, like a Hong Kong or a Switzerland, to stabilize it. There is an airport and it's functioning. My idea was always based on the notion that the Caribbean

was the Mediterranean of the future, and that one of the big four world industries was going to be telecommunications. And telecommunications can be based anywhere you want to put it. What it needs is one beautiful environment so that half the people would want to go there. Belize has the biggest, most gorgeous coast, untouched, anywhere in the world. And two, it has to be a small, independent country, because you want to have your own satellites and you want to have your own government administer itself for the good of your main industry which is telecommunications.

Belize is three hours from here, three hours from New York, it's English-speaking, there's hardly any people there. I really . . . what I was thinking, my fantasy—well, I'm not going to really do this, of course, but in my fantasy life if I were writing a story about it, that's what I would do—I would turn the young people of that country and the young people of the Caribbean and young people in general to video. Give them the tools to do it and then make it a little national industry.

Q: *So you believe in video more than film?*

A: There will not be film in fifteen years except for industrial and biochemical or analysis reasons; it's simply . . . remember what happened to Super 8 black and white, then there was no black and white. Now there is no black and white 35 mm film. Film is already like the horseless carriage; it's not relevant. The thing about film is that it is *so beautiful,* and it's in the apogee of its development, that one can't say that there should be no film. But I'm saying, aside from that, that film is dead, it's finished. Because the new medium is so incredibly flexible and immediate and economical, and *can* be as beautiful.

Q: *It can be?*

A: Oh, sure it can. I mean, basically, when we talk about the beauty, the reason film is so beautiful is because it has occupied our imaginations for eighty, ninety, hundred years and they have learned how to get those emulsions, to carry those little chemical spots, while the electronic medium. . . . If you saw Betamax ten years ago, you wouldn't believe that it exists.

Now I have a camera which is this big and you can put the cassette in it, you can put the video right in it. The high definition television that Sony has developed shows that the physics can accommodate what we're talking about as soon as this enormous world market is going to cave in. You have to realize that one country is one type, another country is another type—countries can't really intercommunicate. The quality is poor, it's monaural, it's small.

This is going to change very quickly, if the little vested interests that control broadcasting will let it. The reason the medium isn't growing is because the people who control it don't want it to change. Usually history tells us that you can't stop that kind of innovation—ten years later or twenty years later, it's going to go. When it goes, it's going to be one standard and everyone in the world is going to be able to see everything in their language. Well, this is going to change the world. It's going to change politics, economics, art—and I assume it's going to change it for the better—since we know that in the past, usually, bad vested interest groups are those who hold the information. So I'm looking at that world, which is the world in which I'm going to be an old man. And I'm giving up on this world, because I can't deal with it anymore.

Q: *Does that mean that Zoetrope, as it's existed in its various forms for the last twelve, thirteen years is a thing of the past?*
A: Well, Zoetrope has always given birth to itself over and over again. It's done it four or five times. We were American Zoetrope because we were very young, we were very sincere, we believed we were American filmmakers and that Zoetrope was the traditional symbol of the cinema. After a while, we realized when we were more cynical that America wasn't going to help at all. That you've got to become international Zoetrope if you want to be anything. Or even more into new dimensions: Omni-Zoetrope for about a month. And then the idea of the studio came up and that really warmed my heart, because what I love more than anything is the theatre. The studio. The commissary, the actors coming, the excitement, staying up all night, getting the script down. We thought we'd have our own Hollywood studio in the image of the old one. And when that wasn't able to support itself, which is where we are now—I think it's about to be reborn; I think it's going to probably be called Zoetrope Corp., and it's going to end up in the Chrysler Building which is going to buy it. . . .

Q: *So far you've been describing all those pasts and all this future in this*
very complicated way—do you have a sense of now?
A: I have no present at all. I live like a flea in between two blocks of
granite, there's no space, it's horrible. I never have time to do anything
I want to do. I feel I'm always basically solving some problem with somebody which is not necessary. I'm always under the gun. I try to be
courteous with people, but there are lots of people! Usually I'm working
on a lot of projects, but when I was most happy in January, February,
and March of this year—it was a period which really fills me with a lot
of hope, when I was supposed to direct *The Pope of Greenwich Village.*
You know, I had some good ideas on it; I had Vittorio Storaro and the
idea of making a kind of George Orwell, down-and-out movie—in
New York. I got excited about that. Then they kept delaying it, partly
because Al was over on his picture, and then it stopped happening.
And I decided, instead of waiting for it or caring, that I would start
work on a new project that I had been thinking about. And I would go
to this cottage that I have—I have a beautiful library in Napa . . . on,
you've seen it. And I would go every day and work on this thing and I
just put out in those two months four-hundred pages of really interesting stuff, and I was working on that when I got the phone call about
The Cotton Club.

Q: *That stuff you were putting out then, can you give us an idea of what it*
was. Fiction?
A: Oh, yeah. My idea is that I would like to pass on to another job
classification. I would like to be a kind of—I don't have a name for it, so
I can only toss out some funny names for it—but I would like to be like
a chromakey novelist. You haven't seen any of the rehearsals, have you?
We now have the means where I can have a group of actors and I can
say, "All right, go out there and you're in a car and etc., etc.," and I can
do that. And the actors play it and when you see it on the screen it looks
like they're on a set. That can be done very convincingly if you know
how to do it. You put it in front of a screen and it would be kind of
invisible and you could do anything you want, but you can do many
sophisticated things, so you can totally create anything you might . . . if
you use live actors . . . you can put live actors . . . so it's not something
artificial or cold; it's just that the scenery is fake.

Q: *It's very like the theatre.*

A: But unlike the theatre, you do it by shot, so you can get the full vision of the cinema and you can make the whole illusion. I want to basically pick up not with the great filmmakers but with the great thinkers and novelists who were my brother's interests: Joyce, Thomas Mann, etc. And try to write a novel. But instead of it being a novel on the written page, it would be written in cinema.

Q: *Would you distribute this in the form of cassettes or discs?*

A: No, film. It prints out as movies. But it can be made in 1/20th of the time. And that's what I'm going to do. Instead of making a regular movie . . . twenty at a time, I'm going to take the same money and make it twenty times bigger. Go the other way. It's called—I'll tell you what it's called—*Megalopolis*. It all takes place in New York. And it's contemporary. It has many characters and it takes place in one day.

Q: *Like Joyce?*

A: Like *Ulysses*. But that's in all our lives, that pressure. *Megalopolis* is like Tokyo . . . but also, New York to me now is the perfect setting for a film which is going to attempt to deal with questions of who are we, where are we, what is the human race at this point? It's based in part on Roman history, because it takes a period in Rome just before Caesar, in which the conditions in Rome were almost identical. Everybody was into death, all the values had turned into a pursuit of money. Society was just spinning itself out. And this is the time of Cicero . . . and I researched this period, taking the incident of the revolt of Catiline, and I want to tell that story in a kind of Plutarch vision of New York as the Roman city, although it's not going to look Roman, it's going to look like New York.

Catiline was a real interesting character. He just wanted to burn everything and kill everybody—just to go down with society; he wanted to destroy it. A very interesting idea, of course. But ultimately, in its biggest scale . . . it has lots of dimensions to it. You know the Bendix takeover . . . it kind of tells itself on a level like that, and also the Steve Ross Corporation . . . it runs through the entire city: through the sewers, the stock market . . . it also shows the city as an organism. I really wanted to make an epic about today that deals with the theme of utopia. I think that utopia is a word whose time has come. We used to make fun of it, and we all know that the word utopia in Greek means nowhere. The way I'm going to do it is in a kind of elaborate, novelistic structure which has an intermission and a very bizarre second half going later and later into the night until the section that deals with three in the morning is really a wild section which ultimately puts forth the basis for the concept of utopia in the course of this mad hallucination that goes on. But I want to make a film about utopia, about what it is. It's been ignored. Everyone just laughs at it. We don't even think about it.

Q: *You were talking about that period earlier this year where you were writing a lot and obviously writing some of the basis for this project, when along came* The Cotton Club. *Can you go back?*
A: Well, *The Cotton Club* happened originally with Bob Evans, whom I don't know very well, but somehow Bob Evans inspires people to want to take care of him—maybe because he's like a reckless prince or something. At any rate, he's gotten in trouble a couple of times, and I've always felt compelled to help him. He called me in desperation with some hokey metaphor about his baby was sick and needed a doctor. Bottom line, I said I'd be happy to help him for a week or so, no charge, to see if I could give him my opinion. I was just thinking that maybe the script was a little screwed up, and quite honestly, I'm always anxious to try out my inventions. And he came up and I looked at it and I saw that there was nothing I could do in a week. There was nothing there, it was a shallow gangster story without any attempt at anything, you know? But in reading some of the research, I started to become more . . . there's a lot going on in that period and it's very rich and very stimulating. It has music, great music, and it has theatre—because it *was* a theatre—and it has beautiful dancers. So ultimately I took a shot at the script, then I reworked it. The whole thing was trying to hold it together for him. He kept offering for me to direct it, and I didn't want to because I'm terrified of being in a situation where I have people second-guessing me. Because my ideas don't sound good when I first say them, and they always sound really good later if I'm allowed to do them. But if I have to fight for everything, like I had to fight for Al Pacino and Marlon Brando, I don't have the energy anymore for that or I'm not willing to put up with it. So I made it very clear that if I were

to do the film, I would need to really control it on every possible level. And then of course I come here and although I have those rights, the same thing goes on. So finally I've just been putting them all in their place, for the sake of the picture.

What happened is that I'm going to do this film, *Interface*, which is very worthwhile, and I sort of fell in love with *Cotton Club*, if I could get to do it the way I see it. It's like an epic in its own way. It *is* an epic. It's a story of the times: it tells the story of the blacks, of the white gangsters, about entertainers, everything of those times, like Dos Passos, and the lives all thread through with "Minnie the Moocher" and "Mood Indigo." You can't lose if you handle that right.

Q: *You obviously knew that Evans was keen that you direct this, and it didn't take too much to see that the screenplay was a bait. When was it that you knew you were going to do it?*

A: Well, you know, my life has been very difficult this last year. I mean, we have the loan and then there's an article in *Newsweek* and we lose the loan. So it's been really like that, and I don't take it too hard. I'm pretty good about that stuff, but it puts you in a state of confusion, and we got ready for bankruptcy and Ellie had to turn over all of her jewelry and they came into the house to do all . . . So this was going on, and I can't say for sure what I am going to do because I don't know what the givens are. The *Pope of Greenwich Village* job was one that would pay a salary that would help, and there were several writing offers, and I almost wanted to work on something just so I could avoid all this chaos. So I said, I'll do *Interface* and *The Cotton Club,* one after another. I figured with that I would deal a devastating blow to my financial problem—maybe even find myself a couple of years . . . a chance to have a rest. I would very much like to have that. I've had no life, my whole life I have never had a vacation; I haven't been able to stay in an apartment or have fun. It's always been this absurd life. And I knew that *The Cotton Club* material was so rich that, if I had control, there was no reason why I couldn't make a beautiful film out of it.

Coppola Carves a Cinematic Elegy: *Gardens of Stone*

PETER KEOUGH / 1987

Francis Coppola was running a little late. Cara, a Tri-Star publicist with a South Carolina accent, guessed that while driving to the hotel from Fort Myer, the director had run into remnants of a massive peace demonstration that had filled Washington, D.C., earlier in the day. He would arrive, she estimated, in about fifteen minutes.

The delay and its reason added to the mood of foreboding. Coppola had just flown into town that afternoon to participate in the world premiere of his new movie, *Gardens of Stone*. He was maintaining an understandable distance from the press. A little less than a year ago, on Memorial Day 1986, during the first week of filming, his twenty-three-year-old son, Gian-Carlo, was killed in a boating accident on the Chesapeake Bay.

The driver of the boat, Griffin O'Neal, son of Ryan O'Neal, was convicted of "reckless endangerment." He had just begun his 416-hour community service sentence the day before the film's premiere. Undoubtedly Coppola would be preoccupied with these dark matters and discussing his movie—a story about the cermonial Army unit, the Old Guard, which buried the fallen in Arlington National Cemetery during the Vietnam War—would do little to dispel the melancholy.

In the film, a Vietnam vet, Sgt. Clell Hazard (played by James Caan), becomes a surrogate father to a rocky recruit, Jackie Willow (played by D. B. Sweeney). Despite Hazard's blandishments, the boy insists on going to Vietnam, and Hazard winds up burying him.

From *Chicago Sun-Times*, 10 May 1987. Reprinted by permission of the author.

There seemed to be no way to avoid uncomfortable moments in the conversation to come. The rococco atmosphere of the Tri-Star hospitality suite, as bright and gay as a canvas by Fragonard, took on the eerie aspect of mourning.

Abruptly, much earlier than predicted, the generous, full-bearded figure of Francis Coppola bounded into the room, vanquishing the gloom in an instant. "I'm starving," he announced, and made a beeline to a buffet table laden with pineapples, melons and wheels of pale cheese. "Halfway through the flight from L.A., they announce, 'This is a special snack flight,'" he explained apologetically. "So all I get is this bag of chips. I just want to get a slice of cheese."

Cutting a tiny bite, Coppola eyed it suspiciously, reconsidered, and took a cup of coffee instead. Sitting on the sofa, he cradled the cup, which was toy-sized in his big hands. His subdued gray suit highlighted the silver in his jet-black hair and beard; his sedate gray and burgundy tie outlined his expansive girth. Wasn't he at least a little anxious with his movie premiering?

"Is it?" He seemed surprised. "I guess it must be. I haven't seen the final cut yet, the print. I'm anxious to see it sitting down, with an audience. When I've seen it before, all I'd do is correct mistakes, saying, 'I need another day!' But I'd like to see it with an audience here. I wouldn't be nervous about it."

The real anxiety, Coppola pointed out, came in an earlier stage in the production. "We take the picture when it is semi-finished, and we preview it very extensively," he explained. "We get our lumps from these audiences, and we try to respond with further creative work. I'm the most nervous at that point, because I don't know what's coming."

What came during the pre-release screenings could not have been too heartening. The distinctiveness of the film is its embrace of the grandeur and pace of ritual and its reliance on character and mood rather than a dynamic story. These were precisely the elements that stymied the preview audiences.

"The issue of the military drill," said Coppola, somberly setting his cup and saucer on a coffee table, "seemed confusing to a young audience— and young audiences are pretty much what you get in these previews. They didn't seem to understand that there was something unique about this. They saw it only as marching. So we had to modulate these drills and let the ceremonies come across with beauty and not just as soldiers marching. And it's not a real narrative. There's not an engaging plot—in the first five minutes you're not on the edge of your seat to find out what's going to happen. It's more a poetic piece about the Old Guard and the characters involved. This means you have to give it a little more beauty to let it be interesting and enjoyable without the benefit of a strong plot."

Coppola deliberately avoided injecting the film with gratuitous excitement or exploiting some of the more spectacular possibilities of the period, the late '6os, in which the film is set. For example, mention is made that Hazard's love interest (played by Anjelica Huston), has been arrested in an anti-war demonstration.

"There was no scene like that in the Nicholas Proffitt book on which the film is based," Coppola said. "I was trying to be faithful to the book. I didn't want to juice the film up with that kind of superfluous plot and conflict. When I see movies or plays sometimes—you can tell when a scene looks like it's hyped up and the people are given a conflict that looks tagged on or readily resolvable. I've always tried to refrain from such formulas, though by so doing, you lose the benefits such more violent turbulence will give you.

"When I first read the screenplay, I had never seen a story about people who do the kind of work the Old Guard does. I thought it was moving and manly and had to do with traditions handed down. The whole issue of the Army as an old institution with lots of powerful traditions—I liked that part of it. I tried to depict that, and it was only halfway through the filming that I realized I really didn't have a story."

Older Coppola fans might find the film's sympathy for the military more disturbing. Perhaps it should not come as a surprise—Coppola, after all, did write the screenplay for *Patton* and *The Godfather, Parts 1* and *2*, and each was immersed in a love for tradition. But the reverence toward the Army displayed in *Gardens of Stone*, a film whose politics producer Michael Levy hedges with the description "pro-military, anti-war" is a little unsettling in comparison with the more radical vision of *Apocalypse Now*.

"I'm sure people will arrive at that comparison," Coppola said, unfazed. "But *Apocalypse* was from its inception a film about morality, almost a surreal epic that was *set* in Vietnam, but was not *about* Vietnam or about the Army. It could have been about the Persian Army in ancient Greece. It was about the spectacle of destruction, of warfare, of men on the brink. No opinion is expressed about the U.S. Army in *Apocalypse*. All those scenes are so flamboyant—surfing in the middle of combat—though there were elements of the Army that did things not unlike that. But I wanted to express a universal theme about soldiers out of control.

"*Gardens of Stone*, by contrast, was an extremely modest, personal story about a particular unit in the U.S. Army. Whether I was attracted to it because I had spent a short time in a military school, and I remember a certain appeal, or because of the uniqueness of these people who bury the dead, I don't know. And when I read the script, I was moved, I almost wept. There was something about depicting men in a way that shows the other side of the macho attitude—showing them loving their women, love in general. Not often do you get a chance to invent stereotypes like that. In *Gardens of Stone*, we were working with the Old Guard in a story about them. And I came to know them for the first time. They were gentlemen, and I ended with a very positive and affectionate attitude toward them."

The desire to show the human, decent and sympathetic side of the military is laudable, but wasn't the emphasis on the beauty of military ceremony, uniforms and memorializing dangerously close to a glorification of war?

Coppola regarded the question with some dismay. "Clearly, I wanted to use the rituals of the Old Guard to accompany their personal lives and the central theme, which seemed to be how we are entrusted to protect our children; we're sworn to protect our children; we want to protect our children, but . . . can't . . ."

He stopped and looked at the coffee cup on the table before him, half-empty and tepid. After a few moments, he resumed with more composure. "I thought it was interesting how when the young lieutenant [Jackie Willow] goes to Vietnam, he writes back, 'We lost three men today. You always lose the good ones.' So the same thing is happening to him that is happening to the Clell character, who tried, but couldn't save him. The Vietnam conflict was an example of one of the many similar, illogical, ludicrous conflicts that are cooked up on the world power front that our youth are sacrificed to. I view the Army as defenders. And if my government chooses to send the Army into some absurd military conflict in a desire for world power, the Army will go, but in itself, the Army is not making the policy, and I'm sure they would rather not. Our Army has for over two-hundred years not been an influence in the government. The military establishment perhaps has been so. But the Army, per se, has been standing there as the defenders of the country, waiting to be called on."

Whether the Army has influenced government policy seemed at the moment a moot point; more pressing seemed the question of how much it had influenced Coppola. The image of Coppola eluding peace demonstrators as he drove to the Tri-Star hospitality suite from Fort Myer, where much of *Gardens of Stone* was shot (and where he was staying as a guest of the Army during his recent stay in Washington), seemed particularly ironic. The U.S. Army had provided assistance in making this film, more so than any other film since John Wayne's *The Green Berets*, according to Lt. Col. John Myers, head of the team of Army advisers who oversaw the making of *Gardens of Stone*. Without this assistance, producer Michael Levy said, the production would have cost twice its actual $13.5 million budget. Given such conditions, wasn't it difficult to avoid making compromises?

"Compromises," Coppola repeated sardonically. "When you have to film a sunny scene and it's raining, you have to compromise. Filmmaking is the art of compromise. There is no question that this film is more conservative because I'm a professional director hired by a company. Whereas *Apocalypse Now* was a film I had financed. But now I don't have the mandate to go as far as I would if it was up to me."

Things have not been up to Coppola since 1983 when Zoetrope Studios, his filmmaking company that he hoped could operate free of the suffocating Hollywood film industry, collapsed into bankruptcy under the combined failures of *One from the Heart* (1982) and *Hammett* (1982). Coppola's debt was estimated at $15 million.

"I have been in the position for several years after I lost my studio where I decided I would just work continuously until I paid off my debt. I would choose something—although it wasn't something I'd written—that touched me.

"And it's true," he noted suddenly, "the movies you work on very much become your life at that time. It always seems like a coincidence, but now to me, it isn't such a coincidence. The movie is part of a process of trying to grow and resolve issues of your own life. I would say, even though I don't understand it 100 percent or even 50 percent, that those movies made after my attempt to found my studio very much show my desire to find out my own place. Where should I go? What should I do? And of course, questions about family, memory, love of friends."

Coppola paused and grew pensive. "But during *Gardens of Stone*, I can't say I was really myself. In fact, during the production experience, I was extremely . . . I was in a dream. I just wanted to get through it. Some nice people got me through that, people I worked with before. That's one of the real beautiful things about having a close crew. When someone gets the flu, the others sort of help him a little. I certainly was not myself. And trying to orchestrate a piece that didn't have as strong a narrative, I felt after a while I was shaving things with a razor not knowing whether I was having any forward motion. . . . But I'm glad we didn't add any phony plots. I'm glad it was poetic, in the spirit of the ceremonies themselves. I wanted to . . .

"Let's face it. I wanted to honor my son. . . . I think that the dead . . . you can't do much for them except honor them, and that's the basis of the Army in honoring . . . their fallen comrades. What else can you do? Try to do the rituals. Save the precious little things. Keep faith with them by honoring them." .

Coppola lowered his eyes. With a broad index finger, he rubbed under each of the lens of his glasses.

After a few moments, he began to talk about recent projects—his experiments in 3-D and his new film, *Tucker* about a maverick '40s car inventor. Coppola grew more animated, and as he spoke, a few people slipped into the hospitality suite. Some sat and listened or whispered among themselves, others picked at the wares piled on the buffet. Among them was *Gardens of Stone* producer Michael Levy, who laughed loudly at Coppola's wisecracks and dialects.

"I did it because it was in 3-D," Coppola said of *Captain Eo*, a wild fifteen minute film he directed for Disney boasting theatrical effects, explosions, spacemen and Michael Jackson. "When we finished. I asked my collaborator, the photographer Vittorio Storaro, what he thought. 'Now we have 3-D,' Vittorio said. 'When I go back to Italy, I make a film, it is only 2-D. I lose one D!"

"The film industry is losing many D's," Coppola said. "I feel like there are more opportunities and possibilities than ever before, but the film industry is entirely in the hands of a management mentality that would rather just keep repeating the same movies and sequels than use the tremendous resources of this country to invent and be creative. The time has come for industry—the entertainment industry, certainly the automotive industry—to let creative people be creative.

"But they won't," Coppola said, his fervor mounting. "Lawyers and managers want to fly around with their secretaries in their Lear jets: Like the guy in my new movie *Tucker*—he got squished in the end! They all do. Everybody does in this country. This is not a place for creative people. Do you think real estate brokers made this country this country? No, it was artists and inventors and . . ."

Cara, the Tri-Star publicist, stepped up to Coppola and pleasantly told him that they were running behind schedule.

"You got me just when I was getting controversial," he said with a laugh. "I hadn't been controversial until now."

He stood up. "Time to get that piece of cheese," he said, and walked to the big table.

Promises to Keep

ROBERT LINDSEY / 1988

Outside, New York City is sweltering in a heat wave. In an apartment on the Upper West Side of Manhattan, an eleven-year-old girl mixes a strawberry daiquiri in a blender, pours a glass for her mother, then sips from her own tall glass of foamy pink fluid.

Just a few feet away, in a high-backed canvas chair, a large, middle-aged man with receding black hair watches the scene on a television monitor that's perched on his right knee like an affectionate pet. With his high forehead, a thick body bordering on plumpness, a heavy dark beard streaked with gray and thoughtful eyes behind thick eyeglasses, he has the look of a kind and learned rabbi.

"This is going to be as bad as the horse's head," Francis Ford Coppola says.

"I know it; people are going to be outraged that I show a little girl who knows how to drink." Then, as if he feels it necessary to defend himself to his cast, he adds: "I think kids who learn about booze are more likely to respect it."

"All I heard after *The Godfather*, was 'cruelty to animals,'" he says a few moments later, referring to the 1972 movie that elevated him to stardom as a film director. He is talking about the scene in which a movie executive discovers a bloody horse's head in his bed, left by Mafiosi pressing him to give an acting job to a singer who's friendly with the Mafia.

"Thirty people were shot in the movie," Coppola says, seemingly confounded by human nature, "but people only talked about 'cruelty to animals.'"

From the *New York Times Magazine*, 24 July 1988. Reprinted by permission.

ROBERT LINDSEY/1988   133

On this morning in June, however, Coppola doesn't seem deeply concerned about the public's reaction to the scene he's filming. (It will be included in his segment of *New York Stories*, three short films by New Yorkers—Coppola, Woody Allen, and Martin Scorsese—to be released early next year.) He is thinking instead about his imminent liberation from Hollywood and what he considers his final Hollywood movie, *Tucker: The Man and His Dream*. On the eve of its release, he says he is ready to embark on a period of "amateurism and experimentation" as a Hollywood dropout.

Coppola has traveled this road before. Once part of the Hollywood establishment, he broke ranks to create his own studio, but failed. Now, approaching fifty, he is an outsider at once angry with industry moguls who stifle "creative people" and unsure of himself in the world they dominate. There are those who wonder if he is destined, like Orson Welles, to be remembered as a cinematic prodigy who never fulfilled his youthful promise, a director who burst onto the scene with originality and a willingness to take risks, snubbed the establishment, and was ultimately destroyed by it, or perhaps by himself.

Coppola prefers to consider his best work still ahead of him. "Two weeks from now," he says, "I'll be done here. I'll be free to do what I want. I'll be able to focus on things I want to do, not what other people want. I've been 'promising' all my life: first, I was a 'promising writer'; then I was a 'promising director.' Well, maybe at fifty, I'll fulfill the promise."

Few film directors have left a greater mark than Coppola on the American motion picture industry in the last twenty years. The first of a generation of celebrity directors whose talents were nurtured not on Hollywood's sound stages but in film schools, he co-authored *Patton*, which in 1970 brought him the first of his five Oscars. Also in the early 1970s, he directed two of the most honored and profitable movies of all time, *The Godfather* and *The Godfather, Part II*.

In Hollywood, where so few are able to divine the capricious tastes of a fickle public, the ability to make financially successful movies translates into power, independence and, ultimately, fear. Coppola's early blockbusters made him a force to be reckoned with in the motion picture business, and he used them to assert his independence from the seven Hollywood studios that finance and distribute most movies.

Like a Mafia godfather flexing his muscle on behalf of the members of his extended family, Coppola also used his clout to advance the careers of a coterie of young film makers, including the writer-director George Lucas, who created the *Star Wars* trilogy, and the directors John Milius and Carroll Ballard.

Movies directed by Coppola or produced by American Zoetrope, the company he founded in 1969, helped establish a galaxy of new stars: Al Pacino, Diane Keaton, Robert De Niro, Robert Duvall, Richard Dreyfuss, Rob Lowe, Emilio Estevez and Harrison Ford, among others. Coppola also helped scores of film editors, art directors, and other behind-the-camera specialists crack the Hollywood scene.

His influence swept through the movie business at a critical time. He had arrived in Hollywood to find an industry operating in a partial vacuum left by the post-war collapse of the studio system—where the major film companies kept legions of actors and directors under contract, and strong producers and studio executives, for better or for worse, controlled the content and budgets of movies. Coppola helped make American movie-making a director's medium, championing the new Wunderkinder and looking on as these disciples delivered high-grossing blockbusters that allowed them to operate, however profligately, without interference from producers. Often swimming upstream against convention and established power, Coppola seemed to be reinventing the rules.

Though on the surface Coppola's fortunes were rising, his vision of film making was changing, and the seeds of future troubles were being sown. *The Godfather* was, by Hollywood standards, a conventional movie: a vividly told story about the Mafia that had a beginning, a middle and an end and was photographed largely as Mario Puzo had written the novel on which it was based. In short, it was a movie that the industry could both marvel at and understand. But inside the director who made the brilliant gangster movie was a visionary aching to get out, aching to make movies that were *different*.

Coppola, then as now, does not like his movies to be bound by restrictions that he deplores with the generic epithet "naturalism." He wants, he says, to exploit the power of film to create works, as do artists in other media, that may deviate from apparent reality but that "explore what we are as a people and a nation and a world."

In 1974, the same year *The Godfather, Part II* was released, his audiences got a taste of this vision in *The Conversation,* a haunting story of a surveillance expert, played by Gene Hackman. In the movie, reality— or so it seemed—blended into fantasy.

As Coppola translated his visions into celluloid during the mid-1970s, some critics began to accuse him of self-indulgence. Studio executives began to close their checkbooks to his more innovative projects. And part of his audience—those moviegoers who wanted literal storytelling from the creator of *The Godfather*—began to desert him.

When Hollywood refused to finish bankrolling *Apocalypse Now,* a surrealistic story that wedded the horrors of the Vietnam War to some of the themes in Joseph Conrad's *Heart of Darkness,* Coppola decided to complete the financing himself. It went wildly over budget, costing more than $30 million in the end, $16 million of which Coppola put up himself. The movie eventually took in more than $110 million, but that took years.

Wealthy from his early successes, Coppola embarked on a daring enterprise that had tantalized Hollywood's hired hands since Mary Pickford, Douglas Fairbanks, Charlie Chaplin, and D. W. Griffith formed United Artists in 1919. He bought his own Hollywood studio, one whose gates he had passed daily as a dreamy and ambitious junior high school student during a time his family lived in Los Angeles. Announcing his intention to employ high-tech electronic editing and processing techniques that would revolutionize film making, he set out to make movies on his own terms.

The enterprise, to understate the case, was not a success. His vision, as exemplified in *One from the Heart* and other costly movie projects that failed, left him $50 million in debt. In 1984, the ten-acre Hollywood General Studios was sold at auction. Agreements were made that allowed Coppola to repay some debts at roughly thirty cents on the dollar and to keep his homes and his production company, which he renamed Zoetrope Studios. Then he went looking for work.

For the last six years, Coppola has played the role of a cinematic hired gun, directing, at a rate of one a year, other people's movies for about $2.5 million apiece, plus 10 percent of the profits. Of these, only one— *Peggy Sue Got Married,* for which Coppola shows little paternalistic pride—was a major hit at the box office.

He recalls the making of *The Cotton Club*, a troubled and critically panned movie set in Harlem that he took over from another director in pre-production, as an "unbelievably unpleasant experience." But, he says, he had to take on the job to help meet his debts and is resigned to the fact that most moviegoers will remember him as its creator.

The description you heard most often, Coppola remembers of his attempt to run his own studio, "was that the inmates had taken over the asylum." It is eight o'clock on a sultry evening in New York. He's sitting in the dining room of his apartment, purchased fourteen years ago at the height of his success, eating penne with bolognese sauce and sipping a glass of red wine from his 1,700-acre estate in the Napa Valley. This corner apartment in the Sherry-Netherland Hotel is one of Coppola's five homes. He considers the Victorian house in the Napa Valley his principal home; the others are in San Francisco, Los Angeles, and Belize.

With him at dinner are his wife, Eleanor, their seventeen-year-old daughter, Sofia, and several friends, including Nastassja Kinski. I had first met the German-born actress in 1981, a year after Coppola brought her to the United States to co-star in *One from the Heart*, his ill-fated, off-center story about love and life in America that cost more than $23 million to make but produced less than $2.5 million in revenues.

"Directors remind me of little boys," Kinski had said then about Coppola. "They say, 'I want this or I want that. It reminds me of a child who says, 'I want a castle built for me,' and they get it. Money does not seem to matter." We were speaking in her dressing room. A few yards away, Coppola had built one of the most expensive movie sets in the history of Hollywood for *One from the Heart*. The lot was a landscape of gray hangers, each containing its own magnificently detailed world. His glittering, surreal re-creation of neon Las Vegas alone cost more than $6 million.

That was the way things went in those days, Coppola observes as he savors a taste of his own wine. "The success of *The Godfather* went to my head like a rush of perfume," he says. "I thought I couldn't do anything wrong."

Born in Detroit on April 7, 1939, Coppola attended twenty-two schools in different parts of the country, a result of his father's travels as a musician. (He was born while his father was playing flute on the *Ford Sunday Evening Hour* radio show—thus his middle name.) But he spent most of his childhood in Queens and considers his roots to be in New York. His Italian-American family, he recalls, was close and warm: "It was kind of like a dream family." In addition to his father, Carmine, he idolized his older brother, August, now the dean of the School of Creative Arts at San Francisco State University, who introduced him to literature and awakened an interest in science and technology that is still a major element in his life. The actress Talia Shire, who plays the mother in Coppola's segment of *New York Stories*, is his sister.

In 1947, Coppola contracted polio and spent almost a year in bed, his legs paralyzed. "When you had polio then, nobody brought their friends around; I was kept in a room by myself, and I used to read and occupy myself with puppets and mechanical things and gadgets; we had a tape recorder, a TV set and things like that." Thomas Edison, Alexander Graham Bell and other inventors became his heroes.

"I became interested in the concept of remote control, I think because I had polio. I'm good with gadgets, and I became a tinkerer. I think what I really am is an inventor."

He decided to invent stories. Alone in his room, after reading works by James Joyce and other authors recommended by his brother, he played with his puppets, listened to *Let's Pretend* on the radio and began to fantasize stories that he might tell.

Later, at Hofstra University, Coppola was determined to become a playwright and plunged into the theater arts program. But after seeing *Ten Days That Shook the World*, the Russian director Sergei Eisenstein's epic movie about the Bolshevik Revolution, he decided motion pictures were the more powerful storytelling medium. He abandoned thoughts of studying at the Yale School of Drama and enrolled in the graduate film department at the University of California at Los Angeles.

At U.C.L.A., Coppola demonstrated a precocious flair for screen writing that caught the eye of Roger Corman, a maverick producer who operated a film-making factory for low-budget, non-union, mostly forgettable movies. Corman hired Coppola, first as a writer and general-purpose set roustabout, then as a director. The first movie he directed for Corman, *Dementia 13*, brought him critical notice in 1962. Five years later, he made

You're a Big Boy Now for Seven Arts studios and was once again noted as a rising young director. "Not since Welles was a boy wonder or Kubrick a kid has any young American made a film as original, spunky or just plain funny as this one," wrote a critic for *Newsweek* in 1967. Then came *Patton*, his phenomenal success with *The Godfather*, the years of independence and experimentation that produced his mountain of debt and finally his descent into the role of a kind of artistic streetwalker.

During the summer of 1987, a few miles from his home in the Napa Valley, Coppola reflected on his varied career during a break in shooting *Tucker*. Life, he said, had demonstrated a curious capacity for paralleling the stories in some of his films. During production on *Apocalypse Now*, a movie about a man's journey into madness, he experienced a period of emotional turbulence some of his friends considered a nervous break-down. In 1986, two weeks into the filming of *Gardens of Stone*, a movie depicting the relationship between an old soldier and a surrogate son destined to die in Vietnam, one of Coppola's two sons, twenty-two-year-old Gian-Carlo, was killed in a boating accident. It is plain that Coppola still grieves painfully for his son, whom he was tutoring as a film maker and whom he recalls as "my best friend and collaborator; he was perfect, like Pinocchio."

Tucker, which opens in early August, reflects a common theme in Coppola's work, a reverence for the binding strength of the family unit. Autobiographical elements are there, too. Yet it is not the picture Coppola wanted to make.

The movie depicts the life of Preston Tucker (played by Jeff Bridges), an industrialist who challenged Detroit after World War II by designing an innovative car. Although he built fifty-one of his automobiles, best remembered for a Cyclops-like third headlight that turned when the front wheels of the car turned, Tucker's company went bankrupt, and he was accused of being a con man who had taken millions of dollars from prospective car dealers under false pretenses.

Just how much Detroit and its political allies contributed to Tucker's undoing has long been debated. Coppola's movie implies that the industry's "Big Three"—Ford, General Motors, and Chrysler—smothered Tucker out of the same arrogance and smugness that later led them to underestimate so gravely the threat of Japanese auto makers.

The parallels between the plot of *Tucker* and Coppola's own life are plain: A creative, if perhaps impractical, dreamer comes forth with a better idea that is quashed by a powerful establishment in order to maintain the status quo. But what also comes through, though unintentionally, is the isolation the creator must endure as his vision is slowly stripped from him.

Coppola's interest in Preston Tucker began as an eight-year-old boy fascinated with machinery and inventors. As he grew older, he never forgot the story of a David-and-Goliath struggle. In 1976, he acquired the rights to film Tucker's life story from the industrialist's family (he also owns two of the forty-six surviving Tucker automobiles), and conceived an ambitious motion-picture musical based on his life and the process of innovation in America.

"It was a dark kind of piece . . . a sort of Brechtian musical in which Tucker would be the main story, but it would also involve Edison and Henry Ford and Firestone and Carnegie," he says.

Leonard Bernstein agreed to write the music, and Betty Comden and Adolph Green were approached about writing the lyrics. They all spent a week planning the musical at Coppola's home in the Napa Valley. But before the project could get off the ground, the economic tailspin at Zoetrope began.

"People no longer felt what I had to offer was of value," he says. "They thought my projects were too grandiose. With the collapse of my studio, everything fell into a black hole—*Tucker*, plus a lot of other things I wanted to do." He says he never called Bernstein or Comden and Green to inform them that the project was dead. "I was too embarrassed."

Then, two years ago, George Lucas, one of Coppola's original Wunderkinder, encouraged him to revive his dream of filming the life of Preston Tucker.

"I thought it was the best project Francis had ever been involved with," Lucas recalls. In a poignant role reversal, Lucas offered to produce. *Tucker* for the father figure who had helped finance *American Graffiti*, the movie that made Lucas famous. But when they sought financing for the $24 million movie, Lucas says, "no studio in town would touch it; they all said it was too expensive. They all wanted $15 million *Three Men and a Baby* movies or *Crocodile Dundee, Part 73* sequels." Lucas decided to finance *Tucker* himself, although midway through production Paramount Pictures agreed to cover much of the investment.

Lucas, Coppola learned, had his own ideas about *Tucker*. Instead of a philosophical inquiry into the nature of invention in America, Lucas wanted an upbeat "Capra-esqe" approach.

"Francis can get so esoteric it can be hard for an audience to relate to him," Lucas says. "He needs someone to hold him back. With *Godfather*, it was Mario Puzo; with *Tucker*, it was me."

The result is a picture with a whimsical, upbeat air in which Jeff Bridges smiles a lot. Some critics may look on *Tucker* as movie-making by committee, but both producer and director say they are pleased with the product of their collaboration.

"I wanted to make it an uplifting experience that showed some of the problems in corporate America, and Francis didn't resist," says Lucas.

"I'd lost some of my confidence," Coppola explains. "I knew George has a marketing sense of what the people might want. He wanted to candy-apple it up a bit, make it like a Disney film. He was at the height of his success, and I was at the height of my failure, and I was a little insecure. I'd made a lot of films, a lot of experiments, but the only one a lot of people seemed to like was *Peggy Sue Got Married*. I decided, if that's what they want from me, I'll give it to them. I'll do *Tucker* in the style of *Peggy Sue*. I think it's a good movie—it's eccentric, a little wacky, like the Tucker car—but it's not the movie I would have made at the height of my power."

Coppola's segment of *New York Stories* focuses on a wealthy child who is sophisticated beyond her years—a kind of latter-day Eloise—who grows up in the Sherry-Netherland Hotel. Patterned loosely upon his daughter, Sofia, who helped write the script, the character, Coppola explains, "is like one of the rich kids you see in New York who have their own credit cards and have lunch at the Russian Tea Room."

He enters a shiny, aluminum-skinned motor home parked outside the Apthorp apartment building on Manhattan's Upper West Side, where part of the picture was filmed, passing two residents who are complaining about the film crew's ubiquitous cable and lighting equipment. The trailer is crammed with television monitors, video recorders and other electronic equipment.

Sitting on a sofa, watching the filming of a minor scene on a television screen and occasionally directing it via a telephone link to the set, Coppola talks about film making and his future. Soft-spoken, at once pensive and candid, he is a man, like Preston Tucker, convinced that he knows a better way of doing things, but frustrated by his inability to convince others to accept it. *Tucker*, he says, will mark his official exit from commercial Hollywood film making.

"My feeling is that cinema is an art form that can have a tremendous amount of variety," he says. "You can do all kinds of styles, like literature, painting or music. But today they want only one type. There used to be room for innovation, but there isn't any more; I find it hard to work in a regulated industry."

He is reminded that the average production cost on a Hollywood feature film has passed $15 million, plus $9 million to advertise and market it. How can a studio be expected to finance a film maker's expensive experiment without confidence that audiences will be large enough to recoup the investment?

Unruffled by the question, he replies that studio overhead and distribution fees account for much of the cost. "It's to their benefit to have big budgets," he says. With *Apocalypse Now* and *One from the Heart*, he proved he was willing to back his dreams with his own money, he adds. Reminded that his own studio failed, producing an economic nightmare it took six years to extricate himself from, he says, "That was a kamikaze attack—I went down in flames by myself."

He points to his string of "hired-gun" movies as evidence that he can, if necessary, give Hollywood what it wants. But it is not what Francis Ford Coppola wants: "I'm almost fifty years old; I have to focus more on what I want to say."

He discusses the specifics of his future projects reluctantly. One prospect is a screenplay he has been working on for four years, a story set in contemporary New York that draws parallels with the decadence and decline of ancient Rome and would be "much more ambitious than *Apocalypse Now*. I think there is a whole other way we can do cinema. It will be like a big, dramatic novel."

To reduce production costs, he plans on future films to employ the electronic systems he has been working on for a decade; some are already being used by his twenty-two-year-old son, Roman, to make low-budget features, the first of which will soon be released. "Although they're shot on film, everything else is done electronically; it's as different from the old way as night and day. We can make a million dollars look like $50 million."

He will finance his projects himself, he says, noting that largely because of recent real-estate inflation, "I'm really quite wealthy and can afford to do what I want." Asked if his net worth exceeds $20 million, he says, "that would be conservative."

Coppola expects this second exit from Hollywood to be permanent, and he insists he won't look back. "The industry needs guys who are willing to make pictures like *Rambo 7* or *Rambo 8*," he says, "I need to be a solo guy, like I was when I had polio. I don't say that with bitterness. I'm just not going to participate any more. I'm going to experiment with my own ideas—experiment without the fear that failure will finish me off."

Francis Ford Coppola Interviewed

GENE D. PHILLIPS/1989

"The trouble with American film making is that producers don't allow
the risk of failure. If a good film can't risk being a failure, it won't be
really good." So said Francis Coppola when he spoke with me at the
Cannes Film Festival, one of the international festivals at which a
movie of his had won a prize. Add to that the five Academy Awards he
has received during his career, and one can see that Coppola's penchant
for making films which, in his words, "depart somewhat from the
ordinary Hollywood fare," has often paid off. When I talked with him
in Cannes, I noticed that his stocky build and full beard made Coppola
an imposing figure. One journalist even described him as a bearded
bear wearing a panama hat. Yet I found him cordial and cooperative
when he shared with me some of his reflections about his movies. The
festival, of course, attracts film directors from around the world, but
Coppola was as unmistakably American as the Queens section of
New York where he grew up and went to school. As a matter of fact,
he has kept his New York accent over the years, despite his living most
of his adult life on the West Coast.

During a conversation he always listens intently to the person
with whom he is talking, as if he stood to gain as much from the interchange as his interviewer. Nothing in his manner implied to the latter
that he was in the presence of a filmmaker whose work had won him
critical acclaim and popular success throughout the world. The material

From *Film in Review* 40, no. 3 (March) 1989. © 1989 by Gene D. Phillips. Reprinted by
permission of the author.

which I gleaned from our conversation will be found spread throughout this article.

Coppola has the distinction of being the first major American motion picture director to emerge from a university-degree program in film making. Moreover, he has since helped other graduates get their start in the industry, including George Lucas (*Star Wars*) and John Milius (*The Wind and the Lion*).

Francis Ford Coppola was born in Detroit, Michigan, in 1939; he received his middle name because he was born in the capital of the American automobile industry, and in Henry Ford Hospital as well. He consistently used his full name professionally for some years, but has tended more and more to suppress his middle name, ever since he got to hear of the old adage which warns that people tend to dismiss as an upstart someone who calls himself by three names.

His high school years began at Cornwall-on-Hudson, a military academy in New York State; but when the script and lyrics he wrote for a school musical were revised without his consent, he angrily quit the academy and transferred to Great Neck High on Long Island, from which he graduated in 1956. He then attended Hofstra University, and, after graduating from college in 1960, he enrolled in the master's program in film at the University of California at Los Angeles.

Coppola gained invaluable practical experience in film making during this period by working for independent producer-director Roger Corman (*House of Usher*) in various capacities, from scriptwriting to film editing. Finally Corman gave Coppola the chance to write and direct his first feature, a low-budget effort called *Dementia 13* (1963), a horror film he shot quickly and cheaply on location in Ireland. The set designer for the movie was Eleanor Neil, who became Coppola's wife when the film unit returned to the States. He was subsequently hired as a scriptwriter by Seven Arts, an independent producing company; and he received a screen credit as co-writer on two 1966 films, on which he worked for Seven Arts: *This Property Is Condemned* and *Is Paris Burning?* He also coscripted *Patton* for Twentieth Century-Fox around this time, although that picture, as it happened, did not reach the screen until 1970.

The experience that the neophyte film maker had gained from making *Dementia 13* and from collaborating on various other movies helped him convince Seven Arts to allow him to write and direct his first important film, *You're a Big Boy Now* (1967), which he shot on location in New York City. In due course, Coppola submitted the finished film to UCLA as his master's thesis and thereby gained his degree of Master of Cinema in 1968. The movie, which he adapted from a novel by David Benedictus, is a freewheeling comedy about a young fellow on the brink of manhood (Peter Kastner) who takes a giant step toward maturity when he finally gets out from under the control of his domineering parents (Geraldine Page and Rip Torn) and endeavors to make it on his own in the big city.

Although the film was not a financial success, it garnered some positive reviews. Consequently Seven Arts, which by this time had merged with Warner Brothers, was sufficiently impressed with Coppola's handling of *Big Boy* that the company asked the promising young director to make *Finian's Rainbow* (1968), a large-scale movie musical starring Fred Astaire. The studio was pleased with Coppola's direction of the picture, particularly his filming of the musical numbers; and the front office was therefore willing to finance the picture he wanted to make next, a modest production based on an original scenario of his own, entitled *The Rain People* (1969).

The plot of this tragic drama concerns Natalie Ravenna (Shirley Knight), a depressed young housewife with a child on the way who impulsively decides to walk out on her husband one rainy morning and to make a cross-country trek in her station wagon. She takes this rash course of action in the hope of getting some perspective on her life. Natalie at this juncture feels stifled by the responsibilities of married life, epitomized by the prospect of having a child. In the course of her journey she picks up a hitchhiker, an ex-football player named Jimmy "Killer" Kilgannon (James Caan), who turns out to be mentally retarded as a result of a head injury he suffered in his final game. In effect, Natalie now has yet another "child" on her hands, and, almost in spite of herself, she gradually comes to care for him more and more as they travel along together.

In a sense both Natalie and Jimmy qualify to be numbered among the rain people of the film's title. The rain people are tender, vulnerable types who, as Jimmy himself describes them at one point, are "people made of rain; when they cry they disappear, because they cry themselves away." Like the rain people, Natalie and Jimmy are easily hurt, and, sadly, they will both end up wounding each other deeply.

For her part, Natalie is touched by Jimmy's disarming vulnerability; but she is also wary of his growing emotional dependence on her and wants to break off their burgeoning relationship. She consequently secures him a job on an animal farm they happen to come across during their trip, in order to be able to move on without him. But the childlike Jimmy spoils everything by releasing all the animals from their cages, because he simply cannot stand to see them penned up. Jimmy is fired, of course, and Natalie is enraged at him for continuing to be attached to her. She accordingly abandons him on the road and forthwith takes up with Gordon, a state highway patrolman (Robert Duvall). Gordon, whose wife is dead, invites her back to the trailer park where he lives with his young daughter, Rosalie.

Jimmy surreptitiously follows Natalie to Gordon's trailer and furiously bursts in on them in order to save her from Gordon's advances. Rosalie also shows up unexpectedly; when she sees the hulking "Killer" Kilgannon attacking her father, she frantically grabs his patrolman's pistol and shoots Jimmy. The movie ends abruptly, with Natalie sobbing inconsolably as she cradles the mortally wounded Jimmy in her arms, futilely promising to care for him from now on. "I'll take you home and we'll be family," she murmurs as Jimmy expires.

For the first time, Coppola's overriding theme, which centers on the importance of the role of a family spirit in people's lives, is clearly delineated in one of his films. "I am fascinated by the whole idea of family," he says, adding that in his films this theme "is a constant." Thus, as Robert Johnson notes in his book on Coppola, Natalie takes to the open road to escape the responsibilities of family life, only to find that she has taken them with her. This fact is strikingly brought home to her when she reflects that her unborn child, the very emblem of her marriage, is always with her, accompanying her wherever she goes. And this reflection in turn ultimately leads her by the end of the picture to reconcile herself to her responsibilities as a wife and mother; for she realizes that in trying to escape the obligations of family life she has brought nothing but misery to herself and others. Hence the movie ends, Coppola emphasizes, with an implicit "plea to have a family."

Coppola assembled a hand-picked cast and crew to make the movie, which he planned to shoot entirely on location. Together they formed a caravan consisting of five cars, as well as a Dodge bus that had been remodeled to carry their technical equipment. "We traveled for four months through eighteen states, filming as we went," he recalls. "We did not set out with a finished screenplay in hand but continued filling it out as shooting progressed. When I spied a setting that appealed to me along the way, we would stop, and I would work out a scene for the actors to play."

Because the script for *The Rain People* was developed in this piecemeal fashion, the story does not hang together as coherently as one would like. As a matter of fact, Coppola is the first to concede that the killing that climaxes the movie is a kind of *deus ex machina* he concocted in order to resolve the movie's plot. The lack of a tightly constructed plot line made for a slow-moving film, and hence *The Rain People* did not win over the critics or the mass audience.

Still there are some fine things in the film, for example, the key scene in which Jimmy liberates the animals from their captivity is a symbolic reminder that Natalie at this point still feels cooped up by circumstances and likewise yearns to be set free from the emotional entanglements in her life. Another neat Coppola touch is having Gordon live in a mobile home, an indication of the transient nature of his life since he lost his wife and, by the same token, a foreshadowing of the sort of rootless existence Natalie is opening herself to if she opts to foresake her husband for good.

Like *The Rain People*, *The Conversation* (1974) was based on Coppola's original screenplay. After making *The Rain People*, he told me, he was thinking of "leaving Hollywood and making low-budget films in San Francisco." One low-budget, high-quality movie he made there was *The Conversation*.

The movie focuses on Harry Caul (Gene Hackman), a surveillance expert, who bugs a conversation between Ann and Mark, as they converse about Ann's husband, the wealthy director of a corporation (Robert Duvall). It seems that the director has discovered their illicit affair and may be planning to kill them.

They are to have a rendezvous with him at a local hotel in order to hash things out. Harry, intent on protecting Ann and Mark from the wrath of her huband, shows up at the designated hotel room—only to find the director dead. He discovers that Ann and Mark arranged to liquidate him, so that they could possess his wealth and power. Too late

Harry realizes that he misunderstood the conversation which he over-heard between Mark and Ann: they were planning to kill the director before he got the opportunity to murder them. Completely shattered by this revelation, Harry is even more distraught when he receives a threaten-ing phone call, in which he is warned, "We know that you know, and we are watching you." The movie ends with Harry in despair, unable to find the surveillance device which has been planted in his own apartment.

Although *The Conversation* was not a box office hit, it went on to win the *Palm D'Or* (Golden Palm), the Grand Prize, at the Cannes International Film Festival, and to become Coppola's favorite among his movies. When I asked him why it was his favorite, he replied that *The Conversation* "is a personal film based on my own original screenplay; it represents a personal direction I wanted my career to take. I have always preferred to create my own story material, as I also did with *Dementia 13* and *The Rain People*," rather than make films derived from literary works.

Because Coppola's early films did not fare well at the box office, he experienced some difficulty in launching film projects. When he won an Academy Award for coauthoring the script for the epic war film *Patton*, however, Paramount Pictures decided to entrust him with the direction of a gangster picture about the Mafia they were going to make called *The Godfather*, based on the bestselling novel by Mario Puzo.

The Godfather (1972) begins in 1945, on the wedding day of Connie Corleone (Talia Shire, Coppola's sister), who is the daughter of Don Vito Corleone (Marlon Brando), the chieftain of one of the most powerful of the New York Mafia "families." The jubilant wedding reception in the sunny garden of the don's estate offers a sharp contrast to the somber scene in his study, where the godfather sits in semi-darkness, stroking his cat and listening to the petitions being presented to him by his associates. He is following a custom which dictates that a godfather must seriously consider any request for help made to him on such a festive occasion.

Vito Corleone is a calculating man who has always run his empire of crime with the efficiency of a business executive. Whenever he encoun-tered resistance from someone with whom he wanted to make a deal, the don simply extended to him what he ominously terms "an offer he couldn't refuse," and he got what he wanted. The awesome Don Vito is, therefore, the object of the envy and the hatred of some other Mafiosi, who fear that he is becoming too powerful. Accordingly an assassination attempt is made on his life, which leaves him incapacitated for some time. Sonny, his oldest son (James Caan), rules in his stead for the duration of his illness. Michael, Don Vito's youngest son (Al Pacino), just home from serving in the army during World War II, is anxious to prove himself to his father. He gets the chance to do so when he convinces Sonny to let him even the score with the family's enemies by killing the two individuals responsible for the attempt on their father's life: a leading mobster and a corrupt cop.

In one of the most riveting scenes in the picture, Michael successfully carries out his plan to gun down both men in a Bronx restaurant. He then escapes into temporary exile in Sicily, in order to be out of the reach of reprisals. While in Sicily Michael meets and marries Apollonia, a beautiful peasant girl. Despite the bodyguards that surround Michael and his new bride, Apollonia dies in an explosion that had been intended to kill Michael. Embittered and brutalized by this neverending spiral of revenge, Michael returns to America, where his tough methods of dealing with other Mafiosi continue to impress his father; and he gradually emerges as the heir apparent of the aging Don Vito.

Friction between the Corleones and the other Mafia clans continues to mount; and the volatile Sonny is gunned down as the result of a clever ruse. Then, when the ailing Don Vito dies as well, the Corleone family closes ranks under Michael's leadership, and the new don effects the simultaneous liquidation of their most powerful rivals by having them all killed on the same day and at the same hour. Coppola intercuts these murders with shots of Michael acting as godfather at the baptism of his little nephew. The ironic parallel between Michael's solemn role as godfather in the baptismal ceremony and the stunning "baptism of blood" he has engineered to confirm his position as godfather of one of the most formidable Mafia clans in the country is unmistakable.

Coppola told me that it was his idea to include the baptism in the film. When Puzo said the script lacked real punch at the end, Coppola responded, "We'll have Michael's enemies murdered while his nephew is being christened." He explains, "I decided to include some Catholic rituals in the movie, which are part of my Catholic heritage. Hence the baptism. I am familiar with every detail of such ceremonies, and I had never seen a film that captured the essence of what it was like to be an Italian-American."

By this time Michael has married again; and the movie ends with his second wife Kay (Diane Keaton) standing in the doorway of the study where Don Vito once ruled, watching the members of the Corleone Mafia family kissing Michael's hand as a sign of their loyalty to him. The camera draws away and the huge door of Don Michael's study closes on the scene, shutting out Kay—and the filmgoer—from any further look at the inner workings of the Mafia.

Coppola's continuing preoccupation with the importance of family in modern society is once again brought into relief in the present picture. As a matter of fact, the thing that most attracted Coppola to the project in the first place was that the book is really the story of a family. It is about "this father and his sons," he says, "and questions of power and succession." In essence, *The Godfather* offers a chilling depiction of the way in which Michael's loyalty to his flesh-and-blood family gradually turns into an allegiance to the larger Mafia family to which they in turn belong, a devotion that in the end renders him a cruel and ruthless mass killer.

With this film Coppola definitely hit his stride as a film maker. He tells the story in a straightforward, fast-paced fashion that holds the viewer's attention for close to three hours. Under his direction the cast members without exception give flawless performances, highlighted by Brando's Oscar-winning performance in the title role. *The Godfather* also received Academy Awards for the best picture of the year and for the screenplay, which Coppola coauthored with Puzo. Furthermore, the picture was an enormous critical and popular success.

Nevertheless, a few reviewers expressed some reservations about the film. The movie was criticized in some quarters for subtly encouraging the audience to admire the breathtaking efficiency with which organized crime operates. Coppola counters that such was never his intent. He feels that he was making "an especially harsh statement about the Mafia at the end of *The Godfather*, when Michael makes a savage purge of all of the Corleone clan's known foes." If some reviewers and moviegoers missed the point he was trying to make, however, he looked upon the sequel, which Paramount had asked him to make, as "an opportunity to rectify that." For in the sequel Coppola would see to it that "Michael was shown to be manifestly more cold-blooded and cruel than his father ever was."

The Godfather-Part II (1974), which was once again coauthored by Coppola and Puzo, treats events that happened before and after the action covered in the first film. The second *Godfather* movie not only chronicles Michael's subsequent career as head of the "family business," but also presents, in flashback, Don Vito's early life in Sicily, as well as his rise to power in the Mafia in New York City's "Little Italy" after his immigration to the United States. As Pauline Kael says, "We only saw the middle of the story in the first film; now we have the beginning and the end."

Godfather-II begins where the previous picture left off: with the scene in which Don Michael's lieutenants pay him homage as his father's rightful successor. Then the movie switches to a scene from the child-hood of Michael's father, when young Vito's own father was murdered for defying the local Mafia don back in the Sicilian village where Vito was born. Vito's mother and older brother were also killed shortly after-ward for attempting to take vengeance on the Mafia chief; and Vito, now an orphan, escaped to America. Back in the present, the film focuses on another youngster, Michael's son Anthony, who is enjoying a big cele-bration in honor of his first Holy Communion. The party is being held on his father's estate at Lake Tahoe, which is now the center of Michael's business operations. Michael, like his father before him, privately con-ducts his business affairs while the festivities are in full swing.

The story continues to shift back and forth between past and present, as we watch Vito (Robert De Niro) return to Sicily briefly in order to gun down the old Mafia chieftain responsible for the deaths of his parents and his brother. In a parallel act of vengeance Michael arranges for the assassination of rival mobster Hyman Roth (Lee Strasberg), who had plot-ted to have Michael slain. Michael also has his weak and ineffectual older brother Fredo (John Cazale) shot when he learns that Fredo, who all along had been jealous of his kid brother Michael for superseding him as head of the Corleone family, had cooperated with Roth's scheme to kill Michael.

Throughout the picture Coppola makes it clear that the higher Michael rises in the hierarchy of Mafia chiefs, the lower he sinks into the depths of moral degradation. His wife Kay is appalled by what he has become and finally comes to the bitter conclusion that Michael will never change his ways and phase out his unlawful business interests, as he has promised her so often that he would. Indeed, it is far too late in the day for Michael to become a legitimate businessman, even if he wanted to.

Because Kay is now as aware of this painful reality as Michael himself is, she finally informs him that she is going to leave him and take their little boy and girl with her. At the climax of their dreadful quarrel, Kay reveals that the miscarriage she had told Michael she had suffered earlier was actually an abortion. She killed their unborn son, she explains, because she would not bring another child into the vicious Corleone world. Michael is shocked to learn of the loss of a second son, who would have helped to keep the Corleone name alive; and he angrily slaps his wife across the face. But, Robert Johnson comments, it is Kay who has delivered the severest blow. Michael orders Kay to get out, but she must leave their children behind.

"That Kay had deliberately aborted the baby was the suggestion of my sister Talia," says Coppola. "Kay is appalled that Michael has gone scot-free after the Senate investigation into his illegal activities." She tells him what she has done as her way of "resisting the terrible evil which is spreading out from the man she once loved. She had the abortion because she knew Michael would never forgive her, and she wanted out of her Mafia marriage."

Once Michael has become permanently alienated from his wife, he is left a lonely, disconsolate man, living in virtual isolation in his heavily guarded compound at Lake Tahoe. Michael may have built the Corleone family into one of the strongest Mafia clans in America, but he has at the same time lost most of his own immediate family: he murdered his only remaining brother, his first wife was killed by his enemies, and his second wife has been banished. In brief, the vile family business has invaded his home and all but destroyed it.

In making *Godfather-II*, "I wanted to take Michael to what I felt was the logical conclusion," says Coppola. "There's no doubt that, by the end of this picture, Michael Corleone, having beaten everyone, is sitting there alone, a living corpse." The final image of Michael, sitting in a thronelike chair, brooding over the loss of so many of his family, recalls the shot in the film's first flashback in which the sickly young Vito Corleone sits in an enormous chair in a lonely hospital room at Ellis Island, right after his arrival in the New World. The lad, we know, came to America because of a vendetta against his family in his own country, and he will grow up to wreak vengeance on the man who slaughtered his loved ones back home.

Years later his son Michael will in turn take it upon himself to avenge the murderous attack on his father's life; by so doing he will inevitably become an integral part of the ongoing pattern of vengeance that began with the massacre of his ancestors long before he was ever born. Hence, Johnson perceptively observes, there is a direct connection between the frail little boy sitting alone in the oversized chair early in the movie and his grown son sitting alone in a majestic chair late in the movie. Coppola articulates that connection when he remarks that in *Godfather-II* his purpose was "to show how two men, father and son, were . . . corrupted by this Sicilian waltz of vengeance."

The second *Godfather* film, like the first, was awarded Oscars for best picture of the year and for the best screenplay. In addition, Coppola also won the best director Oscar; and Carmine Coppola, his father, received an award, as did Nino Rota, for the film's musical score, while Robert De Niro was named best supporting actor. Moreover, *Godfather-II*, like *Godfather-I*, was also favorably received by both critics and moviegoers. What's more, the two films, taken together, represent one of the supreme achievements of the cinematic art.

Although both of the *Godfather* films were productions originated by Paramount Pictures, Coppola continued to maintain his own independent production company, through which he initiated projects that he arranged to finance, shoot, and release in cooperation with various major studios. He initially named this operation, which he established in San Francisco in 1969, American Zoetrope, after the primitive mechanism that was a forerunner of the motion picture projector.

In 1980 he purchased the old Hollywood General Studios in the heart of the film colony, which had all the elaborate technical facilities necessary for shooting a motion picture that his San Francisco setup did not have. He christened his new acquisition Zoetrope Studios and envisioned it as "similar to a repertory theater company, where a group of artists and technicians would collaborate in making movies together."

But after the commercial failure of two major films produced there, an expensive musical entitled *One from the Heart* (1982), which he directed, and a detective movie made by another director, Coppola was ultimately forced to sell the studio facilities in 1982. Nevertheless, the Zoetrope name still survives as the title of Coppola's production company, which is once again based in San Francisco. Under the American Zoetrope emblem he continues to develop projects for filming, which he then carries through in association with some major film studio, just as he did before he owned a studio of his own for a time.

The first film he directed after shutting down his own studio in Hollywood was conceived on a smaller scale than the big-budget movies he had made during the previous decade. *The Outsiders* (1983) was derived from a novel by S. E. (Susan Eloise) Hinton that her devoted teenaged readers had turned into a bestseller. The story revolves around the ongoing feud between two gangs of teenage boys living in Tulsa, Oklahoma, in the sixties. One group is made up of underprivileged lads known as greasers; the other group is comprised of upperclass youngsters. "All of the greasers were orphans, all outsiders," says Coppola, "but together they formed a family"; hence the film touches on family, a common theme in Coppola's work.

In working on the script, Coppola wanted to stick as closely as possible to the literary source, since he respected Hinton as a serious writer. "For me the primary thing about her books is that the characters come across as very real," he says. "Her dialogue is memorable, and her prose is striking. Often a paragraph of her descriptive prose sums up something essential and stays with you."

The movie opens with Ponyboy (C. Thomas Howell), the film's narrator, beginning to write a composition for his teacher about some recent events in which he has figured. We hear him recount what happened, voice-over on the sound track, as the plot unfolds. Ponyboy belongs to the greasers, most of whom are orphans like himself, boys who have consequently formed a surrogate family of their own. The gang member Ponyboy looks up to as a father figure is Dallas (Matt Dillon), a street-wise young fellow who has just gotten out of jail.

One night Ponyboy and his other chum, Johnny (Ralph Macchio), are accosted by some members of the rival gang who are drunk. When the other boys attack Ponyboy, Johnny panics and pulls a knife, stabbing one of them to death. Johnny and Ponyboy run to Dallas for help, and he advises them to hide out in an abandoned country church for the time being. Dallas comes to their hideout later on to tell them that a witness to the fatal stabbing is willing to testify in their behalf, and they decide to give themselves up. Before they can start back to town, however, a fire breaks out in the dilapidated church, and the trio are suddenly called upon to save the lives of some children who happen to be in the old building when the blaze starts. Tragically, Johnny is severely burned during the course of the courageous rescue effort, and he dies shortly afterward.

Later on Dallas, the ex-convict, lapses into his old ways, attempts to hold up a store, and is killed in a reckless scuffle with the police. Reflecting on the loss of his two best friends, Ponyboy hopes to come to terms with this double tragedy by writing down what happened in a composition for his teacher. After all, one of his brothers tells him, "Your life isn't over because you lose someone." And so the movie ends where it began, with Ponyboy writing the essay that forms the content of the film's spoken narration.

The Outsiders was a bona fide blockbuster, despite the fact that some critics dismissed the movie as a minor melodrama unworthy of Coppola's directorial talents. On the contrary, the picture deserves a respected place in the Coppola canon for various reasons, not the least of which is the host of consistently excellent performances he drew from his youthful cast, most notably Matt Dillon, C. Thomas Howell, Ralph Macchio, Tom Cruise, Emilio Estevez, and Rob Lowe as the greasers.

On the technical side, the camera work in the movie, which was filmed entirely on location in Tulsa, Oklahoma, is superb. Coppola employs shots of some incandescently beautiful sunsets throughout the movie to symbolize the brevity of youth. "When you watch the sun set, you realize it is already dying," he explains. "The same applies to youth. When youth reaches its highest level of perfection, you can already sense the forces that will destroy it." Coppola's remark becomes still more meaningful when one relates the golden sunsets pictured in the movie to a poem by Robert Frost that Ponyboy recites to Johnny, in which the poet likens the innocence of childhood to gold. Johnny picks up on the poem's theme by offering his pal this advice: "Stay gold, Ponyboy; stay gold." This is Johnny's way of encouraging Ponyboy not to lose the

fundamental wholesomeness of youth as he grows older and is forced
to face more and more of the grim realities of the adult world.

Coppola next filmed *Rumble Fish* (1983), based on another Hinton
novel. "While I was shooting *The Outsiders* in Tulsa, I said to Susie
Hinton, 'Have you written anything else I can film?' She told me about
Rumble Fish, and I read it and loved it. I said to her, 'On our Sundays off
from filming *Outsiders*, let's write a screenplay of *Rumble Fish*; and then
as soon as we can wrap *Outsiders*, we'll take a break and start filming
Rumble Fish.' And so we did." Coppola shot the dark tale in stark black-
and-white.

In the story Rusty James (Matt Dillon), a disadvantaged teenager from
a broken home, looks up to his older brother, who is known only as
Motorcycle Boy, the leader of a local gang (Mickey Rourke). Motorcycle
Boy is fascinated by the Siamese fighting fish in the local pet shop; he
calls them "rumble fish" because they possess a fighting instinct that
drives them to attack each other. "Motorcycle Boy senses a kinship
between these hostile creatures and the rival gangs, who have rumbles
to fight with each other," Coppola explains.

One night Motorcycle Boy takes Rusty along with him as he breaks
into the pet shop; he opens all the cages and releases the animals. He
tells his kid brother that he intends to set the rumble fish free in the
nearby river. Officer Patterson, who all along has thought Motorcycle
Boy a menace to society, seizes the opportunity afforded by the pet shop
break-in to shoot Motorcycle Boy dead. He is gunned down at the climax
of *Rumble Fish*, just as Dallas was shot in cold blood in *The Outsiders*, in
both instances by trigger-happy cops. Society, Coppola implies, has no
place for rebellious loners like Dallas and Motorcycle Boy.

Coppola was next brought in at the eleventh hour to collaborate on
The Cotton Club (1984). By the time he signed on to rewrite the script
and to direct the movie, the project was plagued with a variety of production problems, as well as with an unviable screenplay; Coppola did
his best to improve matters.

The Cotton Club was designed as a musical about the famed Harlem
nightspot that flourished in the Prohibition Era, where the entertainers
were black and the customers were white. Because the club was run by a
racketeer named Owney Madden (Bob Hoskins) and his cohorts, the
plot at times takes on the dimensions of a gangster picture, thereby

recalling the director's *Godfather* films. The concept of blending the format of the movie musical with that of the gangster movie—the two most popular film genres during the period of the early talkies—seemed like a dandy idea in theory; but it did not work out satisfactorily in practice. Admittedly, *The Cotton Club* has its share of eye-filling musical numbers, featuring the celebrated dancer Gregory Hines, plus some exciting action sequences built around harrowing gangland shootouts between rival mobs of bootleggers. Nevertheless, despite Coppola's conscientious efforts to whip the movie into shape, *The Cotton Club* remains a hybrid, a mixture of two disparate screen genres that, in the last analysis, never quite coalesce into a unified work of art.

In any event, Coppola had much better luck with his next venture, *Peggy Sue Got Married* (1986), a remarkable fantasy warmly applauded both by the critics and the public. Still a fantasy film was not his cup of tea. *"Peggy Sue,* I must say, was not the kind of film that I normally would want to do," he explained. "At first I felt the script—although it was okay—was just like a routine television show." Nevertheless, "the project was ready to go and they wanted me."

The title character is a woman approaching middle age (Kathleen Turner), who passes out at the twenty-fifth anniversary reunion of her high school graduating class and wakes up back at old Buchanan High in 1960, her senior year. But she has brought with her on her trip down memory lane her forty-two-year-old mind, and hence she views things from a more mature perspective than she possessed the first time around. Thus, when Peggy Sue tells her younger sister that she would like to get to know her better, she adds a perceptive remark that could only have come from her older self: "I have too many unresolved relationships."

One relationship she has failed to resolve in her later life is that with her estranged husband, Charlie Bodell (Nicolas Cage, Coppola's nephew), who, of course, is still a teenager when Peggy Sue meets him in the course of her return visit to her youth. She and Charlie married right after high school but have since split up because Peggy Sue discovered that he was cheating on her with a younger woman.

Early in the movie, before she was transported backward in time, Peggy Sue had mused to herself during the reunion celebration, "If I knew then what I know now, I'd do a lot of things differently." But the question is, now that she appears to have the chance of a lifetime to change her destiny by altering her past, will she?

In Charlie's case, when he comes to court Peggy Sue in the course of her return trip to her adolescent years, her sour experiences with him in later life prompt her to break their engagement. "I'm not going to marry you a second time," she tells the uncomprehending Charlie, who cannot foresee the future as she can. Their lovers' quarrel comes to an end when they kiss and make up—and make love; and this occasion turns out to be the time Charlie gets Peggy Sue pregnant, with the result that she does in fact decide once again to marry Charlie. In short, she winds up not doing things any differently the second time around after all, although she promised herself she would!

Back in present time, Peggy Sue had been taken to the hospital in the wake of her fainting spell at the reunion. Charlie is at her bedside when she awakens, and begs her to take him back. Their daughter is there too, and the three of them embrace. For Peggy Sue the high school reunion has proved to be the occasion of a family reunion as well. The reconciliation of Peggy Sue and her husband at the fadeout challenges the viewer with the notion that, as Gene Siskel puts it, "it is a generous and proper idea for us to accept the whole package, faults and all, of the people we care about." *Peggy Sue Got Married* thus reaffirms the need we all have to preserve strong family ties in life, a perennial Coppola theme.

In reworking the screenplay along with the scriptwriters prior to filming, Coppola says that the model he kept in mind was "Thornton Wilder's endearing play *Our Town*, in which the heroine goes back and sees . . . her youth." He wanted to invest the movie with "that kind of small-town charm and emotion." And so he did, for he managed to turn out a touching, sensitive film that ranks high on the list of his best movies.

From the film's opening sequence onward, Coppola demonstrates that he is in total control of his material. The picture begins with a shot of a TV set on which Charlie can be seen doing a commercial for his hardware store. Coppola's camera pulls back to reveal Peggy Sue primping at her dressing table before departing for the high school anniversary party. Her back is to the television set, indicating that she has, at this juncture, turned her back on her philandering spouse. When she arrives at the party, which is being held in the school gym, she is chagrined to see an enormous blowup of a photograph picturing herself and Charlie as king and queen of the senior prom. The photo captures them at a moment in time when their relationship was happy and carefree, rather than sad and careworn, which is what it eventually became.

Visual metaphors of this sort abound in the movie. As a balloon floats upward toward the rafters of the gym, one of the alumni reaches for it, but it gets away. So too, many of the hopes and dreams that Peggy Sue and her classmates nurtured when they were young have eluded their grasp, driven off by the frustrations and disappointments of later life—epitomized, in her case, by her foundering marriage to Charlie. When Charlie himself makes his appearance at the reunion, he is at first barely visible in the shadowy doorway. He is but a dim figure from Peggy Sue's past, someone whom she will get to know all over again, as she relives the past and is thereby able to come to terms with the present.

With Coppola's next film, *Gardens of Stone*, the director returned to a subject he had dealt with earlier in *Apocalypse Now*: the Vietnam War. *Apocalypse Now* (1979) depicts the war itself, while its companion piece is concerned with the homefront during the same period. The first of Coppola's two Vietnam films was a mammoth production, which he shot on location in the Phillipines. The screenplay, by John Milius, Michael Herr, and Coppola, was derived from Joseph Conrad's 1899 novel *Heart of Darkness*, but the setting was updated to the period of the Vietnam War.

Captain Benjamin Willard (Martin Sheen), who is the central character and narrator of the movie, is mandated by his superior officers to penetrate into the interior of the jungle and track down Colonel Walter E. Kurtz (Marlon Brando), a renegade officer who has raised an army composed of deserters like himself and of native tribesmen, in order to fight the war on his own terms. When he locates Kurtz, Willard is to "terminate his command with extreme prejudice," which is military jargon meaning that Willard should assassinate Kurtz. Colonel Kurtz, it seems, has taken to employing brutal tactics to attain his military objectives; indeed, some of his extreme measures have sickened the members of the army intelligence staff who have succeeded in obtaining information about him.

Willard's first reaction to his mission is that liquidating someone for killing people in wartime seems like "handing out speeding tickets at the Indianapolis 500." Besides, even though Willard has been ordered to eliminate no less than six other undesirables in the recent past, this is the first time his target has been an American and an officer. He therefore decides to withhold judgment about Kurtz until he meets up with him personally.

As Willard chugs up the Mekong River in a river patrol boat in search of Kurtz, Richard Blake comments, his journey becomes a symbolic voyage "backward in time" toward the primitive roots of civilization. Near the beginning of the trip Willard and the crew of his small craft witness an air attack on a North Vietnamese village carried out by Lieutenant Colonel Kilgore (Robert Duvall), which utilizes all the facilities of modern mechanized warfare, from helicopters and rockets to radar-directed machine guns. By the time that Willard's boat reaches Kurtz's compound in the heart of the dark jungle, the modern weaponry associated with the helicopter attack earlier in the movie has been replaced by the weapons of primitive man, as Kurtz's native followers attack the small vessel with arrows and spears. In entering Kurtz's outpost in the wilderness, Willard has equivalently stepped back into a lawless, prehistoric age where barbarism holds sway.

In fact, the severed heads that lie scattered about the grounds mutely testify to the depths of pagan savagery to which Kurtz has sunk during his sojourn in the jungle. Furthermore, it is painfully clear to Willard that, despite the fact that Kurtz's native followers revere him as a god, Kurtz is incurably insane.

After he has Willard taken into custody, Kurtz spends hours haranguing Willard about his theories of war and politics, which he maintains lie behind his becoming a rebel chieftain. Kurtz does this, not only because he wants a brother officer to hear his side of the story, but also because he ultimately wants Willard to explain to Kurtz's son his father's reasons for acting as he has. Significantly, even in the depths of his madness, Kurtz has not lost sight of the preciousness of family attachments.

In Kurtz's own mind, the ruthless tactics he has employed to prosecute the war represent in essence his unshakeable conviction that the only way to conquer a cruel and inhuman enemy is to become as cruel and inhuman as he is and to crush him by his own hideous methods.

By now Willard has definitely made up his mind to carry out his orders by killing Kurtz; and Kurtz, who has sensed from the beginning the reason why Willard was sent to find him, makes no effort to stop him. As Willard reflects in his voice-over commentary on the sound track, Kurtz wants to die bravely, like a soldier, at the hands of another soldier and not to be ignominiously butchered as a wretched renegade. Willard accordingly enters Kurtz's murky lair and "executes" him with a scimitar. Afterwards, as Willard leaves Kurtz's quarters, Kurtz's worshipful tribesmen submissively lay their weapons on the ground before him as he passes among them. Clearly they believe that the mantle of authority has passed from their deceased leader to the man he allowed to slay him. But Willard, his mission accomplished, walks out of the compound and proceeds to the river bank, where his patrol boat awaits him.

Coppola was adverse to ending a war film with the usual climactic battle scene, although United Artists, the distributor of the film, urged him to do so. "People are not interested in just helicopters flying by or in seeing big explosions," he explained to me; "they want a good story and some character interaction." Willard has carried out his mission, and so "the film ends with Willard returning to his patrol boat," just as a cleansing rain washes over his body; and he sails downriver to salvation, a sadder but wiser man. "The ending reminded me of T. S. Eliot's 'Waste Land'; I wanted to end the movie, 'not with a bang but a whimper.'"

As the boat pulls away from the shore, Willard hears the voice of Kurtz uttering the same phrase he had spoken just before he met his maker: "The horror, the horror." At the end Kurtz was apparently vouchsafed a moment of lucidity, in which he realized what a depraved brute he had become. To Willard the phrase represents his own revulsion at the vicious inclination to evil he had seen revealed in Kurtz—a tendency that Kurtz had allowed to overpower his better nature and render him more savage by far than the enemy he was so intent on exterminating.

Hence the theme of the movie is the same as that of Conrad's novel. "In *Apocalypse Now* just as in *Heart of Darkness*, the central journey is both a literal and a metaphoric one," writes Joy Gould Boyum; it is fundamentally "a voyage of discovery into the dark heart of man and an encounter with his capacity for evil." In harmony with this observation, Coppola says that he too "sees Willard's journey upriver as a metaphor for the voyage of life, during the course of which each of us must choose between good and evil."

Although some critics found those scenes in which Kurtz theorizes about the motivation for his unspeakable behavior wordy and overlong, most agreed that the movie contains some of the most extraordinary combat footage ever filmed. The battle scene that particularly stands out is the one in which the officer who is aptly named Kilgore systematically wipes out a strongly fortified enemy village from the air.

Kilgore, all decked out with a stetson and gold neckerchief, looks as if he should be leading a cavalry charge rather than a helicopter attack. His fleet of helicopters is equipped with loudspeakers that blare forth Wagner's thunderous "Ride of the Valkyries" as the choppers fly over the target area. "Wagner scares the hell out of them," Kilgore tells Willard, who is observing the operation as a passenger in Kilgore's copter. As a napalm strike wreaks havoc and destruction on the village below, Kilgore exults, "I love the smell of napalm in the morning. It has the smell of victory." It is spectacular scenes like this one that have prompted some commentators on the film to rank *Apocalypse Now*, which won one of the two Grand Prizes awarded at the 1979 Cannes Film Festival, among the great war movies of all time.

There are no such stunning battle sequences in *Gardens of Stone* (1987), Coppola's other Vietnam film, since it takes place stateside. In contrast to king-sized war epic like *Apocalypse Now*, *Gardens of Stone* tells what Coppola calls "a more intimate, personal story." The film focuses on Sergeant Clell Hazard (James Caan), a combat veteran who has become increasingly demoralized as he observes the army futilely waging a war in Vietnam he is convinced is unwinnable. "I care about the U.S. Army," he says to a friend; "that's my family. And I don't like it when my family is in trouble."

After four years in Vietnam, Hazard is now a member of the Old Guard, a special unit that serves as the honor guard for the burials of servicemen killed in Vietnam at Arlington National Cemetery (the gardens of stone). In practice this can involve participation in as many as fifteen funerals a day. Depressed by the continuing loss of so many young lives, Hazard sardonically tells Jackie Willow, a young recruit in the Old Guard (D. B. Sweeney), that burying is their business and business has never been better. Bright-eyed, impetuous Jackie insists that the war is not lost and that the right kind of soldier could make a difference. Hazard, on the other hand, thinks Jackie far too idealistic and tells him so repeatedly. Nonetheless, the rambunctious lad is itching to plunge into the fray, in order to do whatever he can to help with the war.

Jackie in due course is shipped overseas, where he is killed in action just a few weeks before he completes his tour of duty. During the ceremonies at graveside for Jackie, we can hear a couple of the younger members of the Old Guard muttering their favorite jingle: "Ashes to ashes and dust to dust; / Let's get this over and get back in the bus." Jackie no doubt recited this same impish little ditty when he was part of the ceremonial guard.

Hazard, who had become a surrogate father for Jackie during their time together in the Old Guard, feels as if he has indeed lost a son when Jackie is killed. The aging soldier remembers that Jackie had dreamed of winning the Combat Infantry Badge while he was in Vietnam but did not live long enough to receive one. Hence Hazard places his own C.I.B. on Jackie's coffin before the interment, equivalent to a gift from father to son. Hazard also decides, in the wake of Jackie's death, to return to the battleground in Vietnam, in the hope that he can teach other young fighting men everything he knows about how to survive under fire, since he never got the chance to help Jackie in this way.

Coppola explains that he decided to make this muted, elegiac film about the special ceremonial unit of the army, because he has been interested in the role of ritual in army life ever since he attended a military school as a youngster. Besides, he also valued the opportunity "to present an in-depth portrayal of servicemen as a sort of family whose members are bound together by a traditional code of honor and by mutual loyalty and affection." In short, his goal in making the film was "to limn military men, not as conventional movie stereotypes, but as complicated human beings." He accomplished this task quite satisfactorily, as reflected in the solid characterizations of Clell Hazard and Jackie Willow and in the subtle father-son relationship that gradually develops between them.

Coppola experienced a personal tragedy during the making of *Gardens of Stone*. During the first week of filming, his twenty-three-year-old son Gian-Carlo, a technical assistant on the movie, was killed in a boating accident on Chesapeake Bay near the location site. The driver of the speedboat was Griffin O'Neal, son of actor Ryan O'Neal; he was convicted of reckless endangerment and gross negligence. This writer, like numberless people in the film world, extended condolences to Coppola. Later on he commented, "It's true that movies you work on become part of your life at the time. They raise questions about family and friends. I was doing a movie about the burying of young boys and suddenly found that my own boy died right in the midst of it; and his funeral was held in the same chapel where we shot similar scenes of deceased veterans in *Gardens of Stone*. My son is gone, but his memory is not."

His next subject, a biographical film about Preston Tucker, a maverick automobile designer in the 1940s, was one that had been in the back of his mind for more than a decade. Tucker was an inventive designer, but he was never able to obtain sufficient backing to mass-produce an auto based on his imaginative concepts. It is clear in viewing Coppola's "auto" biography, *Tucker: The Man and His Dream* (1988), that, as he himself says, his cinematic imagination was inspired by creating a film "centering on an automaker's technical ingenuity." In essence, since Tucker's car was a mechanical miracle, he wanted his film to some extent also to be a mechanical marvel—a movie that emphasizes a variety of technical effects, from crane shots to split screens (whereby the frame is divided between two parallel scenes, shown on the screen side by side). There are, for example, some super high-angle crane shots of Tucker's dedicated crew putting together the first Tucker car, as well as some tricky split-screen shots—as when Tucker phones his wife, and we see separate shots of each of them on the screen simultaneously, as they converse about his latest inspiration. "I always like my movie's style to reflect the subject matter," Coppola explains.

It is not surprising that a movie maker named Francis Ford Coppola, who was born in Detroit, should be fascinated by someone associated with the automotive industry. (Coppola's elder son, Gian-Carlo, shared his father's fascination: the film ends with the dedication, "For Gio, who loved cars.") Coppola told this writer that Tucker (Jeff Bridges) "developed plans for a car that was way ahead of its time in terms of engineering; yet the auto industry at large stubbornly resisted his innovative ideas." Unfortunately, Coppola commented, "creative people do not always get a chance to exercise their creativity."

Francis Coppola is one creative person who has continued to exercise his considerable creative talent throughout his career. He personally agrees with the tenets of the *auteur* theory, concerning the pivotal role of the director in the film making process; but he also believes that "a film maker must earn the right to exercise artistic control over the movies he makes." Coppola himself has certainly earned that right. The films he has directed over the years have demonstrated that, as *Time* magazine has indicated, he is one of the most gifted American directors to come across the Hollywood horizon since Stanley Kubrick. What's more, he is one of the few directors of his generation whose track record is usually enough in itself to persuade studio officials to finance a film he wants to make.

Francis Coppola is an *auteur* who has used his creative freedom well. The enormous critical and financial success of the first two *Godfather* films encouraged Paramount to extend to him a free reign in creating *The Godfather-III* (1990). In conceding to Coppola a substantial amount of control over the script and direction of *Godfather-III*, the studio in effect "made him an offer he couldn't refuse," to cite an oft-repeated line from *Godfather-I* that has become part of our language.

In order to ensure continuity between the third film of the trilogy and its predecessors, Coppola reassembled most of the members of his production crew. This team of regulars included cinematographer Gordon Willis, production designer Dean Tavoularis, and composer Carmine Coppola. Furthermore, some of the key actors were once more on deck, including Al Pacino, Diane Keaton, and Talia Shire. Working closely with each of his creative collaborators unquestionably enabled Coppola to place on all three films, not the stamp of the studio, but the unmistakable stamp of his own directorial style—which is one of the hallmarks of an *auteur*.

"The thing that is different about *Godfather-III*," Coppola recalls, "is that Michael is different." The third film begins in 1979, twenty years after the close of the second film. Michael is getting ready for death, and he wants to rehabilitate himself. "So I wanted him to be a man who was older and concerned with redemption," Coppola continued. "Michael Corleone realized that he had paid very dearly for being a cold-blooded murderer and was a man now who wanted to make peace" with God. In brief, Michael is aware that his final reckoning is drawing near.

Michael's heir apparent as head of the Corleone family is Vincent Mancini (Andy Garcia), the illegitimate son of Michael's dead brother Sonny (the James Caan character in *Godfather-I*). Vincent cleverly insinuates himself into the family business by methodically liquidating members of rival Mafia clans who are plotting against Michael and by seducing Michael's daughter Maria (Sofia Coppola, the director's daughter). Some of Michael's underworld enemies want him dead, and an assassin attempts unsuccessfully to murder him in the course of an opera performance.

Godfather-III was Coppola's work-in-progress while this article was being prepared for publication. In turning to his next project, he observed that he looks upon the movies he has directed in the past as providing him with the sort of experience that will help him to make better films in the future. "So the only thing for a film maker to do," he concludes, "is just keep going."

Godfatherhood

MICHAEL SRAGOW/1997

In 1972, a thirty-two-year-old Italian-American director, Francis Ford Coppola, made his name with a gangster movie called *The Godfather*. It grossed more money more quickly than any previous film and helped to sweep away the moral cant of its era. But even before he had directed a single film that attracted a large audience or substantial acclaim Coppola made the movie business seem wide open in a way few directors had since the early silents. In the sixties, moviemakers coming out of film programs at places like U.S.C. and U.C.L.A. hoped to revitalize American movies as an art form and overturn the Hollywood status quo. Coppola, as the writer-director John Milius recently told me, was "the rebel envoy, the guy who had gotten into the walled city." Coppola had worked as a writer (notably on *Patton*), as a director (on the musical comedy *Finian's Rainbow*), and as a writer-director (on the horror quickie *Dementia 13*, the frenetic coming-of-age film *You're a Big Boy Now*, and the offbeat woman-on-the-road movie *The Rain People*). He'd cowed his peers and impressed the press as the one member of the "movie generation" who both broke into the studio system and kept one foot outside it. And his initiative backed up his high standing: in the case of *The Rain People*, he shot first and asked questions later, roaming cross-country with a caravan of fledgling filmmakers (including his friend George Lucas).

In 1969 Coppola had institutionalized his outsiderdom. He settled in San Francisco, keeping his distance from the studios and sinking

whatever funds he could find—including seed money from Warner Bros.–
Seven Arts—into a production company called American Zoetrope. The
company swiftly became a magnet for known movie-industry mavericks
like John Korty (*The Crazy Quilt*) and Haskell Wexler (*Medium Cool*) as
well as a cinematic frat house for tyros like Milius, Lucas, and Carroll
Ballard (a U.C.L.A. film-school classmate of Coppola's, who later made
The Black Stallion under his aegis). Coppola's dream was that American
Zoetrope would allow artists to share ideas and equipment, and eventually to transform their native cinema. He infected dozens of other film
post-graduates with his spirit of conquest. Lucas, just five years younger
than Coppola, has said, "Francis was the great white knight. . . . He
was the one who made us hope." Milius, who wrote the first draft of
Apocalypse Now for Zoetrope before establishing himself as an action filmmaker (*Dillinger, Conan the Barbarian*), recalls, "He always said we were
the Trojan horse, but that wasn't quite true, because he was inside opening the gate. None of those other guys—Lucas, Spielberg, all of them—
could have existed without Francis's help. And his was a much more
interesting influence than theirs. Francis was going to become the
emperor of the new order, but it wasn't going to be like the old order.
It was going to be the rule of the artist."

Actually, American Zoetrope had relatively little to do with *The
Godfather*, which celebrated its twenty-fifth anniversary on March 15.
The Godfather was a Paramount picture. And it was just the sort of
project that Zoetrope's would-be mavericks were supposed to shun:
Mario Puzo's gigantic best-seller about the Sicilian Mob in America
blended juicy research and the remarkable central character of Don
Vito Corleone (inspired, Puzo now says, by his mother) with cheesy
roman-à-clef material about Hollywood and Las Vegas. Coppola agreed
to adapt and direct it largely to pay Zoetrope's bills, and then (by his
own admission) risked compromising the movie's final form in an
attempt to keep its postproduction centered at Zoetrope. In interviews
conducted on the eve of its re-release, to be marked by a gala on March 20
at the Castro, San Francisco's old-style movie palace, Coppola's
co-workers continually circled back to his embattled commitment to
Zoetrope. Walter Murch, who was a postproduction consultant on
The Godfather and is responsible for improving the sound for the movie's
re-issue, says, "We knew if Zoetrope was going to survive it was because

this film was going to be made and be good. We had tied our rowboats to a speedboat; we had each intended to take our little rowboats into the lake and make our seven-hundred-thousand-dollar films, like *The Rain People* and *American Graffiti*. *The Godfather* was this huge and early exception. It had such a giant engine attached to it because the book and the head of the studio were involved. It was energizing, in a way. And it was also a little disorienting."

No one was more disoriented than Coppola. His sister, Talia Shire, who appeared in *The Godfather* and its two sequels, was taken aback at his transformation, comparing him to a performer who lands in a defining part: "When you play a role of force, a king or queen, and you have not been by casting or nature that size yet, it suffuses you. You saw Francis emerge . . . not just from people applauding but from something of the epic size of the project and of the central character—a dark character, a Machiavellian character, but a man also appealing."

Yet to this day Coppola hasn't satisfactorily reckoned with the success of *The Godfather*. Its filming, he told me, was, "right up to the end, one of the stories of the thing you think is going to ruin you." He added, "And in some ways it did ruin me. It just made my whole career go this way instead of the way I really wanted it to go, which was into doing original work as a writer-director. It just inflamed so many other desires. After *The Godfather*, there was the possibility of having a company that could one day evolve into a real major company and change the way we approach filmmaking. Suddenly, a lot of things that I didn't have a shot at I did. *The Conversation*, which I did write and direct as an original, was a film nobody wanted me to do, but I got to make it out of the deal to do *Godfather II*. The great frustration of my career is that nobody really wants me to do my own work. Basically, *The Godfather* made me violate a lot of the hopes I had for myself at that age."

Critics tend to date Coppola's descent into creative chaos from the manic-depressive overreaching of *Apocalypse Now* (released five years after *The Godfather II*). In the last few years, he has directed the bombastic *Bram Stoker's Dracula* and the flaccid, commercial *Jack*, and he is currently at work on an adaptation of a John Grisham novel. But from the beginning of his career Coppola almost recklessly mixed aestheticism and cunning and showmanship. What's significant is that a filmmaker so divided against himself and so disdainful of outside authority managed to pull all his impulses together for *The Godfather* and *Godfather II*. He achieved the combination of groundbreaking expression and public acceptance that is a popular artist's holy grail—a relic that, for all its glory, exacts misery from those who seek it, and even from those who find it.

When I talked to Coppola recently in his penthouse office on the eighth floor of the triangular green Sentinel Building, a 1906 San Francisco edifice that serves as American Zoetrope's headquarters, he mused that the stance he took toward the studios in the company's early years was founded on his exploits as a theatre major at Hofstra: "We would launch these ambitious productions, and the faculty would say, 'Oh, that's too much for students,' and we'd do it anyway." But on a day now known in Coppola's circle as Black Thursday (November 19, 1970), Coppola had to report that Warner Bros. was taking over the editing of Zoetrope's first full-fledged production, Lucas's *THX 1138*, and had rejected Zoetrope's future slate. The studio also demanded repayment of the development money for the projects it had spurned. In the meantime, Coppola says, "there was talk that if we didn't pay certain bills the sheriff was going to lock our doors." It was Lucas who persuaded him to consider Paramount Pictures' offer of directing a movie version of Puzo's semi-tawdry bestseller. "Of course George was the key person," Coppola admits. "He is very practical, and he said, 'You gotta do it, you gotta do *The Godfather*, it's going to be good, you'll see.' "

At first, Coppola didn't see how it could be good. Puzo, a respected novelist, set out to write a blockbuster—he initially called it, bluntly, "Mafia." As Puzo told me on the phone from his Long Island home, the manuscript generated interest at both Universal and Paramount when he had written only "about a hundred and fifty pages." Robert Evans championed it at Paramount, where he was then chief of production. Indeed, in his 1994 memoir, *The Kid Stays in the Picture*, Evans says he met with Puzo, liked him, and agreed to pay him enough money for the book to clear his gambling debts. Puzo says that the session never took place. (He also refutes widely circulated rumors that Paramount set him up in an office on the lot to finish the book.) In any event, Evans controlled the movie rights, giving Puzo option payments totalling twelve thousand five hundred dollars ("All the money in the world!" Puzo says), which would escalate to eighty thousand if the film was made. When the novel generated huge sales in 1969, a movie version seemed inevitable. But in 1968 Paramount had released a Mafia film called *The Brotherhood*, starring Kirk Douglas as an old-style don fighting the corporate tides of the postwar Mob. It ignominiously flopped.

Evans and his production vice-president, Peter Bart, approached one director after another, including Costa-Gavras, Peter Yates (*Bullitt*), and Franklin J. Schaffner (who'd just directed *Patton*). They all turned down Puzo's novel. Some had moral qualms about the risk of romanticizing the Mafia; one who didn't, Sam Peckinpah, had two meetings with Bart, but was concerned less with Puzo's material than with a vision resembling (in Bart's phrase) "The Wild Bunch in the Mafia." Evans and Bart thus had to come up with a ploy to sell Paramount's president, Stanley Jaffe, a Sicilian Mob film without a name filmmaker attached. They insisted that *The Brotherhood* tanked because it had a Jewish creative team. (The director, the star, and some members of the supporting cast were Jewish, but the screenwriter was Lewis John Carlino.) *The Godfather*, they vowed, would be Italian-American all the way. This pitch worked; it also led to what Bart, now the editor of *Variety*, calls a major misunderstanding. "The legend became that Francis Coppola was being considered because he was the only Italian-American director I knew," he told me. "The thing was that Francis was not the only Italian-American director I knew but the brightest young director I knew." Bart believed that there was an underlying integrity to Puzo's story-telling. Through conversations with Coppola, he came to see that the novel was a family chronicle as well as a crime story, with the Mob as a metaphor for capitalism. He trusted that Coppola would "present the movie brilliantly to my colleagues."

Coppola demurred. "I had always approached my career thinking that I was going to be a writer-director—that I was one of the few guys that *could* write an original screenplay," he explains. "I had taken a left turn against my planned direction with *Finian's Rainbow*, because musical comedy was something that I had been raised with in my family, and I thought, frankly, that my father would be impressed. And now here was a big best-selling book, which upon my first look seemed to have a lot of commercial sleazy elements." It was only after he scraped away subplots, like the ones about a Dean Martin-like performer's dipsomania and a woman with an oversized vagina, that he realized he could extract a "classical" story about an aging Mob king, Don Vito Corleone, and his potential heirs—the hotheaded Sonny, the emotionally fragile Fredo, and the thoughtful, rebellious Michael.

Coppola's next problem was the script: "It was contemporary, set in the seventies—there were *hippies* in it. By then, I felt there was a good core jewel in *The Godfather*, but it should be set in the forties. And of course the studio felt to do it in period would cost more money." Paramount wanted the film to be made cheaply. Coppola says, "No doubt that's why I got the job—because I was considered kind of a younger filmmaker using what were thought of as more modest techniques, such as handheld cameras."

Evans and Bart had brought in Al Ruddy to produce; he'd acquired a reputation for speed and efficiency with youth movies, like the Robert Redford biker flick *Little Fauss and Big Halsey*. Ruddy arranged for Coppola to meet Evans and Jaffe at Paramount's executive offices, and Coppola, as Bart had predicted, was a spellbinder. Ruddy is still dumb-founded that this young man who'd made nothing but flops operated as if he had the clout of a Mike Nichols or a Stanley Kubrick. Ruddy told me that Coppola was "like Starbuck in *The Rain-maker*": he dragged *everything* into his spiel, "how films should be made, the history of the world, the domino theory, everything. It should have been taped." Coppola persuaded Evans and Jaffe to do a period film despite the rise in budget, from two and a half million dollars to a final cost of more than six million—still a bargain in an era when Paramount turkeys like *Paint Your Wagon* cost more than twenty million. And when it came to rewriting the script, Puzo, who had been treating his chores as a lark, proved a game collaborator. "To this day," he says, "I can't even remember what's mine and what's Francis's. I feel it's Francis's picture."

Coppola's ideas for the cast—Brando, Pacino, Duvall, Diane Keaton—now look classic to us. But the studio considered them wildly unorthodox, and Coppola took this resistance personally. Shire told me that when she asked her brother if she could audition for the role of Connie Corleone Rizzi, "Francis said 'No!,' a very loud 'No!'" Even after a contingent led by Evans offered her the part, and she took it, "Francis said I should have asked him first." Once she realized, however, that his unconventional choices were going to "give everybody terror," she began to think that it might have been "wrong" for her to give him "something else to worry about"—a sibling in front of the camera.

In fact, Shire fit the criteria set by her brother and Fred Roos, his casting director. Roos recalls, "Francis and I tried to make a pact to cast Italian for every role that was Italian, to keep a certain purity to it. And we stuck pretty damn close to it." That's one reason that James Caan, a Coppola favorite, *wasn't* cast, at first, as Sonny; Coppola and Roos had selected an actor named Carmine Caridi, who, Roos says, "looked exactly the way Sonny was described in the book." For the Don, he explains, "We couldn't find a real Italian actor with the charisma he needed to have. There's a lot of talk about the Don in this movie; he permeates the movie even when he's not onscreen, and you had to have someone who could deliver on all this talk. So we started to bring up great actors who could do it as a display of great acting— learn the accent, turn it into a tour de force. We thought of three: Marlon Brando, George C. Scott, and Laurence Olivier, who'd recently played a Russian in *The Shoes of the Fisherman*. But I remember on the day we tried to decide which one should play the Don I said Marlon, and Francis said, 'Of course, Marlon.' "

The first to envision Brando as Don Vito Corleone was Puzo: he had already sent the superstar a letter and talked to him about the role on the phone. But Brando was dubious. "I had never played an Italian before, and I didn't think I could do it successfully," he says in his autobiography. And he warned Puzo that no studio would go for him. Erratic behavior and abysmal box-office returns had turned him into a Hollywood pariah. At a meeting that has been reported with varying degrees of comedy and melodrama for the last quarter century, Coppola pressed the case for Brando. "You have to remember that they were very seriously considering if they had the right director, and I brought up Marlon Brando," Coppola says. "I was told by one of the executives—I shouldn't say which one—'Francis, Marlon Brando will never appear in this picture, and I instruct you never to bring him up again.' At which point, I fainted onto the floor, as if to say, 'How can I deal with that type of statement?' My 'epileptic fit' was obviously a gag, and they got the point. Finally, they recanted and told me that I could consider Brando if I could meet three criteria: one was that he would do the film for 'nothing,' one was that he would personally post a bond to insure them against any of his shenanigans causing overage, and the third was that he would agree to a screen test. And I agreed, even though I didn't even *know* Brando." In an incident that has since entered Hollywood lore, Coppola shot Brando on video metamorphosing into Don Corleone with shoe polish in his hair and Kleenex in his mouth, and the deal was done.

For the Don's favorite son, Michael, Coppola favored a shrimpy New York actor named Al Pacino. "When I read *The Godfather*, I saw Al in the part of Michael," Coppola recalls. "I remember when the shepherds are walking across Sicily I saw his face, and when that happens it's very hard to get out of your head. So right at the front I said 'Al Pacino'—and of course that was not viewed as a possibility." Pacino was primarily a New York stage actor, with only one major movie in the chute, the antidrug film *Panic in Needle Park*. "So they had me do lots and lots of screen tests," Coppola says. "And I tested every talented American actor—Jimmy Caan tested for Michael, Dean Stockwell tested for Michael, Frederic Forrest, everybody." Coppola kept coming back to Pacino, and kept hearing the response that he was a "runt." Coppola now reasons, "I think Bob Evans was a handsome guy, a tall guy, so he tended to see Michael as someone more like himself. He was suggesting Ryan O'Neal or Bob Redford and I was suggesting Pacino. I wanted someone more like me." Pacino's then girlfriend, Jill Clayburgh, had taken to berating Coppola for stringing Al along: "I'd call up and ask 'Please, could Al come back one more time?' and she'd get on the phone crying. 'What are you doing to him? You're torturing him, you're never going to give him the part!'" According to Coppola, the matter was resolved when he was out of the country. He went to England to meet Brando, who was finishing *The Nightcomers*; upon his return, he learned that Pacino *would* play Michael, and James Caan, who was being pushed to play Michael, would play Sonny. "Apparently," Coppola says, "they'd seen a little footage of *Panic in Needle Park*. And I think they also decided that if they weren't going to fire me, they at least would go along with some of my recommendations."

In the meantime, Pacino, assuming he would be rejected, had signed on with M-G-M for a role in *The Gang That Couldn't Shoot Straight*. Evans had to call on his close friend, the late lawyer Sidney Korshak, a

high-level fixer with a notorious Chicago past and connections to the
unions and big business, to wrest Pacino away from M-G-M. Korshak,
in an ironic twist on the movie's subject, solved another critical problem when Coppola's demand that the film be shot in New York
caused mobsters to shut the movie out of locations throughout the
boroughs and Long Island. The production designer, Dean Tavoularis,
recalls, "We looked high and low; somebody would follow us; we'd
strike a deal for a location and suddenly it would unravel." Evans says
that what finally opened up New York "like a World's Fair," complete
with the help of "the garbagemen, the longshoremen, the teamsters"
and security for the locations, was a call or two from Korshak. Evans says,
"I was getting calls at the Sherry-Netherland like 'To kill the snake you
cut off its head,' or 'If you want your son to live longer than two weeks,
get out of town.' " Evans now states flatly, "*The Godfather* would not
have been made without Korshak. He saved Pacino, the locations, and,
possibly, my son."

Coppola, Tavoularis, and the cinematographer Gordon Willis devised
a shadowy look for the film which would profoundly influence period
films for three decades to come, and would confound screening-room
kibbitzers accustomed to ultra-bright Doris Day lighting. Coppola was
searching for a classical style to fit his classical story. Tavoularis testifies,
"We went scene by scene, and determined that we'd have tableau shots,
five or six men in a dark room or in front of Jack Dempsey's restaurant
or in front of the hospital, straight-on shots where the actions unfold
without the camera doing anything." Willis says that he intuited "something about a dirty yellow feel—it seemed organic for me," and he adds
that much of his lighting scheme emerged "from wondering how the
audience would first see Brando—how they'd respond to him made up
in this fashion." He continues, "We used overhead lighting a lot to form
the person behind that desk theatrically. The idea was that this was a
character who didn't always let you see what he was thinking, so
sometimes you'd see his eyes, sometimes not. As the rushes went back
to the studio, the legend became 'You never see Brando's eyes, your
camera is always focussed on the dark.' But if you look at the movie
it's very well structured visually. You have to remember that when
the first Godfather was done, screens were generally so blitzed with light
that you could see into every corner of every toilet and closet on the

set. When the studio people saw what we were doing, their reaction was 'What happened?' I got a lot of criticism because of the juxtaposition of bright, Kodachromey stuff for the wedding with the dark office where sinister things were happening. But in my mind and Francis's the contrast between the happiness in the background and this thing inside was quite clear. We had two rhythms going all the time, and it was not a mistake. But nobody got it in Hollywood. Whatever the studio people tell you now, they weren't cooperative."

For the first three weeks of shooting, Coppola was actively concerned about being replaced. Not only were the images too murky to please the executives; they also thought Brando was incomprehensible. Even Peter Bart, Coppola's biggest supporter in the executive suite, admits that he felt as if he'd worn sunglasses to dailies.

Bart divulged to me that he descended to subterfuge to help save Coppola. "There was a movement to substitute Elia Kazan," he explains. "At a pivotal meeting in Bob Evans' office, I brought in a prominent Hollywood figure; he asserted that he had talked to Kazan and found him to be senile, and was sufficiently persuasive that the idea of hiring him was thrown out. I'm not proud of this—I knew Gadge was not senile— but at every studio there comes a crunch time when you have to be devious." (Coppola says that when he and Kazan met, Kazan told him he'd never wanted to do the film.)

Coppola's first editor, Aram Avakian, is said to have put out the word that the footage was garbage. Gray Frederickson, the line producer, told me that Avakian, who had only one solo directing credit (*End of the Road*), was trying to stage a putsch. Frederickson says that Ruddy and Jack Ballard, the production man whom Paramount had sent to New York, even screened Avakian's movie to see if he was a capable director who could possibly take over. Coppola had Avakian fired, but his queasiness never went away. Frederickson recalls Coppola's quipping that the two of them should form W. U. Productions, for "Washed Up."

As for Willis, he and Coppola found it hard to reconcile their temperaments. "I like to lay a thing out and make it work, with discipline," Willis says. "Francis's attitude is more like, 'I'll set my clothes on fire—if I can make it to the other side of the room it'll be spectacular.' " Willis's camera operator, Michael Chapman, soon to become a renowned cinematographer (*Taxi Driver, Raging Bull*), attests to "marvellous operatic fights" between Coppola and Willis. At one point, Willis walked off the set, and Coppola called for "Chappie" to shoot for him, but Chapman, rather than get between his two higher-ups, ran into a stall in the ratty old bathroom at the Filmways studio and lowered his pants, so that any emissary of Coppola's would have to be really motivated to get him. (Coppola, blowing off steam, reportedly pulverized his own office door.)

If the director was tense, the cast was often loose. Stories of Caan, Duvall, and Brando's competitive jokes abounded during and after shooting; Caan admits to having been shocked when Duvall and Brando mooned the assembled extras for the wedding scene. Caan says that Coppola cemented his working relationship with Brando by being straightforward: "With Brando, all Francis did was talk to him. Everyone wants to conquer Brando—Francis just talked to him."

Coppola does take credit for instilling family feeling in the cast, "through a lot of early rehearsals and improvisations over meals and stuff." But Caan says that this kind of gentle manipulation extended throughout the movie. For example, to nudge Caan into brotherly feeling for Connie, Coppola would make him feel protective toward Shire: "Francis would tell me, 'Someone's bothering Talia,' and it wouldn't have anything to do with the movie, but I'd take care of it. The s.o.b. must have done it on purpose."

Still, Coppola says, "I don't take a lot of pleasure in anything to do with *The Godfather*. I love the cast, and I think the film definitely brought out something, but it was a terrible period in my life. I had two little kids and a third on the way, I was living in this borrowed apartment, and at one point my editor told me that nothing was any good. It was a total collapse of self-confidence on my part; it was just an awful experience. I'm nauseated to think about it."

Didn't Coppola expect that his unconventionality would upset the studio, that it would take the executives time to see what he was doing? "No, because I was just following my nose. I really saw it as an Italian family, and I knew that if I had one asset it was to do things—textures, what have you—that would be like my own family and not like so-called movie Italians. But I thought the movie was a disaster, because everyone was saying it was." Did Coppola realize that lines like "It's not personal . . . it's strictly business" would seep into the culture? "No. I was so frightened and depressed that I just wanted to get through the night and day. I was in so much trouble the first week—they were seeing dailies and didn't like them. To this day, even Peter Bart says, 'Well, the first stuff . . . ' But the first stuff was probably the best stuff in the picture. The scene in the restaurant where Michael kills Sollozzo—that was the Tuesday and Wednesday of the first week. So they didn't *see* it. Really, almost nothing in the picture was reshot, if the truth be known, but they weren't saying, "Gee, good work.' I was being told I was going to be fired up until the end of the third week." Didn't he know that in adapting the book he had transformed it? Consider, for example, how much more nuanced he made the character of Fredo. "Well, a lot of that came from the actor, John Cazale, who was a very magical person. Where the process gets at its best, where it's relaxed and fun, where every single moment becomes an opportunity, you don't even remember who thought of anything."

Coppola says that the first person to offer him any encouragement was the screenwriter (later to become writer-director) Robert Towne. Towne had known Coppola from their days of making quickies for Roger Corman, and had since become Hollywood's premier script doctor. (He received a "special consultant" credit on *Bonnie and Clyde*.) He remembers that he flew to New York to write a crucial summation scene for Don Vito and Michael, and that Coppola screened roughly an hour's worth of material for him beforehand. "I told him it was amazing," Towne says, "and he looked deeply distressed, as if he'd hired someone to help him write a scene and instead he'd got someone on an acid trip. I had already heard from people at Paramount that the picture was not going well; only Fred Roos said, in his quiet, understated way, that 'it's going to be good.' It always is a surprise when footage is so beautiful. I'd never seen footage with that kind of texture related to any so-called gangster movie; Francis had brought so much of himself and of life to it. The wedding! I thought, Jesus, what are people complaining about? But wasn't it Mark Twain who said, 'Thank God for fools, without them none of us would succeed'?"

Towne stayed up all night to write the father-and-son scene. He recalls, "Francis picked me up around six-thirty in the morning, so nervous— he had a little baby with him—and we drove out to Staten Island in a station wagon. We drove for forty-five minutes without saying a word. Then Francis said, without turning around, "Any luck?' I told him

I thought so: I had a clipboard with the scene on it, and showed it to him. 'Yeah, that's good,' he said. 'Let's show it to the actors.' We showed it to Al; he liked it a lot. Then Francis said, '*You* show it to Marlon.' Marlon was in makeup, having his cheeks put in. And Marlon made me read him the scene, both parts. It was extremely intimidating and infuriating. Read Marlon's dialogue to him? I made up my mind immediately to read it as badly as possible, as flatly, to *not* try to act it. There was a long pause, and Marlon said, 'Read it again.' And afterward he said, 'That's not bad. I want you to tell me something. Why doesn't he say anything about Fredo?' 'Because he can't figure out what to say about him at that moment.' 'O.K.' He went through every phrase and comma in the speech. Then he said, 'Would you mind coming on the set?' Francis was naturally relieved. He had no idea what we had been doing."

Besides Towne, Coppola's biggest non-Zoetrope supporters were probably the film editors who replaced the fired Avakian—William Reynolds and Peter Zinner. Respected Hollywood veterans, they went to New York and cut film as it came in. After shooting stopped, they flew to San Francisco, where each would polish half of the movie. Zinner says, "Reynolds and I flipped a coin, and he won—he got to do the first part." Why did that make him the winner? "Because the wedding was stupendous." Indeed, Reynolds considered the opening sequence, which intercuts Connie Corleone Rizzi's marriage party with the Don granting favors in his office, one of the sublime challenges of his career. "Francis knew he had to stage a real Italian wedding," Reynolds explains, "and he did it superbly, but there wasn't any plan as far as the script was concerned about going back and forth. We did it; *I* did it."

Zinner, too, made a signal contribution. In a climactic sequence, Coppola had the stroke of genius (confirmed by Puzo) to intercut Michael's serving as godfather at the christening of Connie's baby with his minions' savagely executing the Corleone family's enemies. But, Zinner says, Coppola left him with thousands of feet of the baptism, shot from four or five angles as the priest delivered his litany, and relatively few shots of the assassins doing their dirty work. Zinner's solution was to run the litany in its entirety on the soundtrack along with escalating organ music, allowing different angles of the service to dominate the first minutes, and then to build to an audiovisual crescendo with the wave of killings, the blaring organ, the priest asking Michael if he renounces

Satan and all his works—and Michael's response that he does renounce them. The effect sealed the movie's inspired depiction of the Corleones' simultaneous, duelling rituals—the sacraments of church and family, and the murders in the street.

The happiest moments for Coppola came during the untroubled location shoot in Sicily and the postproduction time he spent in San Francisco. He applied an S. F. trademark to this L. A.-studio production: the inventive use of music and sound, and sometimes sound *as* music— for example, when the roar of an elevated train mirrors the turmoil in Michael's heart and mind as he's about to commit a double murder. (Coppola regards San Francisco's preeminence in movie sound as a Zoetrope legacy; the company had its own state-of-the-art sound equipment.) But this tranquillity didn't last. Coppola and his collaborators found that the picture ran comfortably at roughly three hours. (The final movie runs two hours and fifty-one minutes.) What came next is the *Rashomon* of postproduction stories. Both Coppola and Evans say they fought for a long version of the film—but they often fought at cross-purposes. Reynolds states the nearest thing to a consensus version of what happened: "Francis didn't have all the muscle that he has now. He said Paramount would never accept it at that length. We did some drastic editing. So we took it down and showed it to Bob Evans when it was probably a little over two hours. Once the screening was over, Bob said, 'Yeah, it's good, but I remember a lot of wonderful material that wasn't in the film.' And Francis said, 'I thought you and Paramount would never accept a film of excessive length,' and Bob said, 'I don't care how long this picture is, put that material back in.' I've often told this story as a bold stroke on Bob's part. And I was there. Bob *was* Paramount at that point, and he said, 'Put it back.' He had a sense of the scope of the picture and how good it was." Zinner, Bart, and Ruddy by and large concur. Bart says, "This was a unique case where the studio production chief said, one, make it longer, and, two, the studio will give up a prime Christmas opening date—and he told the distribution arm as much. Today, marketing and distribution control the process. And Bob was a young studio head. For him to go up against the president of the company took serious testosterone."

The way Coppola sees it, Evans simply wanted to bring the film back to L. A. In his view, the issue behind the editing of *The Godfather* wasn't length but location: "I don't think they wanted me to be cutting the film in San Francisco, but I had my own little facility. And Bob Evans had told me that if the film was any longer than two hours and fifteen minutes he was going to yank it and we'd cut it in L. A." Coppola's solution, he says, was to lift "a lot of non-plot-plot-plot parts," pulling out twenty-five minutes "of stuff I loved" in order to keep it in San Francisco: "I figured, 'I'll show it to them, and little by little I'll get it back in.' But Bob Evans said, 'Well, you pulled out the best parts of the film. We'll bring it to L. A.' They brought it to L. A., Evans ordered me to put it all back, which I happily did, and then he said 'See!' " To Coppola, this meant that Evans wanted the movie back in L. A. at any length. No one I spoke to, including Bart, believes that Coppola resisted the idea of a longer cut—no one except Evans, who says he fired Coppola four times during postproduction, and insists that only his threats brought Coppola back to the editing table. (In his memoir, Evans treats Coppola's takeover of their nightmarish production, *The Cotton Club*, as revenge for Evans's hands-on association with *The Godfather*—a historical interpretation that can cut both ways.)

From Coppola's perspective, "at the bottom of things, there were two creative people who had a different point of view." There were fights over the kind of music and the amount; Coppola and his supporters at Zoetrope believe that Evans wanted to remove Nino Rota's lyrical Italianate score, while Evans says he simply wanted recognizably American music to dominate the sequences in Hollywood and Las Vegas. When Charles Bluhdorn, the chairman of Paramount's parent company, Gulf & Western, asked Coppola to do the sequel, Coppola was so sick of the jousting that he suggested Martin Scorsese instead, relenting only after Bluhdorn guaranteed that he wouldn't have to work with Evans. Yet Bob Towne, who wrote *Chinatown* for Evans before falling out with him in 1985 (over its sequel, *The Two Jakes*), witnessed some of the back-and-forth between Coppola and Evans, and found Evans "more sensitive editorially than I would ever have suspected." In the end, Towne says, "you can't gainsay what happened in the work process," and the finished movie had clearly laid the groundwork for an even braver sequel: "In the seventies, when we felt families were disintegrating, and our national family, led by the family in the White House, was full of backstabbing, here was this role model of a family who stuck together, who'd die for one another.

The real appeal of the movie was showing family ties in a setting of power. It was really kind of reactionary in that sense—a perverse expression of a desirable and lost cultural tradition, filling people with longing for a family like that, a father who not only knew what was best but, if a guy was giving you a hard time, could have someone kill him." Towne continues, "I think Francis sensed that in some way the movie elicited this reaction, and I think *Godfather II* was a self-conscious attempt to show the devolution, the tearing apart of the family, by the very things people thought in the first film held it together. One of the most chilling, heartrending sequences in movies is Bobby De Niro as the young Vito Corleone killing the local Mafia guy, committing this horrifying slaughter, and then holding his son in his arms and saying, 'Michael, your father loves you very much;' at the very instant in his life when he moves to save the lives of his children, he damns himself and, as we'll see, them."

Coppola says he didn't get a chance to savor his achievement. When he went to an exhibitors' screening, he heard "Red Somebody, the 'dean' of exhibitors" say, "Well, it's no *Love Story*." (*Love Story*, of course, had been a victory for Evans as a production head.) And by the time the film was out he was once again chained to his typewriter for a cursed adaptation—this time Evans had wooed him into scripting *The Great Gatsby*.

But Coppola's peers saw that *The Godfather* was what Fitzgerald would have called his "golden moment." Milius says, "I cannot extoll the virtues of Francis in those days enough. A lot of the American Zoetrope people, people who are happy to sell out to George"—Lucas— "felt that in choosing to do *The Godfather* Francis had sold them out, when he did it to keep people afloat, and he did keep people afloat. And when it all gets said and done, he *is* the best director of our generation."

Working on someone else's epic story had given Coppola new lucidity as a writer; working on a big studio project had given him new expressiveness as a director. Against his better instincts, he had become a better artist.

Coppola isn't able to see it that way. By all accounts (not just his own), he was miserable during the shooting of the film. His way of acknowledging its success is to credit the cast, along with his luck at getting handed a story "that a lot of people obviously responded to as a book," to which he could apply "some family stuff in my own life that was the glue, that was unusual, that hadn't been done so much in a believable way in the past." Coppola remembers visiting Las Vegas with Puzo when "some thuglike guy came over and said to me, 'Just remember, he made you, you didn't make him!' I said, 'Fine.'"

INDEX

CONVERSATIONS WITH FILMMAKERS SERIES
PETER BRUNETTE, GENERAL EDITOR

The collected interviews with notable modern directors, including

Robert Aldrich • Pedro Almodóvar • Robert Altman • Theo Angelopolous • Bernardo Bertolucci • Jane Campion • Frank Capra • Charlie Chaplin • George Cuckor • Brian De Palma • Clint Eastwood • John Ford • Terry Gilliam • Jean-Luc-Godard • Peter Greenaway • Alfred Hitchcock • John Huston • Jim Jarmusch • Elia Kazan • Stanley Kubrick • Fritz Lang • Spike Lee • Mike Leigh • George Lucas • Michael Powell • Martin Ritt • Carlos Saura • John Sayles • Martin Scorsese • Steven Soderbergh • Steven Spielberg • George Stevens • Oliver Stone • Quentin Tarantino • Lars von Trier • Orson Welles • Billy Wilder • Zhang Yimou • Fred Zinnemann